Law: Its Origin, Growth and Function

Law: Its Origin, Growth and Function

Being a Course of Lectures Prepared for
Delivery before the Law School
of Harvard University

BY

JAMES COOLIDGE CARTER, L.L.D.
of the New York Bar

BeardBooks
Washington, D.C.

James Coolidge Carter

From the Etching by James S. King

PREFATORY NOTE

THE origin and nature of law, both written and unwritten; its growth and development; its function in the social order; its powerful influence as an effective force in the progress and civilisation of mankind; the importance of distinguishing between the nature of written and unwritten law and, ascertaining the proper and legitimate province of each, were subjects which possessed for Mr. Carter an absorbing interest and to which he devoted much attention, particularly during the last few years of his life, when his retirement from active practice afforded him more opportunity for study and reflection.

The general field of inquiry was not new to him, for at a much earlier period, when still in the full tide of professional activity and burdened by the exacting demands of a large and important practice at the Bar, he had taken the principal part in opposing the adoption by the State of New York of the well known Civil Code, of which the late David Dudley Field was the author; and this task and the inquiries which it led him to make, were pursued by him with the keenest interest.

The arguments which he then framed and addressed to successive legislatures and governors, led to the final rejection of the proposed Code. His

views were published in a series of pamphlets, the
first of which appeared in 1883 under the title *The
Proposed Codification of our Common Law.* Five
years later, he delivered an address before the Vir-
ginia State Bar Association, which was afterwards
published under the title of *The Provinces of the
Written and Unwritten Law*, and later, in 1890,
an address before the American Bar Association
upon *The Ideal and the Actual in the Law*
embodied further views and reflections upon the
same general topics. It was to the study devoted
to these subjects in the somewhat brief periods of
leisure permitted by the demands of his active
professional work that Mr. Carter himself attributed
the deep and absorbing interest which they possessed
for him.

After his retirement from active practice, he
determined to devote a portion of his leisure to
writing a somewhat more important and complete
expression of his views on these topics than had been
contained in his former pamphlets and addresses
but at the suggestion of President Eliot, of Harvard
University, he substituted for this proposed work a
series of lectures to be delivered before the Law
School of that University. I find among his papers
a brief memorandum in his handwriting, evidently
written before this change of purpose and intended
as a suggestion for a preface to the work which he
at first designed to write. It is endorsed "By Way
of a Possible Preface," and is as follows:

It happened to me many years ago to be appointed by the
Association of the Bar of the City of New York upon a Com-

mittee charged with the duty of opposing a bill which had
been introduced into the Legislature of that State, entitled
"An Act to Establish a Civil Code."

This proposed Code purported to be the work of a Legislative Commission which had been created by an Act of the
same Legislature, adopted many years before, and at the head
of which was the late David Dudley Field; but it was in fact,
as he often declared, entirely his own work. This eminent
lawyer was a man of great intellectual audacity, the worthy
disciple in that particular of Jeremy Bentham. He would
not tolerate the suggestion that there was any unsurmount-
able difficulty in reducing into statutory form the entire body
of the law which governs the private transactions of men.
He insisted that the whole of it could be embraced in a volume
of very moderate size and that its adoption would substantially supersede the necessity of consulting that prodigious
record of judicial precedent which fills so many thousand volumes and has been hitherto deemed an essential part of the
furniture of every complete law library. Moved by the
high incitements of conferring upon society a benefit so
prodigious, and, as we may suppose, of achieving for his own
name a renown like that bestowed upon the great law-givers
of mankind, he threw himself into the enterprise of procuring
the enactment of his proposed code with the greatest energy
and prosecuted it for years with the utmost persistency. This
made the task of opposition extremely laborious and the chief
burden happened to fall upon myself.

I was thus led into inquiries concerning the distinctions
between written and unwritten law and was unable to find
that these distinctions had ever been to any considerable
extent pointed out.

I was, however, led to entertain much doubt concerning
the correctness of the conceptions most widely accepted of
the nature, scope, and authority, not only of the written, but
of the unwritten law, and came to think that, notwithstanding
the number of treatises upon the subject, the original sources
and nature of what may be called jurisprudence had never

been sufficiently explored; in particular the definition of law as a *command*, laid down by Austin and carried out into all its logical consequences by him, resting as it does, so far as the unwritten law is concerned, upon a manifest fiction, and confounding, as it also does, the separate provinces of the written and unwritten law, seemed to me to be a fundamental error.

These defects, or errors, as they seem to me to be, in the current theories of our jurisprudence, I impute to an underestimate among the members of our profession of the importance of theoretical inquiries. The most distinguished of our lawyers and judges are prone to regard with a species of disdain any resort in forensic argument to elementary principles, and comparatively little attention is given in our schools of law to the scientific study of the foundations of our legal institutions.

This is very much to be regretted. To eulogise the law as one of the highest of human sciences and yet neglect to inquire what kind of a science it is, whether it rests upon *a priori* conceptions or is the fruit of an induction from the facts of human experience; whether it is the conscious command of a supreme authority or an unconscious growth in the life of human society, is an inconsistency of which professed students should not be guilty.

The interest aroused in me, in the manner above indicated, in the theoretic foundations of our law, and my sense of the importance of such studies, have moved me to publish some of the conclusions which seem to me well founded and the grounds upon which they may be supported. I am not so presumptuous as to think them in any way final or anything more than a contribution to a discussion, which, if sufficiently stimulated, must be fruitful in most important and serviceable truth.

Mr. Carter's sense of the importance of the inquiries which he thus describes, and the strong affection which he always entertained for his Alma

Mater and which led him to adopt for the expression of his ripened and mature views the form of lectures for delivery before its Law School, are touchingly shown by a provision of his will whereby he gave a large sum to the President and Fellows of Harvard College "which," he said, "I now wish may be applied to the establishment and maintenance in the Law School of the University of a professorship of General Jurisprudence for the special cultivation and teaching of the distinctions between the provinces of the written and unwritten law; but I do not intend to control the discretion of the donees in respect to the application of this fund. I mention my present preference." This was in addition to another large gift for the general purposes of the University.

It was Mr. Carter's intention to deliver the lectures in the spring of 1905, and the rough draft of the manuscript was completed only a few days before he was stricken with the brief illness which resulted in his death on February 14, 1905. When he realised that he could never deliver the lectures, he expressed a wish that they be published by his Executors.

The manuscript had never been finally revised by him; but it has been thought best to print this volume from it just as it left his hand, save the making of a few verbal corrections.

L. C. L.

New York, June, 1907.

LAW, ITS ORIGIN, GROWTH
AND FUNCTION

LECTURE I

A COMPLETE study of the law would embrace three successive efforts. The first would be to acquire a knowledge of those rules which make up the law, as mere isolated rules; and this might be sufficient for a considerable degree of skill and proficiency in practice. The next would be to comprehend those rules as parts of a classified and orderly system exhibiting the law as a science; and whoever aspires to be a thoroughly accomplished lawyer must take this step. The third and final effort would be to explore the realms of science which lie beyond the immediate boundaries of the law, and ascertain its origin, its essential nature, the method of its development, the function it fills in human society, and the place it occupies in the general system of human knowledge; in other words, to learn what is termed the Philosophy of the Law.

The means for prosecuting the first two of these efforts have been, in a reasonable measure, already supplied. The decisions of a multitude of tribunals

sitting during successive ages, and diligently re-
corded, furnish abundant material from which to
gain a knowledge of what the law at present is, and,
besides these, we have numerous treatises, many of
them thorough and admirable, together with codes
both of ancient and modern states, all aiming to
reduce the law into a scientific form.

In the third and last stage of legal study, however, comparatively little progress has been made.
There are several reasons for this. In the first place,
there is, in the economic sense, but little demand
for this sort of knowledge. Courts are always eager
to listen to intelligent discussion concerning particular rules, or the general heads in the law to which
such rules should be referred; but their concern is
mainly with practical affairs, and they are inclined
to be impatient of discussions which have but a
remote pertinency, and to them all mere philosophy
is apt to seem remote. Lawyers, even the most
accomplished, feel little inclination towards studies
which seem to afford but a small measure of practical
utility, and most efforts in the field of Legal Philosophy are characterised with a polite sneer as
being *academic*. Moreover this branch of knowledge
being part of the field, not strictly of Law, but of
Sociology, has necessarily been kept in abeyance by
the circumstance that Sociology itself is but a recent
study. Add to this the intrinsic difficulty of the
subject, and we need not wonder at the little progress made in its development.

The criticism that such studies are *academic* is
true, but it should by no means discredit them. It

is their highest recommendation; for it means that they are such as are usually pursued in universities, and it is in such places, pre-eminently, that the highest and most useful knowledge is taught. All university teaching is or should be, scientific and philosophical; and never rests satisfied as long as a further step may be taken or a larger generalisation reached.

But if proof be needed of the immediate practical utility of such knowledge it may be found in abundance in the present condition of *legislation*. I speak of this country, but without meaning to imply that it is worse here than elsewhere. There are a vast number of laws on the statute-books of the several States which are never enforced, and generally for the reason that they are unacceptable to the people. There are great numbers of others the enforcement of which, or attempts to enforce which, are productive of bribery, perjury, subornation of perjury, animosity and hate among citizens, useless expenditure, and many other public evils. All these are fruits of the common notion, to correct which but little effort is anywhere made, that a legislative enactment is necessarily a *law*, and will certainly bring about, or help to bring about, the good intended by it, whereas such an enactment, when never enforced, does not deserve the name of law at all, and when the attempted enforcement of it is productive of the mischiefs above-mentioned, it is not so much law as it is tyranny. Among the evils which oppress society, there are few greater than that caused by legislative expedients undertaken

in ignorance of what the true nature and function of law are, and the effective remedy—at least
there is no other—lies in an effort to correct this
ignorance by knowledge.

This neglect of the problems underlying our legal
systems has left important points in our judicial
literature in much confusion, and this is very manifest in the multiform definitions which have been
given of *Law*. It might be thought that the oldest
and most necessary function of human society, and
one which from the dawn of speculation has
engaged the attention of the most superior and disciplined minds, would have received a final interpretation commanding general assent; but the case is
quite otherwise. The various definitions exhibit the
greatest diversity, both in expression and in substance. They are generally vague and uninstructive,
sometimes conflicting and irreconcilable, and scarcely
any will endure a close scrutiny.

I may illustrate this diversity by instances, most
of which I gather from Prof. Holland's recent work
on *The Elements of Jurisprudence*. Cicero, who, with
other Roman jurists, was wont to regard what was
termed the Law of Nature as the foundation of all
law, in one place thus defines it[1]: "*Lex est recta
ratio imperandi atque prohibendi*"; in another thus
"*Lex nihil aliud nisi recta et a numine deorum tracta
ratio, jubens honesta, prohibens contraria.*"[2] Such
definitions can hardly be said to define anything.
Assigning to the law a divine source and authority,
and identifying it with "right reason," is but a con-

fession of inability to define or explain it. It is but saying that law is so far the product of our highest reason that no human origin can be assigned to it, and therefore that its source and authority must be divine. And to say that the law is what commands the honest and just to be done is but moving in a circle, for if we were to inquire what is honest and just the only answer would be what the law commands. A definition by Hooker is very concisely expressed, but marked by the same vagueness: "That which reason in such sort defines to be good that it must be done."[1] What is this *reason* from which law thus proceeds, and where is it to be found, and how does it act in determining what is good? Men may have different conceptions of reason, and be led by them to very different conclusions concerning law. The German philosopher Kant defines law as "the sum total of the conditions under which the personal wishes of one man can be reconciled with the personal wishes of another man, in accordance with a general law of freedom."[2] But while this definition exhibits a profound insight into the purpose, or function, of law, it is otherwise vague and indefinite. What is the nature of the "conditions" here intended? Are they found in the nature of men and things, or imposed by some external human authority, and if the latter, by what authority? Savigny, the most accomplished philosophical jurist of his time, at once profound and practical, describes the law as "The rule whereby the invisible

[1] *Eccl. Pol.*, I. c. 3, c. 8.
[2] *Rechtslehre, Werke*, vii., p. 27.

border line is fixed within which the being and the activity of each individual obtains a secure and free space."[1] This language, however vague and obscure, describes law, or rather its function quite accurately, but it does not inform us of the origin of the rule, or the nature of its authority, matters quite necessary to a complete description.

These instances are not given by Prof. Holland as attempted definitions of any law actually administered; but of that general body of rules to which it is supposed that human conduct ought to conform, even though not enforced by the direct action of the State,—rules derived from what is called the Law of Nature, or from the general code of morality. He is a follower of the celebrated John Austin, and would restrict the name of Law to those rules which a fully organised State recognises and enforces, and which he, adopting the language of Mr. Austin, distinguishes by the term Positive Law. He cites many instances of what, in his view, are attempted definitions of this law, besides giving his own. Among them is that of Demosthenes: "This is Law, to which all men should yield obedience for many reasons, and especially because every law is a discovery and gift of God, and at the same time a decision of wise men, and a righting of transgressions, both voluntary and involuntary, and the common covenant of a State, in accordance with which it beseems all men in the State to lead their lives." This definition, however, seems limited to those rules which are formulated by learned jurists from

---

[1] *Systema des Rechts*, i., p. 332.

the precepts of morality, and scarcely embrace the edicts of a tyrant, or the arbitrary enactments of a legislative body however rigorously they may be enforced. Another is that of Xenophon: "Whatsoever the ruling part of the State, after deliberating as to what ought to be done, shall enact, is called a law." This defines well enough written or statutory law, but no other. Another is that of Hobbes, the champion of arbitrary power, which also defines nothing but statutory law: "The speech of him who by right commands something to be done or omitted." Another is that of Bentham, who believed that legislation should embrace the whole field of law: "A portion of discourse by which expression is given to an extensively applying and permanently enduring act or state of the will, of a person or persons in relation to others, in relation to whom he is, or they are, in a state of superiority." It requires no small amount of intellectual effort to understand what this means, but it is phrased with studied precision to express what the author thought law ought to be. John Austin, in his well-known work on *The Province of Jurisprudence Determined*, limits that province to what he designates as "Positive Law," which he defines thus: "Every positive law, or every law simply and strictly so called, is set by a sovereign person, or a sovereign body of persons, to a member or members of the independent political society wherein that person or body is sovereign or supreme,"[1] and he denies that any other so-called laws fall within the scope of jurisprudence. He,

[1] John Austin, lecture vi., vol. i., p. 116.

like Bentham, whose disciple he was, thus makes the most important element of law, its authority, to proceed from the sovereign power, and pronounces the most profound judgment of an Eldon or a Marshall and the tyrannical decree of the most unscrupulous despot as equally entitled to the august name of law. And yet the theory of Austin has received, both in England and America, a wider acceptance and adoption among juridical writers than any other. There is in the other definitions I have referred to a basis of general truth, however insufficient they may be, but that of Austin seems to me to be radically and mischievously erroneous. This will clearly appear if the views I shall hereafter endeavour to maintain be at all well founded. The definition of a German jurist, Dernberg, is very concise. It is: "That ordering of the relations of life which is upheld by the general will." We would scarcely think that this writer was speaking of the same thing which Bentham and Austin sought to define. Austin, however, could cite Blackstone in his favour, whose definition is: "A rule of civil conduct prescribed by the supreme power in a State commanding what is right and prohibiting what is wrong"; but this, besides being open to much the same criticism as the definitions of Bentham and Austin, is subject to another, namely, that we are not told where we are to find the "right" and the "wrong" which the law enjoins or prohibits, except in the injunction or prohibition itself. Prof. Holland's own definition is, I think, while far from being perfect, one of the best: "A law, in the proper sense of the term, is a general rule of human action, taking cognisance only of external acts, enforced by a determinate authority, which authority is human, and, among human authorities, is that which is paramount in a political society."

Sir Frederick Pollock, to whose disciplined mind and wide learning we might look with confidence for a satisfying definition, thinks one impossible at present, and says: "No tolerably prepared candidate in an English or American law school will hesitate to define an estate in fee simple; on the other hand, the greater a lawyer's opportunities of knowledge have been, and the more time he has given to the study of legal principles, the greater will be his hesitation in face of the apparently simple question, What is Law?"

In this diversity of view two opposing tendencies are discernible. One of them may be described generally as an ideal tendency seeking to enthrone over human affairs a rule of absolute Right.

The ancient jurists, the administrators and students of the law, recognised the sense of justice or right felt by all races and classes of men, and perceived that there were rules of human conduct constituting a rational system the enforcement of which satisfied this universal sentiment. Whence the sentiment came, or the rational precepts which accorded with it, they did not diligently inquire, but they perceived that a like order pervaded all the phenomena of the moral and physical world, that the heavenly bodies moved and the seasons succeeded each other in accordance with some unyielding law, and that, in general, virtue was rewarded and vice punished, in accordance with some law equally imperative. They could not help believing that the universe, moral as well as material, was under the guidance of some All-powerful Mind, the Creator and Ruler of all, whom, expressing their ignorance rather than their knowledge they named indifferently Jove, God, or Nature. Their conclusion was that there was a real and true Law towards which all human law approached, and good men everywhere aspired, capable, in part at least, of being apprehended by our reason, which was a part of universal Nature, and an emanation of the Divine Mind, and to this they gave the name of the Law of Nature.

This conception fell in with the philosophical tenets of Stoicism, which was the school in which the Roman jurists were chiefly trained. It furnished a foundation for the *jus gentium*, a body of law which grew out of the necessities of justice in dealing with the relations between citizens of Rome and the people of her conquered provinces; and it thus found a place in the Roman Jurisprudence, and has been carried with it into the judicial literature of the modern nations of continental Europe which have adopted that system as the basis of their law. It was a favourite theme with Cicero in his legal writings, and he kindles into eloquence whenever he touches upon it. His nobly phrased panegyrics have often been quoted.

Nor is this law of nature a stranger to the juridical writers of England. I might refer to many who recognise it, although all may not understand it alike. I content myself with a citation from Blackstone. He says: "This law of nature being co-eval with mankind, and dictated by God himself, is, of course, superior in obligation to any other. It is binding over all the globe in all countries, and at all times; no human laws are of any validity if contrary to this; and such of them as are valid derive all their force, and all their authority, mediately or immediately, from this original."[1]

This lofty conception of law can scarcely be regarded as scientific. If there were no other objection to it, it would be enough that we know of no certain means whereby we can pronounce what the law of nature is. Blackstone, indeed, says that it may be reduced to one "paternal precept, 'that man should pursue his own true and substantial happiness.'"[2] And while he thinks the task would be "pleasant and easy" if our reason were "as in our first ancestor before his transgression," he admits that in our present state it is encumbered with difficulties, except where Divine Providence "hath been pleased at sundry times and in divers manners, to discover and enforce its laws by an immediate and direct revelation."[3] But the difficulty of gaining any true knowledge of it is quite insuperable. The law of God must be absolute like himself, and before we can know his laws we must be absolute— that is, equal with him. We can know the absolute in no direction, and science could scarcely find in

[1] Blackstone, book i., p. 41.
[2] *Ibid.*   [3] *Ibid.*

the Sacred Scriptures rules of conduct which it was the duty of the State to enforce.

The other tendency in these diverse definitions is the one represented by that of Austin. Others, like him, impressed with the uncertainty which marks what is called the Law of Nature, and dissatisfied with the rhetorical language in which the vague conceptions of it are clothed, go to the opposite extreme and refuse the name of law to everything which is not prescribed in definite language by the sovereign power of the State. With these everything which the so-called supreme power of the State commands, whatever its character in point of right, is law, and nothing else is entitled to that designation. And thus while the one tendency would enthrone Right, the other would erect Force, as the arbiter of human conduct.

The inquiry naturally arises whence this vagueness, confusion, uncertainty, and error concerning subjects which have engaged the attention of the most powerful minds from Aristotle to Bacon, proceeds. Is the law incapable of definition? If so, it must be for the reason that it can not be known, or is not known; for whatever is known can be defined Or do the confusion and contradiction spring from the fact that truth has not been reached for the reason that the proper methods of investigation have not been adopted? In all the physical sciences it has long been recognised that little can be gained by indulging in hypotheses and conjectures, and that the true method of inquiry is to fix the attention upon the field of actual phenomena to which the inquiry relates, and arrange our knowledge of the facts according to the order in which they stand related to one another. Science deals with facts alone, and where there are no facts there can be no science; and where there are facts no progress will be made in erecting a science which shall embrace them until these facts have been diligently studied.[1]

The two diverging tendencies to which I have alluded seem to me to have arisen from a failure to recognise these truths. In viewing the law as a body of rules proceeding from a supposed Law of Nature —an invisible fountain of right—we are simply indulging in hypothesis. No such thing is open to our observation, and, consequently, not to our knowledge. So, too, when we ascribe all law to the command of the supreme power in a State we are simply contenting ourselves with an assumption. That extremely small part, comparatively, of the law consisting of statutory enactments may be thus defined with some approach to truth, but the great bulk of the law, that which is unwritten, does not

[1] NOTE.—Since writing the above some observations of Prof. Maine, of a similar nature, have been brought to my attention. He says: "There is such a wide-spread dissatisfaction with existing theories of jurisprudence, and so general a conviction that they do not really solve the questions they pretend to dispose of, as to justify the conviction that some line of inquiry necessary to a perfect result has been incompletely followed or altogether omitted by their authors. And indeed there is one remarkable omission with which all these speculations are chargeable, except perhaps those of Montesquieu: They take no account of what law has actually been at epochs remote from the particular period at which they made their appearance." (*Early Law*, p. 174.)

It is to be regretted that Prof. Maine did not devote himself to a systematic and sustained inquiry throughout the promising field here suggested instead of accepting the hypothetical conclusions of Austin.

appear to fall under the definition. This is conceded by Austin, and his mode of meeting the difficulty is the short and easy one of *assuming* that the Sovereign *adopts* the unwritten law as it is declared by the courts, an assumption not only unproved, but unprovable. It is a pure hypothesis.

I know of no difference between the physical and the moral sciences so far as their methods are concerned. In the one as well as in the other there must be a field of actual and observable fact, and wherever there is such a field a science is possible. Where there is none, there can be no observation, and therefore no science. The world of fact open to our observation is not, indeed, limited to the external and material world; our own thoughts and feelings are equally matters of fact made known to us by consciousness, and therefore parts, or susceptible of being made parts, of our scientific knowledge.

My first endeavour in these lectures will be to find an answer to the question which has evoked so many different opinions, and which Sir Frederick Pollock deems it impossible at present to answer— What is Law?

There is certainly a region of fact with which the law is concerned. The common description of law upon which all are agreed is that it is "a body of rules for the regulation of human conduct," and whether we look to the exercise of the power of legislation, or to the action of judicial tribunals, we find that in every instance the thing, and the only thing, sought to be affected by law is human conduct. Of course in connection with human conduct everything which directly bears upon it, including especially the nature and constitution of man, and the environment in which he is placed, becomes part of the field of fact to be studied, for these are causes constantly operating upon conduct and affecting it. Human conduct, therefore, with everything bearing upon and restraining it, constitutes the arena of fact which the student seeking for a knowledge of the true nature of law must explore, and an attentive survey of this field, and a just arrangement of its contents can, I think, scarcely fail to clear up much of the confusion and uncertainty which now obscure our conceptions of the origin, nature, and function of the law. It may possibly be found that human conduct is in a very large degree self-regulating, and that the extent to which it can be affected by the conscious interference of man is much narrower than is commonly supposed.

Inasmuch as the whole field of human conduct is to be explored, we should naturally begin with the earliest exhibitions of it to which our knowledge extends—that is, to conduct and its regulation in primitive society. There is another reason for turning our attention at first to primitive society. We can more easily learn the real nature and function of any complex instrumentality, whether it be a piece of mechanism like the steam-engine, or an institution like the law, if we begin by studying it in its original and simplest form. We thus perceive more easily what is essential, and the numerous additions or modifications necessary to adapt it to varying circumstances do not confuse us or divert the attention.

It is not, indeed, possible for us to gain any direct knowledge of the social condition of pre-historic man. Our earliest records carry us back a few thousand years only, and these exhibit man at a considerably advanced stage of progress. We do not know how long he has been upon the earth; but we have sufficient reasons for the belief that he has been here for a period measured by millions of years. What progress may have been made during that period prior to any time of which we have any knowledge, we can not know with certainty.

There are, however, numerous tribes of men now living who are nearly destitute of arts and industry, who do not cultivate the earth, who subsist wholly upon its wild products, who have only the simplest implements and dress, rudely fashioned from wood, stone, and the skins of beasts, and archæology brings to our knowledge the existence of implements of similar character which must have belonged to men living in geologic periods long anterior to our own. We know, moreover, that the ancestors in historic times of the civilised races now upon the earth used similar implements for presumably similar purposes. We are safe, therefore, in the conclusion that the social conditions open to our observation of barbaric man are really those, or resemble those, of primitive or pre-historic man.

The tribes of men lowest in the scale of civilisation of which we have any knowledge are those which subsist upon the wild fruits or products of the earth, without other labour than that required to gather or capture them. They are huntsmen who pursue their game on land or water with the rudest implements and at the same time gather wild honey, yams, cocoanuts, or other wild fruits. They are usually more or less unsettled, wandering not widely, but from place to place, as the needs of their existence require. Those who subsist mainly by the pursuit of wild animals upon the land roam through limited regions. Those who live upon fish, or where wild fruits are abundant, are more settled. Of these are the inhabitants of Terra del Fuego, the Patagonians, some tribes of Australia, the Bushmen of South Africa, the Wood Veddahs of Ceylon, the Andamanese in the Bay of Bengal, the Abipones of South America. They may dwell in caves or hollow trees, or in the rudest huts made of the trunks or branches of trees. They go, in some instances, naked, in others with very slight clothing, and in others, where the climate is severe, they are more completely clothed in the skins of beasts. They have no arts or industries save such as are necessary for the manufacture of their weapons or the construction of their rude habitations. They have scarcely any language. The relations of the sexes are different in different tribes. In some monogamy, in others polygamy, and in others promiscuity obtains. These societies are small and generally inclined to be peaceful, hostilities with neighbouring tribes being comparatively rare. They are usually gentle and kind towards each other. The only things in the nature of property which they possess are their

2

weapons and implements, their clothing and habitations, and the right of property in these things is recognised. They have no laws or organised government. There is no headship in the tribe except on those occasions when hostilities, offensive or defensive, with neighbouring tribes arise, and then the most capable is selected as chieftain to lead the rest. But his authority declines when the occasion for it has passed. There is no council of elders or other body clothed with public authority. All the members of the tribe are equal and independent.

And yet in these societies there is a constant restraint upon conduct. This consists simply in the obligation felt by each one to do as others do—that is, to conform to custom. Every one knows that if he does violence to another, or steals his property, he will excite the resentment of the other, and probably receive from him, and those who will aid him, bodily punishment. He will provoke retaliation. He will lose the approval and friendship of his fellow tribesmen. He will be made in various ways to suffer. These are the consequences, known beforehand, of a failure to conform to custom, and they are sufficient to secure conformity, not indeed in every instance, but in the great majority of instances. The prime requisite of human society, that without which it cannot subsist, is that each member should know what to expect in the conduct of others, and that fair expectations should not be disappointed. When he knows this, and only when he knows it, he knows how to act himself. This requirement is supplied by conformity to custom. The obedience does not proceed from any conception of a principle of right. It is not felt to be a crime to steal the property of a member of another tribe, or to do violence to his person, or even to murder him. Such acts indeed are often regarded as virtues and applauded as such. The custom is obeyed unconsciously in most instances because there is no temptation to depart from it, and where the temptation arises self-restraint is exercised through fear of the consequences. Custom, therefore, is the only law we discover at the beginning of society, or of society when first exposed to our observation. The word itself imports its main characteristic, namely, its persistency and permanency.

The manner in which a compliance with such customs is enforced is shown in the case of the Australian tribes above referred to. We are told that among them "the holiest duty a native is called upon to perform is that of avenging the death of his nearest relative, for it is his peculiar duty to do so; until he has fulfilled this task he is constantly taunted by the old women; his wives, if he is married, would soon quit him; if he is unmarried, not a single young woman would speak to him; his mother would constantly cry, and lament that she had ever given birth to so degenerate a son; his father would treat him with contempt, and reproaches would constantly be sounded in his ear."

It is important to observe that the establishment of a custom requires time, and long periods of time, and as all conduct is preceded by thought, it also involves a long series of similar thoughts—that is, of long-concurring common opinion. Custom rests, therefore, not only upon the opinion of the present, but upon that of the past; it is tradition passing from one generation to another. We know no primitive horde even without this inheritance, and this circumstance, and the respect and veneration for ancestors which we everywhere find in primitive peoples, contribute to make custom more venerable and binding. I can not do better than borrow the authority and the words of Mr. Herbert Spencer in describing at once the existence of custom among primitive tribes and the force it derives from its transmission from prior generations beyond the reach of observation.

"It needs but to remember the painful initiation which at a prescribed age each member of a tribe undergoes (submitting to circumcision, or knocking out of teeth, or gashing of the flesh, or tattooing)—it needs but to remember that from these imperative customs there is no escape; to see that the directive force which exists before any political agency arises and which afterwards makes the political agency its organ, is the gradually formed opinion of countless preceding generations; or rather, not the opinion, which, strictly speaking, is an intellectual product wholly impotent, but the emotion associated with the opinion. This we everywhere find to be at the outset the chief controlling power.

"The notion of the Yukis that 'if they departed from the customs of their forefathers they should be destroyed' may be named as a definite manifestation of the force with which this transmitted opinion acts. In one of the rudest tribes of the Indian hills, the Puans, less clothed than even Adam and Eve are said to have been, the women long adhered to their bunches of leaves in the belief that change was wrong. Of the Korana Hottentots we read that 'when ancient usages are not in the way every man seems to act as is right in his own eyes.' Though the Damara chiefs 'have the power of governing arbitrarily, yet they venerate the traditions and customs of their ancestors.' Smith says: 'Laws the Araucanians can scarcely be said to have, though there are many ancient usages which they hold sacred and strictly observe.' According to Brooke, among the Dyaks custom simply 'seems to have become law, and breaking the custom leads to a fine.' In the minds of some clans of the Malagasy 'innovation and injury are . . . inseparable, and the idea of improvement altogether inadmissible.'

"This control by inherited usage is not simply as strong in groups of men who are politically unorganised, or but little organised, as it is in advanced tribes and nations, but it is stronger. As Sir John Lubbock remarks: 'No savage is free. All over the world his daily life is regulated by a complicated and apparently most inconvenient set of customs (as forcible as laws), of quaint prohibitions and privileges.' Though one of these rude societies appears structureless, yet its ideas and usages form a kind of invisible framework for it, serving rigorously to restrain certain classes of its actions. And this invisible framework has been slowly and unconsciously shaped during daily activities, impelled by prevailing feelings, and guided by prevailing thoughts, through generations stretching back into the far past.

"In brief then, before any definite agency for social control is developed, there exists a control arising partly from the public opinion of the living, and more largely from the public opinion of the dead."

Let us next glance at the conduct of man at a slightly advanced stage of progress, namely, the *pastoral* state, in which he seeks his subsistence from herds of tamed animals, and must, therefore, roam with them wherever food for them is to be found. Unlike the primitive savage, instead of killing whatever animals he captures and consuming them in immediate enjoyment, he tames them

and takes only their increase; he practises absti-
nence, and endures labour in the hope of a greater
happiness in the future. It is in this more than in
anything else that we find the promise of progress
and civilisation; for whenever man has learned to
postpone present enjoyment to a future good he has
taken the first step in individual and social progres-
sion. But the life of the shepherd is still a wandering
one. The communities are small, and present, in
general, so far as the government of conduct is concerned, no features essentially different from those
of the other less wandering tribes. The persistency
of custom and its dependence upon environment
may be well illustrated by a reference to one of these
societies. The Bedouins of the Arabian desert,
although the individuals have greatly advanced in
consequence of contact with civilised peoples, still
exhibit collectively the manners and customs which
distinguished them three thousand years ago.

The chief characteristic which marks the next
stage in social advancement is the adoption, wholly
or partly, of permanent abodes in place of a wandering life, and with it, necessarily, the cultivation of
the earth. The numbers grouped together now
become larger, but the increase is brought about in
two different methods, and they present one of two
widely different aspects according as the tendencies
are to a militant or to a peaceful life. If the society
has the former tendency, it increases by the conquest of neighbouring tribes and consolidating them
with itself; if the latter, the increase is manifested
by the natural increase of its own population largely

accelerated by the diminution in hardships which follows from its abandonment of the wandering life and by the increased care of children.

Confining our attention first to the warlike societies, we find that they exhibit what the primitive groups first noticed lack—some organisation of the State. In war there must be a leader, and absolute power must be reposed in him in order that war may be made effective. Internal quarrels in the warrior bands must also be repressed, and the power bestowed upon the chieftain is employed for that end. The most skilful warrior acquires this chieftaincy and it becomes paramount in him, and develops into kingship. This power, supported, in peace as well as in war, by bands of warriors, becomes absolute, and the chieftain is able to choose his successor. He naturally chooses his son, and thus arises the tendency to hereditary monarchy.

In order, however, that the king may maintain his authority over the tribes he has conquered, he selects a company of favourites from his subordinate chiefs, the leaders of his warrior bands and the heads of the conquered tribes, who are made rulers similarly absolute over such tribes, though subject to him, and through these tributes are exacted and levies of warriors made from the local populations. The land is everywhere distributed among those who have distinguished themselves in battle, or otherwise secured royal favour. Prisoners taken in war are made slaves to cultivate the land, and thus classes are created in the State, all except the slaves enjoying privileges over those beneath them, and dependent for the enjoyment of such privileges upon the favour of the sovereign; and thus the kingdom becomes consolidated into a powerful tyranny. The African kingdoms of Dahomey and Ashantee are typical instances of such societies.

How is conduct regulated in such groups? We do not find any legislative bodies organised to enact laws, nor does the sovereign either by himself or through ministers declare any designed to affect the ordinary life of the people. The different tribes of the kingdom already, when conquered, had their customs, as we have seen, the silent growth of long periods of time, and these continue as before with all their sanctions. The tyrant could not change them, with all his power, even if he would, for, as we have seen, they are unchangeable except in the ways by which they were formed; but he does not wish to change them. All tyrants are unqualified advocates of the maintenance of things as they are. These barbarous sovereigns, indeed, are personally above the customs, and plunder, rob, and murder at their will. Their tyrannical authority is sustained by favour and fear, but public peace and order beneath them it is their interest to promote. The ancient customs are supported by the ancient sanctions, except in the case of slaves who are left at the mercy of their masters. There is indeed an additional sanction. The State is organised, although rudely. It has a political form; the sovereign and his subordinate chiefs are clothed with power in the bands of warriors whom they command, and the weak, when injured, appeal to them, and they enforce redress. Violations of custom are punished by the public authority, and thus a beginning is effected in the public redress of private injuries; in other words, what we know as the public administration of justice begins, although in a very crude form. But whether an act is a public crime, or a private injury, depends as before upon its conformity, or nonconformity, to custom. The advance, for such we must regard it, furnished by this new sanction of custom, is one of the results of the integration of small primitive tribes or hordes into a larger society, and, though effected by war and violence, is in itself beneficent. If we are to have absolute tyrannies, it is well when a number are swallowed up in one.

LECTURE II

TURNING now to the other division of early societies first exhibiting the beginnings of political organisation, namely, those characterised by peaceful dispositions, and which extend themselves, not by the conquest of adjacent tribes and their territories, we find, although not universally, tendencies towards democratic instead of monarchical organisation. This consists usually in the establishment of a council composed of elders of superior wisdom and moderation in which the public authority is lodged. We find examples of such societies among the barbarous tribes of Germany in early ages. Although nearly all these tribes possessed warlike qualities which made them formidable in battle, they did not engage in war generally for the sake of extending their own sway by the conquest of the territory of adjacent tribes, but for plunder, or retaliation, or glory, and some of them were naturally inclined to peace, not taking up arms except in defence against hostile attack. Other instances of substantially similar societies are found among the islanders of the Pacific, such as the Tahitans, the Tongas, the Samoans, and the inhabitants of the Sandwich Islands, although the external conditions are different.

The characteristics of these tribes are, in general, an increasing scarcity of wild game, the possession of a fruitful soil, yielding a large product for moderate labour, some increase in the density of the population and consequently some advance in co-operation by means of a division of employments and exchange of services. These conditions greatly enlarge the intercourse between individuals and multiply their relations with each other. The necessity thus arises for a more extended regulation of conduct. We do not, however, find that any new instrumentality is employed. No laws are made by the kings, or the local chiefs acting under their authority, or by councils composed of chiefs or elders. This cannot be wholly in consequence of ignorance of the art of writing, for laws orally promulgated may be enforced and may be perpetuated by tradition. The only way in which conduct is regulated at this stage is, as before, by custom. The change from the sparse numbers of primeval tribes living upon the natural fruits and products of the earth has been very slow and gradual, and as the changes occur new customs grow up to answer the new needs, but custom is still the only law. There is less and less resort to forceful and violent redress of injuries and more and more of appeal to public authority for justice. This justice is administered by various persons or bodies; sometimes by the King, sometimes by his officers surrounding him, sometimes by local chiefs, who have the government of districts, sometimes by a council of chiefs or elders. But in such cases they act judicially; the rights they enforce and the wrongs they redress are such as derive their character as rights or wrongs from the existing customs. There is now what did not exist in the wandering horde, a society more or less efficiently organised, and a public administration, however imperfect, of justice or rather something which points towards, and may eventually become, an administration of justice. These conditions have subsisted in many parts of the earth from our first acquaintance with them down to the present time. This earliest assumption of functions in their nature judicial by the chiefs or councils, in societies which have become somewhat settled and organised, does not, at once, supersede the other agencies by which violence and disorder were previously repressed, such as private vengeance, the unfriendly opinion of tribesmen, or the superstitious fear of evil coming from the ghosts or spirits of the departed, but it reinforces those agencies. Their united power in restraining conduct is often very great. Tacitus says, speaking of the German tribes, that their good customs were of greater power than the good laws of other people. "*Plusque ibi boni mores valent quam alibi bonæ leges.*"

Nor is there as yet any conception of justice other than as of an obligation to obey the injunction of custom and tradition which in most, if not in all, tribes is assumed to be imposed by some great ancestor or ancestors, or other disembodied spirits, exercising from an unseen world their authority over mundane affairs. The profoundest enquirers into the internal factors which make up the primitive man everywhere find a belief in the existence of a world other than thè visible one, inhabited by gods and demigods, and by the spirits of man's own ancestors as well—beings who hold and exercise a mysterious power over the lives and fortunes of the living. Offences against the customs and usages are offences against them, and from them proceed the commands to obedience. The interpreters of this Divine Will, sometimes under despotic rulers, were the king and the priesthood; in more democratic societies, the elders or wise men, together with the priesthood. This spiritual power is wielded by those who come to be regarded as in communication with the unseen world, and thus constitute a priesthood. They act in alliance with the public authority, and afford powerful assistance in the maintenance of peace and order.

Another feature, characteristic of this as well as of all the preceding social stages, while it operates in some ways to enlarge violence and make strife more deadly, yet on the whole restricts it. This is the family tie. The family appears as the unit of society. Its members stand by each other in all fortunes. If strife breaks out between some individuals of the family itself, the others compose it; but if a member of one family is slain by the member of another, or otherwise injured, the quarrel is taken up by the respective families, irrespective of right or wrong. Retaliation is the immediate impulse; homicide is offset by homicide; robbery by robbery; an eye for an eye and a tooth for a tooth is the maxim of action. We are not to suppose that all the members of a family welcomed the opportunity which an offence given by one of its number afforded to engage in strife with another family. On the contrary, these quarrels were so likely to result in bloodshed that they were dreaded, and the commission of an unprovoked injury which would compel the kinsmen of the guilty person to risk their lives in his defence was an injury also to the family to which he belonged. The family might punish him themselves, or even abandon him for punishment to the family he had wronged.

As the tribe becomes more settled, and industrial pursuits become more established, bringing with them some accumulations of property, some division of labour, some trade and commerce, and consequently some increased complexity in social life, the necessity for increased peace and order becomes more deeply felt, and the want can be supplied only by the adoption of some more peaceful method of redressing grievances. So long as there was little or no property, and disputes arose more from mere passion and accompanying violence, the intervention of the chieftain, or the priesthood, was probably the best agency for bringing about peace and order; but on the springing up of industry with its accompanying contractual relations and accumulations of property, new customs arise, and with them more distinct conceptions of what is due to one from another as the reward of service, and the want necessarily becomes felt of some more intelligent and just decision of controversies. When men enter into contractual relations with each other, *expecta-*

tions are immediately raised, and when these are disappointed trouble arises until some satisfactory redress is afforded. This can come only from a decision by those acquainted with the grounds of the dispute and able to decide it in such way as to afford reasonable satisfaction; in other words, from a decision by *experts*. What is demanded at this stage of human progress is, not some new *law*, for the conception even of legislation does not as yet exist, but some properly qualified *judge*, and some method of compelling the appearance of an adversary before him—that is to say, *a method of procedure*. An existing dispute between men must, of necessity, consist of a difference of opinion concerning the *conduct* which one is *entitled to expect* from the other, and the expectation of either party can be justified only by an appeal to what he supposes to be the *existing* rule or custom applicable to the case. Neither party will assert a *new* rule, for that would, of itself, condemn him. Accordingly we find that the first step in the way of improving the administration of justice is to establish a tribunal for the sole purpose of determining controversies. This is the beginning of Procedure, and *procedure* presupposes an already existing law, or something standing in the place of law, which is to be administered by it.

This stage of society, that of increasing industry with its accompanying trade and commerce, is also the one in which writing becomes necessary, and in which it is first found to be employed. Judicial tribunals could not, indeed, be so established as

to effectively answer their purpose without the aid
of writing, and therefore I shall roughly regard the
creation of such tribunals as nearly contempora-
neous with the introduction of the use of writing,
which, I believe, will be found upon historic inquiry
to be probable.

A conjecture of Blackstone is not unnatural that
the dominance of custom in the governing of conduct at the period under consideration may be
owing to the fact that there could be no written
law until the art of writing had been acquired, and
the existence of some very ancient codes, like the
laws of Solon, may suggest that as soon as men had
discovered an instrumentality by which they could
frame laws they employed it for the purpose of
providing themselves with more fixed and certain
rules of conduct than mere custom could supply.
But the conjecture seems not very probable, inasmuch as writing is supposed to have been known
about 1500 B. C.—many centuries prior to any
authenticated instance of its use in the making of
laws. It may, however, have been employed for
purposes the knowledge of which has not come down
to us; but the important question is, whether it
was employed for the purpose of supplanting custom. I must pause, therefore, to scrutinise the earliest well-known instances in which writing was
employed for the purposes of legislation, with the
view of seeing how far, if at all, this may have been
the object, or whether custom still remained, notwithstanding this new instrumentality, the only
source from which rules of conduct could be de-

rived. We may feel sure that if writing were ever in early times employed to supplant custom, that purpose would clearly appear in the most ancient codes of which we have any knowledge.

Omitting any reference to the Code of Draco, of which we know little or nothing, the first considerable employment of writing in the composition of laws was in Athens by Solon some time about the year 594 B.C. For a long period prior to this, Athens had been a large populous State, and had reached a high stage of civilisation. Its citizens were extensively engaged in commerce and in various forms of industry, and a regular government, with an archon, or archons, for chief rulers, had existed for several centuries. It was the age which just preceded the most glorious period of Grecian history, the period of Thermopylæ and Marathon. Moreover, intellectual cultivation had advanced to a considerable elevation. Thales was already indulging those philosophical speculations which two centuries later were carried forward with a power and subtlety never since surpassed, by Socrates, Plato, and Aristotle. In such a society, with such pursuits, the law of contract must find a most important place, and there is indeed occasion for a juristic system approaching, though not reaching, in extent and refinement that which we find in the advanced period of Roman civilisation, or in the cultivated societies of modern times.

What, then, was the principal motive which induced the people of Athens, under the guidance of Solon, to seek to embody their will in written lan-

guage? Was it that they believed that a law existing
only in the public consciousness and evidenced only
by custom, was insufficient for the ordinary purposes of civil society at the stage which society had
then reached, and that it was expedient that all
their customary rules of a juristic nature should be
reduced to written formulas, or was it that there
were special exigencies causing disturbances in
society and bringing customs into doubt and conflict,
and making it necessary, in some measure, to recon-
struct the social and political organism on some
basis of reconciliation? We shall find that the
latter of these two questions suggests the true answer.
Following what has just been said of the condition
of Athens at the time, we may add the observations
of an intelligent scholar upon the same points:

"It was a time of fermentation in society; Psammetichos
had opened the Nile region to the Greeks (B. C. 666); the first
money had been coined in Ægina; navigation took all at once
a gigantic stride forward; young adventurers gained in a few
years great riches, and those parts of the communities engaged in trade took form as a new middle class, and stood defi-
antly opposed to the ancient families; property in land was
outstripped by movable capital; around Athens on all sides—
in Argos, Corinth, Sicyon, Megara—the old system of things
had been broken, the ruling families had been overthrown,
and through the downfall of the constitutions single tyrants
had come to power, who shone by their riches, employed mer-
cenary troops, and pursued a narrow policy of self-aggrandise-
ment. In this revolutionary time, spite of all splendor, the
best possessions of the nation were endangered—namely, the
free citizen class and the sovereign authority of the law."[1]

[1] Ernst Curtius, in *Johnson's Encyclopædia*, sub verbo, "Solon."

All this indicates conflicts of custom in the interior of society, a destruction of that concurrence of public sentiment upon which the stability of custom reposes, and a social conflict which could be repressed only by overwhelming physical force, or by a reconciliation based upon popular assent.

Passing to the contents of the legislation of Solon, this view of the condition of society and of the purpose of the new laws is confirmed. Solon played the part of mediator between the contending parties. He lightened the burdens of the debtor class, enabling the poor to escape from the grinding tyranny of their creditors, took the political power from the ruling families which had theretofore exercised it, gave all citizens a share, though not an equal share, in the enactment of laws, redistributed the burdens of taxation, and generally gave a more democratic form to the political constitution of the State. All this imports a sudden settlement of pre-existing conflicts in popular customs, and one which can be effected in two ways only, either by over-powering force, or by social agreement, and in the latter case written law seems to be a necessary instrumentality. By no other means can the points agreed upon be defined by a permanent memorial to which appeal can be made at all subsequent times.

Turning now to the history of legislation in ancient Rome, we find that the earliest considerable employment of writing was in the enactment of what is known as the Twelve Tables, in the year 451 B.C., the 302nd year of the foundation of the city. The condition of Rome at that period resembled in many particulars that of Athens at the time of the enactment of the Code of Solon. Rome was a large and populous State with a government in many respects highly organised. It had a population of several hundred thousand, a large commerce, and a consequent minute division of employments and large aggregations of wealth. There was a large debtor class which shows that in the course of social development the stage of contract had long been reached. In every rude society from the first beginnings, the governing power, together with the administration of justice, is lodged either in a king or with the older and more prudent members. These, as society advances and wealth accumulates, become the most wealthy, and the powers of government, including the interpretation and enforcement of the customs, are naturally wielded more or less in favour of the interests with which they are lodged. It was so in a high degree in Rome, and this condition had been the source of dissatisfaction and unrest for a long time prior to the adoption of the Twelve Tables. The royal government, which under seven successive kings lasted two hundred and forty years, had been overthrown and a government somewhat republican in form, with Consuls as the chief magistrates, established in its place. The Consuls were, after a few years, displaced by a Dictator, and his authority was soon afterwards transferred to a body of ten called Decemvirs. The people were divided into two principal classes, the patricians and the plebeians, and the constant complaint of the latter was that the powers of government, both executive and judicial, being lodged with the patricians, were exercised in favour of their own order and to the oppression of the plebeians. The latter class had become so powerful and its frequent rebellions so dangerous that its demands could no longer pass unheeded, and the Decemvirs were charged with the duty of reorganising the political government and framing such laws as would reconcile the conflicting elements of the State. They were engaged in this work for two years, in the course of which they sent a commission to Athens to examine the governmental framework and the laws devised by Solon, and their work in the form of Ten Tables was accepted, and, with two additional ones, subsequently adopted, remained, professedly at least, the basis of the Roman jurisprudence until the age of Justinian.

The use of writing had, we may safely presume, been carried from Greece to her colonies soon after she had acquired it, and would thence pass easily to Rome. It must have been known in that city for centuries before the Twelve Tables, and there is reason to believe that during this period it was occasionally employed in the enactment of some particular laws, but the Twelve Tables were the first instance of its employment upon a considerable scale.

The important features of this review of the early legislation of Athens and Rome, to which I wish to call attention are these: First, that a high degree of social advancement, displaying large populations, division of employments, development of industry and commerce, and highly organised governments, was reached and maintained without the employment of written laws; second, that the chief motive of the first resort to such law was internal conflict among the different elements of the State threatening revolution, a conflict which could not be terminated except by the complete subjection, by overwhelming force, of one of the contending parties to the other, or by the faithful observance of a reconciling agreement. Such an observance would scarcely be possible unless the terms were permanently embodied in written law. Custom is effectual only when it is universal, or nearly so. In the absence of unanimity of opinion, custom becomes powerless, or rather does not exist.

I now return from this incidental consideration of the early employments of writing for the purposes of legislation to the further treatment of that stage of social progress marked by enlarging industries and consequent efforts to substitute in place of the violent redress of injuries the peaceful method of judicial tribunals, and the steps successively taken until the establishment of such tribunals. Any exact tracing of the progress, or of the order, in which the successive steps were taken would be impossible. In the civilisations of Greece and Rome the process had become far advanced at the time of the beginning of the known history of those nations; nor does the history of the States of modern Europe throw more than a feeble light upon the precise nature of this early process; but if we put together the scattered pieces of information which are still within our reach, and draw from them their full significance, we may trace the general features of the progress, and this is all that is necessary. The main difficulty in this study is to rid ourselves of the notion that in these remote times men had the same objects and interests in view and were moved by the same desires as we are conscious of ourselves. We may do something towards removing this obstacle by attempting to form a rude picture of early society, beginning with barbarian times, times even preceding those of increased industry, such a picture as all of them present with greater or less similitude, but which is best furnished to us by the accounts we have of the German tribes, our own ancestors. We are to imagine a tribe of men living in fixed habitations, and subsisting mainly by the rude cultivation of the earth. Substantial equality among the freemen is to some extent broken by the presence of some elevated above the others by superior prowess, or character, or accumulations, or the possession of priestly qualities, but there is a head of the tribe, an elected chief or king. There is no permanent political organisation for any public purpose. There are meetings, some regular, and others special, of the freemen, at which matters involving war or peace with neighbouring tribes and any other important matters interesting to the whole tribe are considered and determined. There are many slaves consisting chiefly of captured enemies, and their descendants, and the more powerful members of the tribe are usually those having the largest possessions of land and slaves. Property and marriage exist. The unit of the tribe is the family, the members of which live together and stand by each other. These institutions rest upon custom alone. There is no ethical conception of a *right* except some vague belief that some unseen power will punish one who violates custom. To plunder from the members of any neighbouring tribe is no crime. Custom, as the word itself imports, is generally obeyed, but there are frequent departures from it, and consequently much violence and turbulence among tribes composed of the more warlike men; but among the more peaceful groups the observance of custom may be even more complete than obedience to law in modern societies. The only security for person or property among those who are warlike is to let each man know that he can invade neither without losing his life or suffering punishment at the hands of him whom he injures. The path of safety is to follow custom. When this is done expectation is not disappointed and resentment is not provoked. Turbulence and strife arise from many causes; but the principal ones are: (1) the mere love of fighting, the disposition to quarrel upon slight offence, the passage from words to blows and weapons and consequent homicide. The family of the slain are angered and seek revenge upon the slayer who takes refuge in his own family, and they stand to their arms in defence. A pitched battle may ensue, and other lives be sacrificed, and a family feud occasioned which may not be cured for a generation. (2) Disputes about land. Titles, resting much upon occupancy or tradition, are subject to much doubt. One man charges another with being a trespasser and demands that he leave the disputed territory. A refusal is nearly certain and a fight to death ensues. (3) A man is found in guilty intimacy with the wife or daughter of another. An injury like this provokes instant vengeance. We have survivals in our own country at the present time of these ancient modes of redress.

But the progress of industrialism is not consistent with the retention of these methods. The man who has begun to long for increased possessions does not wish to keep himself and his retainers in arms to defend them, and he comes to dread the personal peril; and the one who labours has less leisure for quarrel. The desire for peace is more and more felt, but it must be "peace with honour." It must not be allowed to be thought that an injury can be inflicted with impunity. The point is how to get out of the trouble without fighting. The way to attempt it is obvious enough; it is not to *begin* fighting; in other words, to parley, and parleying means negotiation and possible compromise. This usually involves calling in the aid, or accepting the proffered intervention, of the bystanders or other third parties, and thus the efforts of many are enlisted to compose the strife. If a man has been slain in mutual combat provoked by both parties, the resentment is not so deep; but the family of the victim have a feeling that the slaughter of one of their members must be avenged. If they may save their honour without retaliation they are satisfied.

The payment of a sum of money or delivery of other property means that the aggressors have purchased peace from the friends of the victim and thus acknowledged their power. Accordingly, we find a custom established everywhere in barbarous society of the payment of a certain fixed sum by the family of one who has slain another to the family of the victim by way of compromise for the injury. It would be nearly true to say that we know of no race or tribe of men in the past who, or whose ancestors, in the case of civilised people, did not have this custom, or any now barbarous tribe which does not have it. We do not indeed find it in existence at the time of the earliest historical accounts of Greece and Rome which have been preserved to us; but those accounts do not reach back to the really barbarous times of those nations. The Laws of Solon and the Twelve Tables of Rome were regulations for peoples who had for centuries emerged from a state of barbarism, but we can not doubt that if light were thrown upon the antecedent periods we should find that this method of composing strife and preventing bloodshed preceded, among them, the selection of magistrates to declare and execute law.[1] There are in the poems of Homer many evidences that such was the fact, and lexicographers inform us that the Greek word ποινή and the Latin *poena* originally signified the price, or composition, by which crime was expiated. The Germans, our own ancestors, were found in this condition of barbarism within historic times, and Tacitus informs us that all crimes were

[1] Koenigswärter, *Développement de la Société Humaine* Part ii., ch. i.

compounded by the payment of cattle.[1] The annals of the Jews do not carry us back to the times when they were barbarians, yet that the practice of compounding was once prevalent among them is manifest from passages in the old scriptural writings.[2] Among the savages and barbarians of our own day, the custom of individuals or families to avenge their own wrongs and to accept compensation as the price of forbearance may be said to be universal. Mr. Alexander Sutherland, in his interesting and valuable work entitled *The Origin and Growth of the Moral Instinct*, has especially pointed out the payment of compensation for violent injuries as being the first step from the indulgence of retaliative vengeance towards a more peaceful redress. He says: "Somewhere about the level of the higher savages, or more generally of the lower barbarians, the increase of settled life, and the possession of huts and crops liable to destruction in war, produce a greater appreciation of the advantages of peace. Feuds are now avoided by the payment of compensation. According to Morgan (*League of the Iroquois*, p. 331), if an Iroquois committed a murder, a feud was at once established between the two families, unless, as was sometimes done, the relatives of the murderer refused to stand by him; or unless, as was far more often the case, they agreed to make a payment in wampum or other property, to the family of the murdered man. Galton tells us that among the Damaras a murder will commence a feud unless the family of the mur-

---

[1] *Germania*, 12. [2] Num. xxxv., 19.

derer pays two oxen to that of the person slain. Of the Maoris, Thomson says (i., 123): 'Revenge was one of a chief's first duties; an insulted New Zealander would rush to his tribe and relate the injury he had suffered; then, if payment were refused, war might ensue.' Land and women were the chief causes of strife. They were cautious of rushing into wars, and in every dispute mediations were gladly accepted until blood was actually shed. Every offence but murder had some pecuniary equivalent.

"Guinnard states that the Patagonians (or Araucanians) 'put to death the enemies of a slain person, unless they agree to pay a heavy ransom,' (p. 179) and among all the more primitive negro races, with no exceptions that I have noticed, murder can be atoned for with a sufficient payment. Brookes says that among the Dyaks the ordinary compensation for murder is worth about eight pounds sterling; and St. John says that adultery is compounded for by a customary fine to the family that has been aggrieved. Some barbarian races, more vindictive or less avaricious than others, are with greater difficulty induced to forego the blood penalty for a payment; but there is none, so far as I know, in which it is not more or less customary to accept compensation and avoid a feud." Mr. Sutherland's book, which fell under my notice when I had nearly completed these lectures, contains a very instructive chapter on "The Growth of Law"[1] from which the above passage is taken and in which I am glad to find a confirmation of my own views.

[1] Vol. ii., p. 163.

Prof. Cherry, in his lectures upon *The Growth of the Criminal Law in Ancient Communities*, compares the stage of barbarism in four ancient peoples widely separated in time and geographical situation, and finds in each of them the same practice of redressing injuries by private retaliation, or self-help, tempered by composition on the payment of a ransom. These four peoples, some of them embracing large parts of the human race, were the ancient Irish, the Hebrews, the Mahometans, and the early English. He might have included in the range of his observation numerous societies of barbarians now living in which the same methods of repressing internal strife are employed.

But the evidences are numberless, and the fact may be regarded as universal and admitted.[1] Nowhere does the practice appear more conspicuously than among the barbarian conquerors of Western Europe, including England. That it was the only, or principal, form in which violence and crime were repressed is manifest from the fact that the Laws of the Barbarians are, to a very large extent, occupied in enumerating the various compensations which are to be paid for injuries done to person or property, and the Laws of Alfred present the same feature.

But it must not be supposed that the custom of accepting compensation, even when the amounts were fixed by what was called the law, such as the Laws of the Barbarians and of Alfred just mentioned, really amounted to what is properly called *law*.

[1] The chapter in Koenigswärter contains the fullest information. Part ii., ch. i.

These so-called laws were not *laws* in the modern
sense of written law—that is, *commands* which
would be enforced by the State in a formal manner.
Of such law there was at the time none, because
there were no tribunals to declare, interpret, and
enforce it. The very fact that the compensation
was resorted to as the only means of preventing
violence and bloodshed is complete proof that no
other law than private vengeance or self-help
existed. If any tribe or people had the power to
compel the acceptance of compensation for murder,
it would have had power to prohibit murder directly
and to enforce the prohibition by effective punishment. The object of the laws fixing the amount of
the *wergild* was to supply an indefiniteness of custom.
Inasmuch as the compensation was the fruit of a
parleying between the combatants, there would be
contention about the amount, and such amount
would exhibit wide differences according to the
nature of the offence and the character of the
parties. Where there was a willingness to accept
a compensation there would still remain a difference
about the nature and amount of it. The aggrieved
party could honourably accept an amount provided
it was fixed by some one other than his adversary.
The laws just mentioned assumed to determine the
sums for every description of offence, and this decision would be eagerly accepted by a party who
wished to save himself the peril of deadly strife,
and thus the amounts, with the aid of the laws,
would come to be established by custom. Compensation, therefore, was no certain preventative of

violence. It was the recognised right of the injured party to refuse to accept it, if he chose; and what would then happen? Manifestly as the attempt to prevent a fight had failed, it must take place, and the parties must stand up for it. The *right* of a party to redress an alleged wrong by his own arm is evident from the fact that when all efforts for a pacification had failed, rules were made for conducting the inevitable fight. This was the origin of the judicial trial by battle, of which Gibbon says: "It was not as a mode of proof that the combat was received, but in every case the right to offer battle was founded on the right to pursue by arms the redress of an injury." However, with the progress of industrialism the effort to prevent violence would increase, and if an injured party refused to be pacified after his adversary had offered the customary redress, the remonstrances of the fellow-tribesmen would be employed, and if these failed, intimations, or a plain declaration, would follow that the tribe was determined upon peace, and if the obstinate party persisted in his purpose, he would encounter a force which would render the strife dangerous only to himself. He must do something, and the question is what he shall do. There is but one answer to this: he must leave it to some third person to say what he shall do, and this is *arbitration*, the sole possible resort which the parties to a deadly strife can have, and preserve the point of honour, when one refuses to accept the redress offered by another, and is made aware that persistence in his purpose to take revenge upon another will cost him a sacrifice he is not willing to make. This is a lesson which has been taught to contending individuals or families through many ages in the past. Nations are beginning now to learn it.

The person or persons selected as arbitrator or arbitrators would of course be of the class supposed to be grave, impartial, and familiar with the customs, for it would be expected that the decision would be based upon comparing the conduct of the disputants with the established customs. This arbitration of quarrels is a near approach to the establishment of a court. All that needed to be added to constitute a court was to create permanent arbitrators and compel disputants to keep the peace and provide a mode by which they should be forced to submit their differences to the decision of the tribunal. That judicial tribunals came to be established by taking this step is open to little doubt; but a long period was occupied in reaching the end. Why was it that an expedient apparently so obvious was not more speedily adopted? Simply for the reason that it is a direct advance abolishing *self-help* by substituting public help; and this requires the conscious action of society as a corporate whole. It must have a corporate will and a corporate power—that is, it must become a living intelligent organism. Some individual, or some selected individuals, must be capable of commanding the physical force of the body of society, must be able to contribute methods of compulsory arbitration, and have the power needed to enforce them. This condition will not arise until the demand for it becomes sufficiently strong, but the demand will come as soon as the industrial spirit seeking increased possessions and more perfect peace in order to increase them, and to hold them, has created the social conviction of a necessity for the improvement. The step may be facilitated by accident. War with neighbouring tribes may bring forth a military chief who will be able to make his power permanent and thus erect himself into a king or civil chieftain, or a civil council may be voluntarily chosen, and a head thus given to society capable of discerning and supplying public needs; but such as these can not originate out of their own heads a scheme of improvement and impose it upon society regardless of custom. There are no Law-givers such as are reverenced in history. Moses, Lycurgus, and Solon took the customs of their time, and gave them form and furnished better methods of securing their enforcement. Solon, according to Plutarch, when asked why he did not give the Athenians better laws, answered that he gave them the best they were fitted to receive. Niebuhr informs us that "no one in the ancient world took it into his head to make a new system of laws. In the Middle Ages, also, a legislation merely springing from the will of a law-giver is scarcely to be traced anywhere"; and the same view is well expressed by Coulanges, who says "that legislators did not exist among the ancients. Nor did ancient law originate with the votes of the people. In early days the laws present themselves as something even then venerable and unchangeable."[1]

[1] Coulanges, *The Ancient City*, p. 250.

For obvious reasons, as already observed, the passage from self-help, including arbitration, can not be traced in the history of Greece or Rome. At the times to which our earliest accounts of those nations reach, courts of some description were already established, the age of barbarism having been long anterior, but the description of the *Legis Actio Sacramenti*, the most antique form of Roman procedure, and the parent form of all subsequent civil actions, as preserved to us in the Institutes of Gaius, bears upon its face the marks of its origin. The form of proceeding is thus described by Prof. Maine: "Two armed men are wrangling about some disputed property. The Prætor, *vir pietate gravis*, happens to be going by, and interposes to stop the contest. The disputants state their case to him, and agree that he shall arbitrate between them."[1] The *Legis Actio Sacramenti* was compulsory, but the record in it, embracing the above statement, clearly shows that the Prætor, the Judge, was the successor of a private citizen to whom two disputants had voluntarily submitted their difference.

The corresponding stage in the social history of Western Europe is, for similar reasons, enveloped in equal obscurity. History affords rare and obscure glimpses of the details of life, although there are large masses of documentary matter still unexamined which would probably furnish much additional light. But such evidences as are available agree in making it probable that the first step in repressing the private redress of wrongs among Western Euro-

[1] *Ancient Law*. p. 376

pean peoples was in bringing about an arbitration of quarrels. Prof. Maine has pointed out a very significant correspondence between the functions of the Druids as described by Cæsar in his *Commentaries on the Gallic War* and those of the ancient Brehons as they are revealed in the translations of the ancient so-called "Irish Laws" published not many years ago. Cæsar informs us—I give the language of Prof. Maine—

that the Druids were supreme judges in all public and private disputes; and that, for instance, all questions of homicide, of inheritance, and of boundary were referred to them for decision, . . . that the Druids presided over schools of learning to which the better youth flocked eagerly for instruction, remaining in them sometimes (so he was informed) for twenty years.

Prof. Maine further says, referring to the newly published "Law-Tracts," relating to the ancient laws of Ireland :

The extensive literature of law just disinterred testifies to the authority of the Brehons in all legal matters, and raises a strong presumption that they were universal referees in disputes. Among their writings are separate treatises on inheritance and boundary, and almost every page of the translation contains references to the 'eric' fine for homicide.

We have here convincing proof that in the widely separated divisions of the Celtic societies at substantially the same social stage there was a class of persons who made the customs of their peoples the subject of especial study and were habitually employed as arbitrators in disputes. This employment of arbitrators must have been voluntary, for there was, at the time, no organised society capable of enacting laws or contriving other social arrangements. The Brehon laws, so-called, do not purport to be the enactments of any public authority, but collections of the legal maxims and rules adopted by the Brehons in performing the judicial functions voluntarily bestowed upon them. The fact that among these ancient peoples there were *classes* of persons devoting themselves solely to what may be called the law—that is, the rules and customs observed by their tribes, proves that there was a demand for their knowledge and services as the arbiters of disputes, and that such demand had existed for long periods. They could have no authority except such as was derived from the assent of disputants, and such assent must have been habitually given; for otherwise there would not have arisen the demand for such a class. The custom, therefore, was brought about of displacing the bloodshed and violence of self-help with the peaceful method of arbitration. The fair inference is that all the well disposed of the tribes resorted to these customary methods of settling disputes, and that those who refused to do so were those vicious and depraved members who habitually defied custom—that is, the lawless class. Arbitration could not be literally *compelled*, for its very existence implied that there was no organised public authority which could compel anything; but custom supplied a powerful force in bringing it about, and other compelling influences were added to custom. Among the Celtic tribes described by Cæsar, if a disputant refused to obey the decision of a Druid he was, as Sir

Henry Maine gathers, *excommunicated*, by which we are to understand that he was excluded from the protection and shut off from the fellowship of his tribe, and this substantially made him an outlaw, which was regarded as the severest of penalties. Where the rule of the priesthood is strong, as it was among the tribes of Gaul, and must necessarily be where the priests exercise judicial functions, this deprivation of privileges operates as a heavy punishment. The Brehons do not appear, at least after the conversion of the Irish to Christianity, to have been a priestly class; but they were always closely allied to the chief or king of the clan, and could bring their influence to aid in enforcing their decisions.

There is less evidence of the settlement of quarrels by arbitration among the German tribes and the other ancestors of the English people. There was originally among the Germans what stood for a rough public administration of justice by those popular assemblies which seem to have been universal among those tribes. Our knowledge of their customs is derived mainly from the *Germania* of Tacitus, and he informs us that these assemblies took cognizance of all judicial matters. There could have been little uncertainty in the enforcement of the judgments of these bodies. Their authority was unlimited. Every freeman was bound to be present, and could be obliged to answer any complaint. The rude clashing of shields and brandishing of spears in the hands of the judges, which announced a decision, sufficiently indicated that it must be unhesitatingly obeyed. It may well be imagined that such a body would listen to no trifling complaints, and that self-help must still be the main reliance for defence against minor injuries, and also that the parties to any important dispute who preferred not to fight would exhaust every means of pacification, including arbitration by a third person, before they provoked the rough justice of armed warriors. The German conquerors of England of course carried their customs with them, and we find the Court of the Hundred, the legitimate successor of the popular assembly, the first well-known judicial institution in the history of England. It there exchanged its tribal for a territorial jurisdiction, and until the further integration of society under a more complete recognition of royal power it was the chief method for avoiding the violence of self-help by the substitution of judicial action. But the rude instrumentality of a popular court constituted of the great body of freemen, is a very insufficient guaranty of that peace and order which advancing industrialism requires. It may punish great offences, but the minor wrongs will still be left unredressed, except by private punishment, and while this may moderate and tend to repress the worst forms of violence, no general peace can be brought about except by producing peace in small localities, and this can be done only through the instrumentality of a political organisation of localities providing means by which quarrels and disturbances may be prevented; in other words, courts must be brought into existence, and voluntary arbitration be superseded by the exercise of compulsory jurisdiction.

LECTURE III

IN giving a general view of early judicial tribunals, I can best direct attention to England, partly because I have never studied this part of the history of other nations, and partly because the course of social progress elsewhere has not, as I suppose, in substance been different from that exhibited in England. To make this view intelligible we must glance at the general condition of society at the time.

The tribal organisation of the Anglo-Saxon conquerors, such as had obtained in the forests of Germany, had become superseded, and that equality in the holding and enjoyment of the land which was one of the features of that organisation, had passed away with it. England was a conquered country. It had been acquired by the skill and valour of bands of warriors, and a great part of the land, as happens in all such cases, was awarded to the victors in proportions assumed to correspond to the various degrees of rank and worth. The leader of the host became the king and received the largest share; next came those of noble birth, or superior prowess, who composed his immediate retinue, the thanes or nobles, to whom extensive awards were made; and lastly, the common warriors. These, with the remnants of the vanquished Britons, became the people of England. At first there were several kingdoms, but these were eventually consolidated, as a consequence of war, into one. In place of the tribal organisation a territorial one was established embracing the whole kingdom, and this constituted a unity of which the king was the head. His power did not, however, like that of a Roman emperor, extend to the making of laws. The traditions of the personal independence of the German tribes still remained, and no unacceptable authority under the name of law could be enforced by the king against the powerful thanes, the great landholders of the kingdom, without the aid of a standing army such as he did not possess. Industry, although it had become greatly extended beyond that of a barbarian tribe, was still very limited, the principal occupation being that of the cultivation of the land. Of education and knowledge there was scarcely any. England had become Christianised, and with it the authority of the Catholic Church had been extended over the land, and whatever there was of learning at the time was mainly to be found among the members of the priesthood. The actual condition of society was principally determined by the nature of the ownership of the land. The large proprietors cultivated large portions, and committed the possession of other large portions to tenants for cultivation by them, for rents or other services. Those who had no land, villeins, or slaves, were the tillers of the soil. Any such occupation of land is essentially feudal in its nature, although it may lack the precise forms which strict feudalism exhibited as it developed itself on the continent. The land-owners were the men of independence and power. The landless were dependent upon them for their support, and for nearly everything else. Their condition approached that of slavery, and many of them were slaves. All the responsibilities of society devolved upon the landholding class, and it really ruled whether with or without the instrumentality of courts. The large landholder exercised an authority of a paternal nature over his tenants and workmen; and when the rigid feudal system became established, he wielded it through the instrumentality of a seignorial court, such as the court baron in England after the Norman Conquest. Violence and its accompanying crimes, theft and robbery, such as a society advancing out of barbarism first seeks to repress, were committed principally among the lower classes, and the business of the courts, such as we find established, consisted in efforts to repress and punish these. The same condition which has been found in the early history of all known nations was exhibited here. As has been observed by Prof. Maine, the first step in the public enforcement of law is the constitution of some sort of a tribunal with something in the nature of a procedure for the punishment of offences. These rude tribunals we find established in the earliest history of England, in the principal divisions of the territory. There was the Court of the Hundred, and the Court of the County, and perhaps other petty tribunals. Of the precise origin of these courts we have no knowledge, and but little of their actual constitution and proceedings. We know of no legislation or other public act creating them. Certain persons, the sheriffs and other

officials and the whole body of free landholders, were
required to attend them, and were called the suitors.
They constituted the judges.   Over these tribunals
the King exercised some supervision, exerted principally through the sheriffs, who were his officers.
There was little of purely private litigation, for there
was as yet but a feeble development of civil rights,
and this little mainly arose out of disputes concerning the possession of land.   Other business than that
of a judicial nature was transacted at these courts,
such as the making of transfers of land.   There were
no professed lawyers attending them, and their proceedings were extremely rude and simple.

Besides these local tribunals, the King himself held
a court.   The head of a State must necessarily be
the fountain of justice, and, after the establishment
of courts, the final arbiter in all important disputes.
The King's Court, as we first find it, was held at no
particular place, but wherever he might be.   It was
held by the King himself, or by some high official
deputed by him.   It punished any crime committed
in his presence or upon his lands, and it took cognisance of all controversies voluntarily submitted to
him.   The great nobles and landholders were not
inclined to submit their disputes to the rude local
tribunals held by ignorant men, but the King's Court
possessed an authority and dignity which commanded their respect.

No radical change in the constitution of these
courts was effected at once by the Norman Conquest.
The introduction of the feudal system brought with
it the establishment of the baronial courts, and the

privilege of holding these and courts of the manor was very often embraced in grants of land by the King; but the jurisdiction of these was confined to the particular manors or baronies, and to disputes between the tenants living upon them relating to the land and probably to some petty offences.

The important question which concerns us is, What was the *law* administered in these tribunals and where was it to be found? The answer is very plain. It was *custom*. There was as yet no legislation, and consequently no *written* law. Nor were there any judicial precedents which could be invoked, nor any treatises of writers of greater or less authority concerning the law. Some of the great ecclesiastics attached to the court may have had some knowledge of ecclesiastical law and through that, of the Roman law, but this could be of but little direct use in the disposition of the matters brought before tribunals other than the King's Court. All complaints by one man against another, whether of a civil or criminal nature, arose from the fact that something had been done *contrary to the complainant's expectation of what should have been done;* and as every man expects that others will act according to custom, the complaint would be in fact, if not in form, that an act contrary to custom had been committed to the injury of the complainant. If the party against whom the complaint was made denied the accusation, he necessarily asserted that what he did was in compliance with custom. The dispute therefore necessarily turned, if the act was admitted or established, upon the question what the custom was, and these rude tribunals held by the principal and most intelligent men were well adapted to determine that question. The judges in these acted in accordance simply with their sense of what was right, which was necessarily determined by what they thought to be customary. The great institution of property already existed, not by virtue of legislative creation, but it had grown up as a consequence of the customary action of men long before the establishment of any court. The goods and chattels which any man held he was permitted to hold in peace, because such was the custom, and because every one knew and felt that if he should attempt to take them it would cost him a fight, and an unsuccessful one, inasmuch as all the social forces, rude as they were, would be found on the side of the possessor. So also with the security of the person. Men refrained from attacking and injuring others, because such was the habit, and an infringement of it would bring punishment upon the offender. And the same thing was true of the institution of the family and the rights growing out of that. None of these rights grew originally out of the establishment of courts, or any other exercise of governmental power; on the contrary, courts came into existence for the purpose of affording better protection to them. Custom, therefore, at this stage of social progress is, as we have found it to be in the preceding stages, the only law.

This view is confirmed by the legal antiquarians who have sought to discover by direct inquiry the original sources of our law. Blackstone says, speaking of the early laws by which society in England was governed:

"I therefore style these parts of our law *leges non scriptæ*, because their original institution and authority are not set down in writing, as acts of parliament are, but they receive their binding power, and the force of laws, by long and immemorial usage, and by their universal reception throughout the kingdom. In like manner as Aulus Gellius defines the *jus non scriptum* to be that which is *tacito et illiterato hominum consensu et moribus expressum*." [1]

He further informs us that

"about the beginning of the eleventh century there were three principal systems of laws prevailing in different districts. 1. The *Mercen-Lage*, or Mercian Laws, which were observed in many of the midland counties, and those bordering upon the principality of Wales, the retreat of the ancient Britons; and therefore probably intermixed with the British or Druidical customs. 2. The *West-Saxon-Lage*, or Laws of the West Saxons, which obtained in the counties to the south and west of the island, from Kent to Devonshire. These were probably much the same with the Laws of Alfred above mentioned, being the municipal law of the far most considerable part of his dominions, and particularly including Berkshire, the seat of his peculiar residence. 3. The *Dane-Lage*, or Danish Law, the very name of which speaks its original and composition. This was principally maintained in the rest of the midland counties, and also on the eastern coast, the part most exposed to the visits of that piratical people." [2]

Out of these three laws, Roger Hoveden and Ranulphus Castrensis inform us, King Edward the Confessor extracted one uniform law or digest of laws, to be observed throughout the whole kingdom, and the author of an old manuscript chronicle assures us likewise that this work was projected and begun by his grandfather, King Edgar. And, indeed, a general digest of the same nature has been constantly found

[1] *Bl. Com.*, bk. i., p. 64   [2] Ibid., p. 65.

expedient, and therefore put in practice by other great nations, which have been formed from an assemblage of little provinces, governed by peculiar customs."[1]

Blackstone further says: "These" (the laws or customs above mentioned) "are the laws which gave rise and original to that collection of maxims and customs which is now known by the name of the common law."[2] I do not concur in the opinion of Blackstone that our present common law rests entirely upon these ancient customs, but I cite the passages to show that, in the opinion of a profound student of the history of our law, these customs were the only law administered or known by the courts at the time of their establishment.

The next period to which I shall call attention is that embracing the improvement and perfection of legal tribunals. I need not say that this work of improvement must proceed *pari passu* with social progress. That progress is manifested in increasing peace, order, and industry. Such increase involves new forms of conduct, new conceptions of right, and demands better methods of legal enforcement, and such better legal methods in turn react upon, improve, and advance the conceptions of right.

There were several modes in which these tribunals in England were improved and perfected. The improvement, of course began at the top, and the impulses received there were communicated throughout the system. In the first place, itinerant justices came to be appointed by the King, who journeyed

---

[1] Roger Hoveden, p. 66.   [2] Ibid., p. 67.

throughout the realm, and took cognisance of the proceedings in the courts and of the sheriffs and other officials. These judges were selected from the retinue of officials surrounding the King, and were often men of considerable learning and skill. They compelled a better performance by the inferior courts of their functions, and served to give instruction to the judges holding them. In the next place, the King's Court itself, held by the most learned men of the time, some of whom were of really superior abilities, continually enlarged its sphere of action by assuming a larger original jurisdiction over controversies and developed into branches which eventually became the several courts known in later times as the Exchequer, King's Bench, and Common Pleas. Whatever was done in the King's Court was everywhere recognised, followed, and obeyed, and what was called the *custom of the King's Court* became everywhere accepted as law. Again, the advance of society constantly developed new forms of conduct founded upon new convictions of right, and this created a demand for new action by the courts in the way of relief. At first the forms in which relief was obtained were very few, and to meet the new demands it was necessary to devise new forms. This was done in some instances by ordinances of the King and his Council, such as the celebrated Assize of Clarendon, out of which arose several forms of action, the principal of which was the Assize of Novel Disseisin. This furnished for one who had been wrongfully ejected from his lands an easy means of recovering the possession without resort to force. Such improvement was in the nature of legislation. But the principal means by which the administration of justice was improved was by the device of the issue of new writs under the authority of the King, through which new or more complete judicial relief was obtained. Where a sense of right had become clear, that is, where custom had become fixed and clear, but there was no form of action adequate to give effect to it, application was made to the royal authority reposed in the Chancellor. It was there considered, and if it seemed well founded, that is, if the case was one in which relief ought to be granted, a writ was devised which required a court to take cognisance of the case. The issuance of such a writ was practically tantamount to a new determination of law, and the complainant under it received relief upon proof of the facts upon which it was granted. New writs of this character were from time to time issued, each constituting some new cause of action, until the list became exceedingly numerous, and a case could scarcely arise in which an injury could not be judicially redressed. The assumption by the Chancellor of judicial functions in the direct cognisance and hearing of controversies for which no suitable writ at the common law could be framed completed the system of judicial relief.

There was another very important method of procedure which has given to English law, in my estimation, a certain measure of superiority. By degrees, the pleadings in actions became so framed as to lead to the clear and separate ascertainment of matters of *fact* to be tried and determined by a jury. This enables the judge to consider calmly and without distraction what the law is arising upon a given state of facts, and leads to the creation of an orderly system of the Law of Evidence.

In these modes, the principal of which I have indicated, the rude tribunals of England and the system of procedure in them were improved until they reached the condition in which we find them there and in this country three centuries ago. The time occupied in this improvement was more than three centuries, but the particular question to which I direct attention is—What was the law and where was it to be found, which these tribunals recognised and enforced during this period? The answer, I apprehend, must still be the same. It was custom, and custom alone. It must have been so, inasmuch as there was no other source from which the law could be derived. There was no legislation creating law, or next to none. An occasional enactment, like the article in the Great Charter, that no one should be deprived of his freedom without the judgment of his peers, may be found, but for the great bulk of the law administered in these tribunals during the period under consideration, no source or authority can be found save that of custom. It is indeed the period in which judicial precedents come to be known and regularly followed, but what was precedent in the first instance? It was simply a judicial declaration of custom, and it was followed, not so much because it was precedent, but because it was satisfactory evidence of custom. A precedent is but *authenticated* custom. It is like the coin of the realm. It bears the public stamp which evidences its genuineness.

5

We accept a coined piece of gold, not in reality because it bears the public stamp, but because it is believed, from the stamp, that it contains a certain quantity of gold. Its currency would at once be lost if there were no certainty upon this point. The characteristic in early and rude societies—it is so to a much less extent in enlightened society—is that customs, in many respects, are not settled and are in conflict. A judicial decision determines them so far as it extends. If it be a correct one—that is, if the true custom is chosen, (and by true I mean the one most consistent with the largest usage), it is accepted, and conduct is regulated accordingly, and the conflicting practices are discredited and pass away. This is the reaction of the judicial power upon custom, one of the great instrumentalities of social progress. At this stage, therefore, of our investigation, custom is still the law.

We now come to the last stage in our inquiry concerning what has actually governed the conduct of men in society. This is the stage of full enlightenment, such as is exhibited in Europe and the United States at the present day, when the legal tribunals whose progress I have been tracing have reached a condition of high development and efficiency. It is the stage of high development in industry and the arts of social life. Our immediate point of attention is the character of these tribunals and the actual nature of the work they perform. I take up for examination the courts of England and the United States, for the reason that we are best acquainted with them, and because we may be sure that the condition of courts in other countries, however varying from that of these, is not fundamentally different.

We find that they are of various sorts, according to the matters of which they take cognisance, and according as they exercise an original or appellate jurisdiction. We find them held by men who have received a special professional education in the law and who possess in general the highest character for ability, learning, and integrity. We find also a class of lawyers of similar education who attend to the interests of the suitors seeking the judgment of the tribunals, and whose business it is to endeavour to persuade the judges of the rightfulness of the conduct of their clients in the cases brought before the courts for adjudication. And we find these courts taking cognisance both of controversies between individuals and controversies between individuals and the State. Their judgments, except when held in suspense by appeal, stand as the voice of the law, and the execution of them is enforced, when necessary, by the physical power of the State. We find among the instrumentalities employed, both by the judges and lawyers, to aid them in their duties, many thousands of volumes of Reports of previous proceedings in the courts of various jurisdictions, in recent and prior times, and other thousands of volumes of treatises professing to expound and make known the law.

Looking at the prodigious amount of matter contained in all these volumes, of what do we find it to consist? It consists, first and mainly, of statements of the whole mighty multitude of the transactions, that is, of the conduct, of men in their relations and dealings with each other, so far as those transactions have been made the subject of controversy during a period extending backwards for centuries, and of the judgments of the courts pronounced thereon; and, secondly, of the statements of the conduct of men in their relations, not with each other individually, but with the general body of society, so far as such conduct has been challenged for illegality, and of the judgments thereon. The matter first described will be recognised as pertaining to what is called *Private Law*, and that secondly described as pertaining to what is called *Public Law*.

Reserving for the moment, the consideration of the matter falling under the head of Public Law, and directing our attention to Private Law alone, we find, upon looking into the reasons given for the particular judgments pronounced by the courts, that a large number of them declare that the particular transactions described are like, or substantially like, some other transactions which had previously engaged the attention of the courts and had been decided in a particular way, and the like decision is therefore made in the particular case under consideration; in other words, the case is decided by an appeal to known precedent, or to known precedents. Now the precedent, or precedents, thus invoked as the ground of decision we know to have been, in the first instance, the approval and enforcement of some existing custom of men having no force or authority except from the fact that it was a custom, and therefore we perceive that the decisions made upon the basis of precedents were really made upon no other basis than that of *authenticated* custom. The operation, therefore, of the tribunals has consisted simply in scrutinising the features of the transactions and placing them in some already determined class in which they belonged, the judgment pronounced being nothing but the legal consequence of the fact that they belonged to a particular class.

Each of these precedents is, in effect, an assertion that the law arising upon a state, or grouping, of facts, such as that presented by the precedent, is what the court pronounces it to be. This state of facts has been determined either by the agreement of the parties, as where a defendant demurs to the declaration or complaint of the plaintiff, or where a jury has found what the fact is. These various groupings of fact, thus presented by the various transactions which have been drawn into question, we find, on consulting the digests and treatises in which they are arranged, to be very numerous, and to embrace examples of most of the ordinary transactions of life, and as they are arranged in classified order in such books, it is easy in most instances of dispute to find a class of cases which the disputed case so nearly resembles that it is properly disposed of at once by declaring that the same rule of law applies to it as that which distinguishes the class to which it belongs, and, be it observed, all the particular cases fall under one or the other of two ultimate classes composed, the one, of things *approved*, and the other of things *condemned*, by the law. Now we find that cases are continually occurring of transactions which appear to resemble in most of their features an already established class, but which have some new feature not belonging to such class, and never before presented, and which, it is urged before the court, calls for a different disposition. Let us suppose that an action is brought upon a policy of marine insurance to recover for the loss of a ship by a peril of the sea. It is proved that the insured had private intelligence that there had been very heavy weather on the seas over which his ship was sailing, and that he procured his policy without disclosing his information. Now I am speaking of proceedings in court at the present time, but I may suppose, for the sake of the illustration, that this was the first occasion upon which the effect of *concealment* in the law of insurance arose. If there had never been any custom that the applicant for insurance of a marine risk disclosed, at the time of the application, whatever knowledge he had of matters material to the risk, the defence of concealment would have been to no purpose, and the underwriters would have been condemned to pay the loss; but in the case supposed, the insurer proves that underwriters had so long been in the practice of asking what knowledge the applicant for insurance had concerning the vessel he wished to insure, that applicants had been in the habit of communicating their knowledge, whether asked or not, and that all underwriters acted upon the supposal that they possessed all the information the applicant had received. The court leaves the case to the jury with the instruction that if they find that there was a custom of disclosing material facts such as alleged, they find a verdict for the defendant, otherwise for the plaintiff, and this ruling is approved by a court on appeal, and a precedent is thus created which will afterwards be followed. This precedent, it will be observed, created a new class. The contract contained in the policy belonged to the class of actions approved by the law, that is, to the class of contracts, and the obligation of these rested upon no ground, originally, other than that of custom. I know of no reason why men were in the first instance compelled to perform their contracts except that such performance was in accordance with custom. It has often been said by the most approved writers that custom is *one* of the sources of law, and indeed Blackstone views the body of our unwritten law as being custom, or founded upon custom; but the sort of custom thus intended is *ancient* custom, reaching so far back that its beginning is not known. Such a limitation of custom in the making of law seems to me to be without foundation, and the object in giving the last illustration is to show that *present* custom, provided it is established, is as efficient as if it were centuries old. But I must endeavour to make this still more clear. Let me take the example of a second succeeding action in all respects like the one just under notice, except that the information concealed was derived from widespread public accounts of a great hurricane. The underwriter claims exemption from liability on the ground of concealment, and relies upon the decision made in the former case. The insured insists that the former case should not be regarded as a governing precedent, for the reason that this one presents a new feature which effectually distinguishes and takes it from the class of contracts of insurance invalid because of concealment, or rather prevents it from being assigned to that class. He is asked if he has any evidence to prove that it is not customary to disclose notorious facts, and he answers that he has none; that the question has never before arisen. Here we reach a very interesting point in considering the question what law is, and where and how it is found, or, as some say, *made*—at all events how it comes to be known. We are at the very bottom of the matter and considering an operation which is going on every day before our eyes and subject to the clearest observation. Our closest attention should therefore be given to what is really done. The court, we may suppose on appeal, remarks that the case is novel, and must be decided upon *principle*—a vague expression, but correct enough. It says it can hardly see how the underwriter can justly claim exemption; true, the assured failed to disclose his information, but the only effect of a disclosure would have been to give the underwriter knowledge of the peculiar peril, which knowledge he already had derived from other sources; he would have taken the risk even if the disclosure had been made, and therefore he had not changed his condition in consequence of the disclosure. For these reasons the decision is against the underwriter. Was this case decided by custom? Some would say it was not, because, avowedly, there was no precedent, which is authenticated custom, nor any evidence of actual custom not to make disclosure of notorious information, and they would declare that it was a clear case where the judges had *made* the law out of their own heads, upon a simple consideration of whether the failure to disclose was right or wrong. That the decision was based upon the consideration whether that action was right or wrong is, in a sense, true; but whose notion of right and wrong was it? It did not come from on High. It was not sought for in the Scriptures, or in any book on ethics. The judges in considering whether the act was right or wrong applied to it the method universally adopted by all men; they judged it by its *consequences;* they considered that the underwriter, in all probability, and therefore presumably, knew of the special peril, unless he was utterly negligent of his business, which could not be supposed; that therefore he had lost nothing by the act, nor in any manner changed his position. If we went no further it would be manifest that custom decided the case, for to determine whether it was right or wrong by the *customary modes* of determining right and wrong is to determine it according to custom. The court, indeed, declared that its decision was made upon *principle;* but what is meant by this? What is the import of this word "principle"? It has various meanings, but as here employed it denotes a proposition very widely true, and the truth of which is universally admitted. The court in this case judged of the character of the act of concealment as we all, from the very constitution of our nature, judge of all conduct, *by its consequences.* It found that the underwriter had suffered no harm in consequence of the concealment, because he would have taken the risk, even if the knowledge had been disclosed, and that it was a principle of law that a man could not fairly complain of the act of another unless he had suffered injury from it; but this was a principle of law only because it accorded with the universal custom of men. In the view of logic the method by which the conclusion is reached is by first affirming that one can make complaint of the action of another only when he is injured by it. This is dividing all human actions into two classes, those which injure and those which do not injure others. The next step is to affirm that this particular act of concealment did not injure and therefore does not belong to the class of acts which can be made ground of complaint. The final proposition is, that an act by one of the parties to a contract which cannot be made a ground of complaint by the other cannot be used by such other to relieve him from the obligation of the contract. This intellectual process is the employment of what is called the reason, and has been sometimes supposed to be peculiar to the law. This is really why Cicero pronounces the law to be right reason—*recta ratio*—existing from eternity, coeval with the Divine mind, but it belongs no more to the law than to any other branch of intellectual activity. It does, indeed, exist from all eternity, or at least ever since man existed, for it indicates the mode, and the only mode, in which the human mind acts when it engages in reasoning. It observes the *consequences* of acts, and places them in different classes according to their respective consequences, which consequences are the *qualities* of the acts. This is what mere children begin to do, and the mightiest scientific mind does but little else.

I dwell with greater minuteness on the proceedings of courts at the present time; because the technical language in which they are conducted tends to keep out of sight the real grounds upon which they proceed. It will not be a useless repetition, therefore, to employ additional examples to illustrate and confirm the truth that present custom constitutes the guide of action in all cases depending upon the unwritten law. We may take the case in which the plaintiff seeks to recover a piece of land to which he claims title. He produces a deed, and the question is whether the language of that instrument is sufficient to transfer the title. It therefore turns upon the interpretation of that instrument. The court decides in favour of the plaintiff on the ground that the language employed in the deed, according *to the ordinary use of language*, is sufficient to effect a passage of the title. This is the rule observed in the interpretation of all written documents, and thus we perceive that that important branch of the law is but an enforcement of present custom. Whenever the question is as to the meaning of writing, custom determines it.

Take the case of an action upon a promissory note where the defence is that the note was given for a particular purpose, and was without other consideration, and that the person to whom it was given perverted it from the intended purpose to another use, and that the plaintiff when he acquired it had notice of the special purpose for which the note was given. There is much contradictory evidence, let us suppose, concerning the way in which the plaintiff came into possession of the note, and the judge leaves the case to the jury with the instruction that if they should find that the plaintiff came by the note in the *ordinary course of business*, without notice and for value, he is entitled to a verdict in his favour. Present custom is here a turning-point of the case. Again: a husband defends an action brought against him for dresses furnished to his wife, on the ground that they are excessive and extravagant beyond all reason, and the court leaves the case to the jury with the direction to find a verdict for the plaintiff, provided they are of the opinion that the goods furnished were such as were *customarily* worn and used by women of a station in life such as the defendant's wife. Custom thus supplies the rule by which the liability of the husband is regulated, and the same is the case with the liability of an infant.

Take an instance from the largest class of cases which now engages the attention of courts, that in which the plaintiff makes a claim grounded on an assertion of negligence on the part of the defendant, and it becomes necessary for the court to instruct the jury concerning the nature of negligence and to lay down the rule of law for their guidance. Negligence will be defined as "the omission to do something which a reasonable man, guided by those considerations which ordinarily regulate the conduct of human affairs, would do, or doing something which a prudent and reasonable man would not do."[1] Now what is meant by a "reasonable" man? It is a man whose

[1] Alderson, B., in *Blythe vs. Birmingham Water Works Co.* 8 Exc., 781.

conduct is guided by what is called *reason*. But what is *reason* in the matter of conduct? It is the observation, common with all men, of the consequences of conduct and the government of future conduct in accordance with the teaching of such observation. What are the "considerations which ordinarily regulate the conduct of human affairs" here spoken of? They are that men should so act in relation to others as not to justify their displeasure or resentment, and the fact that if men act according to the fair expectations of others, they will not awaken displeasure, and that if they follow ordinary custom they will be secure from harm. What a judge really says to a jury, therefore, when he instructs them in a negligence case that the defendant was bound to do all those things "which a reasonable man, guided by those considerations which ordinarily regulate the conduct of human affairs, would do," is that he was bound to act according to custom. All, laymen as well as lawyers, would feel if a judge should instruct a jury that the defendant was bound to take precautions greater, or less, than are usually taken in a case such as that upon trial, that the law had been incorrectly laid down.

The question will arise with those to whom these views are for the first time presented, how the citizen is to inform himself of customs which he is required to obey, and how judges themselves, in the absence of precedent, find out what custom is. A large part of the answer is that every one acquires a knowledge of custom as fast as there is need of having the knowledge. A man can hardly live in society without knowing how men act—that is, what custom is. He knows what to do and what not to do, as well as what to wear and what not to wear. Custom is of all things the one most universally known. No one needs to be told that he must not injure the person of another, or take his property, or violate his engagements when he has induced another to part with something upon the strength of them.

Of course there are cases, absolutely very numerous, but small when the whole body of human activity is considered, in which men honestly differ as to what ought to be done, that is, as to what custom requires, and other cases, also very numerous, in which men refuse or neglect to do what they well know that they ought to do. When a man is honestly ignorant concerning any matter, the natural recourse is to some person or persons likely to be better informed than himself. In the earliest and simplest societies we know anything about, if there was a dispute between different members, and they cared to settle it without fighting, they called in the aid of the oldest and most respected members of the tribe, who had had the largest experience in life, and who enjoyed the reputation of taking just views of things. We do the same thing to-day. The judges of our courts fill the place occupied by the seniors of the savage tribe. This is the answer given by Blackstone. He says, after assigning established custom as *one* of the foundations of the common law (he should have made it the only foundation) :

But here a very natural, and very material, question arises: how are these customs and maxims to be known, and by whom is their validity to be determined? The answer is, by the judges in the several courts of justice. They are the depositaries of the laws, the living oracles, who must decide in all cases of doubt, and who are bound by an oath to decide according to the law of the land. Their knowledge of that law is derived from experience and study; from the '*viginti annorum lucubrationes*' which Fortescue mentions; and from being long personally accustomed to the judicial decisions of their predecessors.[1]

But the law needs not only to be declared, but, where necessary, it is to be enforced, and part of the constitution of a court is the presence of one of its own officers or an officer of the law, the sheriff, who may command the whole power of the State to execute the mandate of the court. The judge to whom is intrusted the office of declaring what custom is, finds out the fact, for the most part, in the same way that other men do, by his senses; but this means is supplemented with him by his knowledge of the work of his predecessors. What makes the accomplished lawyer more fit than other men for the work of ascertaining and declaring custom, is the fact that custom is a government of conduct *according to its consequences*. This is the proper study of the lawyer, if he makes the best use of his time. The reports, which are the books containing all the disputed cases of conduct in the past, and the affairs of the present day, are supposed to be thoroughly known by him. The judge permits no witness to be called to enlighten him as to what custom is (I do not speak of *particular* customs). He is required to take judicial notice of it;

[1] Blackstone, book i., p. 69.

but the word *judicial* might be omitted, for every one in the ordinary business of life is required to take the same notice at his peril. And here we have another proof that custom is law, for how could men be justly required to obey rules which they had not the easy means of knowing?

But if the law laid down by the enlightened tribunals of the present day be nothing but custom, what, it may be asked, is meant when courts declare certain customs *bad*, and disallow them? It is true that language like this is often employed, but the phraseology is misleading. There are *particular* customs, that is, customs prevailing in certain localities, or in certain branches of business. These are allowed, when they are allowed at all, for the same reason that custom generally is taken to be the law, that is, because the particular conduct in question has been governed by it. But the question always arises whether the particular custom relied upon finds a place in the large category of universal custom. If it be found to have any element taking it out of that category, it is not really an instance of custom, but is a departure from custom. It is not enough to make conduct customary that the instances of it are frequent and numerous. Thefts are extremely frequent, but they are, like all crimes, departures from custom—mere bad *practices* which true custom condemns. Let it be supposed that a milkman brings an action against his customer for the price of milk furnished to him, and the customer asserts and proves as a defence to the action, in whole or in part, that the milk was *watered*. The milkman seeks to meet this defence by asking to be allowed to prove that milkmen generally water their milk, and that every one knows, or has reason to suspect, such to be the custom. If the judge should ask him if he proposed to prove that he and all other milkmen *openly* watered their milk before the eyes of their customers, he could scarcely answer in the affirmative. The act was done in secret with the view of concealing it from customers. Now the sale of milk is but an instance of a contract, and the general custom is that contracts are made and performed openly and in good faith. The distinguishing characteristic of customary conduct is that it is what all parties affected by it *might fairly expect*, and this at once stamps the watering of milk as a violation of custom—a mere bad practice which might with propriety be treated as a crime.

6

LECTURE IV.

CONTINUING our scrutiny of this great history of the treatment of human conduct by the enlightened judicial tribunals, we find that transactions have been brought before them which are in all substantial respects the same with some one or more previously decided, and yet one of the parties is not satisfied with that decision, and insists it was wrong, and it appears from the discussions that the previous decisions have not been acquiesced in generally, and that transactions of various kinds are continually occurring not in harmony with the decisions—that is, that human conduct does not actually govern itself in accordance with them. In such cases we find that the courts have re-examined the prior decision, or decisions, which had thus been questioned, and have sometimes declared that they were erroneous and would no longer be followed, and if we look closely to see in what the confessed error consisted we shall find that it was in a wrong classification of the transaction adjudicated upon—that is to say, that it was classified as being against the approved customs of society when in fact it was, upon a just view, in accordance with them, or as being in accordance with them when it was in fact against them. Here we observe two things: first, that human conduct follows its own inherent laws uncontrolled, except in minor matters, even by the deliberate judgments of courts, and that if some piece of conduct really in accordance with custom is declared by the courts to be otherwise, society will, if the matter be one of grave importance, pursue its own course, regardless of the decision. It will follow the fundamental law which governs conduct, namely, that custom is the controlling power. In the next place, we shall observe that the courts themselves recognise, tacitly, at least, this fact, and when they perceive that a rule of law as laid down by them is not generally accepted, that is, that it fails to control conduct, they change the rule. Now, the real thing to which the courts look for a guide in such emergencies is the actual customs of society. If they see that conduct which they once pronounced wrong continues to be repeated, not in exceptional instances merely, but generally, they see that such conduct is one of the ways of society; that the business of life could not be conducted in the way in which it actually is conducted except upon the assumption that such conduct is right; in other words, that it is actually in accordance with custom, and that their previous classification of it as otherwise was erroneous. We have here a further proof that a judicial precedent is nothing but a supposed custom authenticated by the public official stamp; that such stamp may be placed erroneously, and that in such cases it loses its power and authority. If a base coin were, by error, to receive the public stamp declaring it to contain so much gold, that stamp would be ineffectual to give it value after the truth had been discovered. A judicial precedent is not law *per se*, but evidence of it only. The real law is custom.

I must emphasise a principal feature observable throughout the proceedings of judicial tribunals in the enlightened stage under consideration. This is that they are engaged in a *conscious* effort to administer true justice; and that they seek to accomplish this by studying the features of the particular transactions brought before them and assigning them to one or another of the vast multitudes of classes or sub-classes which make up the structure of the law, or adding to that structure by forming new classes, or correcting it by a re-formation of previous classifications. This is the same kind of work which is performed in astronomy, geology, ornithology, and all other sciences. The law thus appears in its true character as an Inductive Science. The difference between it and other sciences is that the classifications of the latter are subsidiary to the purpose of arranging knowledge into orderly form, with a view to its better comprehension and to its further increase; while in the law the classifications are made, not for the mere purposes of scientific knowledge, but to compel men to do or to suffer what it is right that they should do or suffer. This classification, however, made for the practical purposes of life, is really, at the same time, the true one for scientific purposes.

I must also observe here that Law in this, its scientific aspect, embraces only that part of law which consists of the enforced customs of society—that is, *unwritten law*, and that the operation of this law is in large measure, though not wholly, confined to the province of *Private Law*, that is, the law which governs the ordinary private transactions of men with each other. It is the law for which the Roman word *jus* is the best expression. And it is well to keep constantly in mind that this law, being tantamount to the customs enforced by society, is an *existing fact*, or body of facts, and that the courts do not make it, or pretend to make it, but to *find* and *ascertain* it, acting upon the true assumption that it already exists.

Before passing from the evidences which show that in all stages of social progress the private law is identical with custom, I must call attention to a striking feature observable in the condition of a subject nation which has been conquered by another possessing a different law. It may be the desire of the conquering nation to supplant the law of the people which it has subdued by the introduction of its own, and yet no instance can be found in which this has been done. The Romans did not abrogate the existing law of the numerous nations over whom they imposed their political dominion. The Western Barbarians did not uproot the law they found prevailing in the Roman provinces which fell under their sway. The German conquerors of England did, indeed, nearly destroy the ancient laws of the Britons, but not until they had as nearly exterminated the Britons themselves. The United States adopted and enforced in their various conquests in Mexico, Porto Rico, and the Philippine Islands, the laws and customs of the native peoples. An exception is to be made in respect to such laws of the conquered nations as are in their nature inconsistent with the maintenance of the new Sovereignty and to such laws as the conqueror may find it necessary to impose in order to maintain his supremacy; but these are *public* laws. The private relations of the conquered people with each other remain subject to the same government as before. Accordingly it is a principle of universal public law, everywhere recognised by courts, that in the case of the conquest of one nation by another the laws of the conquered nation remain in force, except so far as they are inconsistent with the supremacy of the conquering nation, and so far as the conquering nation has positively substituted different rules in their place. This is a significant proof that the private law is self-existent and irrepealable in custom.

I now come to consider another feature observable in the proceedings of judicial tribunals still under consideration, and which forms a large and interesting figure in those proceedings. We find many transactions considered and adjudicated upon by the courts in which their action is determined, not by reference, in the first instance at least, to precedent or to custom, but by direct reference to what the legislative power has, by some written enactment, commanded or prohibited to be done, and we find, consequently, that human conduct is governed, to some extent, not by custom, but by the expressed will of the State—that is, by Legislation. It is obvious that these two methods are radically different. When courts apply the law founded upon custom, they do not *make* rules. They find rules already existing, *unconsciously made* by society, the *product*, as it were, of its life; but the written laws which they enforce are rules *consciously made by men* clothed with the legislative power. I have hitherto purposely endeavoured to leave Legislation out of view in order that we might contemplate custom and its operation upon human conduct, uninfluenced by the consideration of other causes affecting it. I did, indeed, find it necessary to treat briefly of the first employments of writing in the making of laws, in order to show that the omnipotence of custom as the guide of conduct was not to be imputed to ignorance of the art of writing, and for that purpose spoke with some detail of the early employment of writing among the Greeks and Romans, but now that we find in scrutinising the proceedings of courts in enlightened society that there is a much larger appearance of written or enacted law, some greater and closer attention must be given to it.

What the real nature of Legislation is, beyond the fact that it is, in form, in writing, and purports to express the command of the sovereign power, and how far it is wise or expedient that we should attempt to govern conduct through its instrumentality, are interesting questions which I shall hereafter discuss. Thus far I have been confining my attention to the causes which, *in point of fact*, have governed and do govern conduct. I am still prosecuting that inquiry, and now come to consider to what extent Legislation has, in different places and in different ages, been, *as a matter of fact*, the source of rules for the government of conduct.

We found, in considering the first employments of writing in the making of laws of which history gives us any considerable knowledge, namely, the laws of Solon in Athens and the XII Tables in Rome, that these acts of legislation were not intended to supersede the previous customary laws of those States, but to furnish better methods of executing those laws, and to effect an adjustment of internal political disputes which had arisen between different classes of citizens; in other words, that the object, substance, and nature of those written laws was not *juristic*, but *political*. I shall briefly glance at the subsequent employment of writing for the purpose of law-making in the early history of different countries down to and including the present time.

The first of these subsequent employments is that presented by what are called the Codes of the Barbarians. They were promulgated at various times during a long period covering parts of the fifth and sixth centuries of the Christian era; but the occasions which produced them, and the purposes they were designed to serve, and their contents, are so far similar as to justify their reference to a single class. In order to gain even the most general knowledge of the nature of these laws, which indeed is all that is requisite for our present purpose, it is necessary to glance at the political and social condition of Western Europe at the times when they were promulgated The martial valour of the Romans and their ambition for extensive empire had, at the time of Augustus, brought under their dominion the greater part of the known world. His advice

to his countrymen to check the career of conquest
and to consolidate the vast possessions they had won,
was accepted by them, and they displayed a genius
in the arts of pacification quite as conspicuous as
their renown in war. They sent out colonists,
especially through Italy, Gaul, and Spain, who
mingled with the native inhabitants, carried with
them habits of industry, gradually induced the natives to devote themselves to agriculture, the arts,
and commerce, and gave them an improved administration of justice and better local governments.
Moreover, they did not attempt the impossible task
of violently substituting their own laws in place of
the native customs, but allowed the latter to be in
large measure retained. They sought in other ways
to attach their new subjects to their authority, committed to their hands many of the functions of local
government, encouraged them to enlist in the Roman
armies, and finally bestowed upon them the proud
title of Roman citizens, with all the privileges pertaining to it. There was, however, at all times, a
gentle pressure for the adoption of the Roman law,
and its vastly superior adaptation to the purposes
of a people seeking to acquire the arts and blessings
of civilisation served to facilitate its reception.

Under these influences the Roman provinces,
especially in Europe, made in the course of five centuries from the time of their subjugation great advances in civilisation, wealth, and knowledge. Hundreds of cities, many of them large and populous,
arose, great accumulations of wealth were gathered
and the magnificence of the imperial city was

emulated in baths, temples, and forums. Schools were established, and some of the great names in the classic literature of Rome were those of provincials. Seneca, for instance, was a Spaniard.

But a great peril at all times threatened the security of these flourishing provinces. The vast regions lying on the North and East were inhabited by rude barbarians, warlike and adventurous, ready to engage in any arduous enterprise promising the rewards of plunder and spoil. To repel the inroads of these terrible warriors the provinces had no military strength of their own. They were not permitted to indulge the military spirit and to raise and maintain armies under their own control with which to resist invasion. There was too much danger that these might be employed against the imperial authority. Rome herself undertook to defend her provinces, and this task was for centuries efficiently performed by her disciplined legions stationed along the whole frontier. Upon the fall of the Empire this safeguard melted away, and the barrier being removed, the barbarians broke in upon all sides. There being no military power to expel them, and no inducement to voluntary return, they gave terms to the vanquished inhabitants, established themselves in permanent occupancy of the territories they had conquered, and with no further enemies to subdue, they gradually settled into peaceful pursuits, together with the peoples they had conquered, and began their march along the pathway of civilisation and progress which those peoples had before trodden after their subjugation by the Romans.

And now there arose some anomalous legal conditions. Similar ones may have been exhibited before and since, when one nation has been subdued by another, but never, in known history, upon a scale so conspicuous. Here were the original inhabitants of the conquered provinces living under a modified Roman law, which tolerated the existence, to some extent, of the prior customs of the provinces. Over them came the barbarians with their rude tribal organisations and customs. They could not, if they would, abrogate the law under which the people they had conquered were living. This law could not be at once abrogated without destroying the customs which it represented and enforced. As we have already seen, customs can not be destroyed at a stroke. To change them is a slow and gradual work. Nor, probably, did the barbarians desire wholly to abrogate them. They wished to make friends, not enemies, of the people among whom they intended to dwell permanently, and in no way could they better effect this purpose than by suffering them, so far as possible, to retain their laws and customs. Still less could they renounce their own laws. The attachment of their own followers to their customs was as strong as that of the native people to theirs. Necessity, as well as policy, pointed to the expedient of allowing both systems to stand side by side to such an extent as to permit the conquered populations to have the benefit of their own laws and customs, so far as concerned transactions between themselves, while the barbarians might assert theirs wherever their interests and supremacy were concerned. This expedient was adopted, or, rather, it came about naturally, of necessity; but to carry it into better effect it was needful to promulgate the laws of the Barbarians in order that the conquered peoples might be apprised of what they were to obey when the two systems might happen to come into conflict. The political power would be in the hands of the Barbarians, and through this they would be enabled to assert the supremacy of their own customs whenever occasion might require. Prior to this time and before they started upon their career of conquest, they were governed by the unwritten rules of conduct; their affairs were discussed and settled in councils composed of the freemen of the tribes. Their kings were elected at these, and at these were determined, by the rude clashing of their weapons, the questions of war and peace, and a rude justice was administered. The purpose of the promulgation of the Barbarian Codes was to settle the conflict thus arising between different systems of custom, and they gave rise to the anomaly of two systems of law co-existing with each other, one territorial in extent, and applicable to the native people inhabiting the conquered territory; the other, *personal*, applicable to the Barbarians, and carried with them wherever they went.

Among these Barbarian Laws, and the most important, was the Code of the Salian Franks, a powerful confederacy of German tribes, who, with their neighbours, the Ripuarian Franks, had reduced substantially the whole of Gaul to subjection and inaugurated the first dynasty, the Merovingian, of the French kings. Others were the Codes of the Burgundians, of the Ostrogoths, the Visigoths, and the Alemanni, and there were still others.

The conflict between these codes and the Roman law of the provinces did not prove so embarrassing as might be supposed. In the case of the rudest of the Barbarians, the Franks and the Burgundians, the characteristics of the provisions were that they related very largely to political organisations and to the crimes of violence. They fixed the *weregild*, or sum required to be paid by a man to the kin of one whom he had slain, and corresponding sums for robbery and other injuries. Among violent and warlike people having no industries, all that is needed is the repression of those offences which disturb the internal peace of the tribe. They have no occasion for resorting to a cultivated jurisprudence, and the Barbarians might well, having the military and political supremacy, insist upon the adoption of these simple provisions for offences and leave the regulation of the other conduct of the peaceful native inhabitants to that system which was already performing that function.

The aspect, therefore, which these conquered countries exhibited was that of rude barbarians living among peaceful inhabitants, and each under laws of their own, growing out of, and fitted to, their respective characteristics and with growing internal harmony.

In the country subject to the Franks, the Salic Law was established for the Franks, and the Theodosian Code for the Romans. In that subject to the Visigoths a compilement of

the Theodosian Code, made by order of Alaric, regulated disputes among the Romans; and the national customs, which
Euric caused to be reduced to writing, determined those
among the Visigoths.[1]

The pride of the conquerors was sufficiently gratified
by the privilege which they enjoyed, like the posterity
of Mahomet, of carrying their laws with them wherever
they went, whereas the laws of the provinces remained local and territorial. The two systems were
left to compete with each other, and the result of
the competition was not doubtful. The Barbarians
themselves, gradually changing their habits from
those of warlike and predatory tribes to those of peaceful and industrious citizens, would soon find that their
rude laws contained no rules applicable to their
changed condition, while the Roman law of the provinces, penetrated by the spirit of a jurisprudence built
up by a thousand years of civilisation, embraced provisions which would justly regulate every transaction
of life. It was inevitable that in these subjugated
countries the original inhabitants, while receiving
from their conquerors a new infusion of independent
and martial feeling, would in their turn subdue the
ferocity of their masters, and allure them into the
peaceful paths of industrial advancement. As this
change progressed, the rude codes of the Barbarians
would silently sink into desuetude and the cultivated
jurisprudence of Rome re-assert its supremacy.

This cursory review of the circumstances attending
the promulgation of the Barbarian Codes enables us
to perceive the purpose of this employment of

[1] Montesquieu, *Esprit des Lois*, vol. ii., book xxviii., ch. iv.

writing in the framing of laws, and we immediately
see that here also it was not *juristic* but *political*.
It was political in the main, in both the instances
we have before considered, those of Athens and
Rome; but there it was for the purpose of re-organ-
ising the political arrangements in order to reconcile
internal conflicts between different classes of long
established societies, and inasmuch as those conflicts in part arose from dissatisfaction with the
public administration of justice, the written Code,
especially in Rome, reduced to writing some of the
ordinary law. But the case was otherwise with the
Barbarian Codes. There were no internal dissensions within the bodies of the tribes. Such internal
peace as barbarians can exhibit prevailed. The
motive was in great part to preserve for triumphant
bands of savage warriors, in the midst of peaceful
provinces which they had subdued, their supremacy
over the vanquished by retaining those prerogatives
and privileges which are becoming to conquerors.
They were not unwilling that the provincials should
preserve, for the regulation of their own affairs, the
laws and usages which then prevailed among them.
In some instances, indeed, the Barbarians caused
some brief codes of Roman Law to be prepared for
their use; but it was not their purpose to subject
themselves to such laws and usages. To have a
personal law which a man can claim wherever he
goes is a most conspicuous mark of superiority, and
this prerogative the conquerors chose to retain. A
permanent memorial which could at any time be
appealed to was needed in order to acquaint the

vanquished with the conditions which their masters chose to impose. This apparently anomalous existence of a personal law with a different territorial system is well sketched by Messrs. Pollock and Maitland in their *History of English Law*:

As the Frankish realm expanded, there expanded with it a wonderful "system of personal laws." It was a system of racial laws. The *Lex Salica*, for instance, was not the law of a district; it was the law of a race. The Swabian, wherever he might be, lived under his Alamannic, or as the expressive phrase tells us, he lived Alamannic law (*legem vivere*). So Roman law was the law of the Romani. In a famous, if exaggerated, sentence Bishop Agobard of Lyons has said that often five men would be walking or sitting together and each of them would own a different law.[1]

Turning now to Great Britain, we find the first known instances of the employment of writing for the purposes of legislation to be of a somewhat different character. The original inhabitants of the island were Celts. The Roman conquest, although followed by four centuries of occupation, is but an episode in the history of Great Britain. The occupation was confined, for the most part, to fortified places and their neighbourhood, while the main bulk of the territory was still in the hands of the natives. The recall of the Roman legions at the downfall of the empire was the signal for the reassertion by the natives of their power. The Roman inhabitants, conscious of their inability to withstand this pressure, resorted to the dangerous expedient of calling outside Barbarians to their aid. Those

[1] Pollock and Maitland, (1899) vol. i., p. 13.

most available for this purpose were bands of free-booters from the promontory of Jutland who were harrying the coasts of England and France. They defeated the British Barbarians, and then turned their arms against the Romans. Fresh bands from their native Jutland and from the neighbouring Saxons poured in to join them, and wars ensued which ended in the extermination of both Roman and Briton, and thenceforth the Angles and the Saxons were to be the undisputed masters of English soil. They brought with them their customs and usages, which bore a resemblance to those of the Barbarians who made themselves masters of the Roman provinces upon the continent. These were personal independence and liberty, and popular assemblies in which kings were elected for their valour to act as military chieftains, and in which justice and other affairs were administered. As the tribes pressed in upon the Roman provinces on the continent their customs and usages were left to compete with the very different ones which had grown up under Roman dominion, and which con-stituted a law substantially Roman. We have already observed that as the Barbarians became softened and civilised by contact with the greatly superior numbers of the conquered provincials, and by degrees came to cultivate the arts and industries of peace, they required a more cultivated system of law, and they found it already at hand in the Roman-ised jurisprudence of the peoples whose masters they had become. They were as nations swallowed up in the bosom of the old populations, and their customs and laws, like their language, became gradually Romanised. The establishment of the Holy Roman Empire of Charlemagne, united with the growing papal authority, gave another impulse to this tendency, which was again caught up in later times by the revised study of the Roman law consequent upon the discovery of the Pandects at Amalphi, and thus in the end all the Western nations of the continent adopted the classic Roman law as the basis of their jurisprudence. And with their juridical system went also the political. The freedom and independence of the German tribes were lost in imperialism, and monarchs became absolute.

The course of legal development proceeded otherwise in Great Britain. The German conquerors, having nearly exterminated both the Roman and the native populations, their customs and usages had no competition to struggle against, and were left to their own natural development. The enlarged territorial dominion, the increasing population, and foreign wars demanded more stability of rule, and the elected chieftain gave way to the sovereign by inheritance; but his authority was always limited in some form by popular safeguards, and the historic origin of our own liberties may be thus traced to our German ancestors.

It would be in vain for us to seek among the originals of English law for any instance of the employment of writing for the purpose of law-making at any time from the completion of the Saxon conquest, near the close of the sixth century, to the Great Charter of King John in the thirteenth, corresponding

in significance or importance with the legislation of
Solon in Athens, the Twelve Tables of the Roman
Law, or even the Barbarian Codes. The genius of
Alfred, patriot, soldier, statesman, and scholar,
fitted him indeed for the task of lawgiver, had such
a mission been acceptable to the people over whom
he ruled. Our legal antiquarians have indeed bestowed upon him the appellation, borrowed from imperial Roman jurisprudence, of *legum Anglicarum
conditor;* but his title to this distinction rests, not
upon any laws written or enacted by his authority,
but upon a compilation, made under his direction, of
certain rules and customs obeyed and enforced in
the various parts of England in his time, and variously styled Alfred's Laws, or Dome Book, and
which has been unfortunately lost.[1] Permanent
kingship was a new experience with Saxon peoples,
and though necessary for their defence against the
hostile elements to which they were opposed in
their new settlements, did not include in their minds
the prerogative of dictating laws. For the purposes
of legislation there must be a sovereign whose authority to enforce his laws is undisputed throughout his
realm, or an assembly regularly constituted and recognised as really representative. Neither of those
conditions existed in England under the Saxon kings,
and though numerous documents have been preserved purporting to be laws, or *dooms*, of the Saxons,
they consist chiefly of attempts to give certainty to
the sums of money, payable by way of voluntary
redress for murder and other injuries. They have

[1] *Bl. Com* , bk. i., p. 65.

never been appealed to in subsequent times as constituting part of the law of England, nor have they been incorporated into any of the authoritative publications of statute law. The authorities seem to agree that the Great Charter constitutes the first appearance of genuine written law in the juridical history of England. Says Professor Lee in his recent work on Historical Jurisprudence:

It is with the Great Charter of 1215 that the distinction between written and unwritten law became certain and accepted. Before that date the enactments of national councils, however important they might be, were not preserved as statutes of the realm. They belonged to the *jus non scriptum*.[1]

Messrs. Pollock and Maitland, in their learned and elaborate work, express the same view: "That charter takes its place as the first chapter of the enacted law[2]"; and Mr. Green, in his *History of the English People*, says:

It is in this way that the Great Charter marks the transition from the age of traditional rights, preserved in the nation's memory and officially declared by the Primate, to the age of written legislation, of Parliaments and Statutes, which was soon to come.[3]

And yet the Great Charter when rightly considered, in the light of the occasion and the motive which led to it, was not a reduction of customary to written law for the sake of the supposed advantages possessed by the latter as law. King John had been for years playing the part of an absolute monarch, and setting

[1] *Historical Jurisprudence* p. 479,
[2] Vol. i., p. 78.
[3] Vol i. p. 245

at defiance every limit upon the royal prerogative. His oppressions, while weighing heavily upon the body of the people, were felt more keenly by the barons, and had at length brought them into open war with their sovereign. He was obliged to yield, and the Great Charter was simply the treaty which he was compelled to sign in order to conclude the war.[1] It was the record of the conditions under which he was to be permitted to continue to wear the crown. The prior law had not in any manner failed because it was not in writing, but because the king himself had set it at defiance. It is, indeed, a proof, if proof were needed, that a written contract embracing many provisions is superior, in form and efficacy, to a verbal one, but it proves nothing more.

I have yet to refer to the most significant and instructive instance of the employment of writing for the purpose of legislation. I mean that of the law of the Church of Rome, what is commonly called the Canon Law. The Roman Catholic Church, originally a small religious society, by degrees, in the face of persecution, had extended itself throughout the Roman Empire until in the reign of Constantine it was acknowledged and accepted by that empire as the only authorised spiritual power, and prior to the Reformation the whole European world had accepted its faith and acknowledged its authority. Its organisation became more and more elaborate, refined, and complete as its numbers and power increased. The fundamental conception upon which it was founded was that of a hierarchy instituted by

[1] Stubbs, *Con. Hist.*, vol. ii., p. 2.

Christ himself through the apostle Peter, and maintained by his successors, the Bishops of Rome, as the visible vice-regents of the Almighty upon earth. The society constituted by it is not limited by the boundaries of nations, but embraces the whole body of believers, wherever found. Absolute obedience is due to it by every member, from the king to the peasant, and even by the corporate nationalities which profess the Catholic faith. It claims an empire not only over the minds and consciences, but also over the actions of men, and if it has failed to assert authority over all their actions it is because reason or policy has advised the abstention. It need not be said that pretensions like these can have no limitation except such as are self-imposed. The Divine authority must necessarily be absolute and supreme over all merely human power. These claims on the part of the Church have never been wholly acceded to in any nation except the Papal States of Italy before the abrogation of the temporal power of the Popes; but they were at an early period admitted to a considerable extent. The conduct of the clergy, the regulation of church property, the administration of the personal property of decedents, marriage and divorce, the punishment of heresy, etc., were conceded to the jurisdiction of the spiritual courts, and many traces of this concession are still to be found in the jurisprudence of England and even of the United States. The legislative authority included within these claims is vested in the supreme pontiff and the general councils of the Church, and by its exercise from time to time, a vast body of law has been created and reduced to a highly refined and logical system. The Code, the Novels, and the Pandects of Justinian, constituting the Corpus Juris Civilis, are paralleled by the Decretum, the Decretals, and the Extravagantes, constituting the Corpus Juris Canonici. Its commands are enforced by many weapons drawn from the spiritual armoury, of which excommunication is the most effective, and when these have failed, the temporal power has often lent its aid. This law, assuming to be an expression of the will of the Almighty, communicated through his vice-regent on earth, is embodied in writing, and is, in theory, the most perfect exemplification of written law. Not being of human origin it cannot be created by custom, though human custom may be, and often is, recognised and sanctioned in its administration. If it were universally and completely enforced in harmony with its pretensions, it would entirely answer to Austin's definition of law, as being a command addressed by a superior to an inferior. The authors, however, whose labours built up the Canon Law, being ecclesiastics, were, in general, the most learned persons of their times, and their system exhibits the first efforts, subsequent to the downfall of the Roman Empire, to apply scientific principles to the composition of law, and the civil law of the Middle Ages is largely indebted to the Church for many of its improvements. This beneficial influence proceeded not only from the text of the Canon Law, but also from the direct work of the ecclesiastics who were frequently employed as ministers of State and members of the judicial tribunals.

But in answer to the question how far this system of written law has at any time come to govern the actual conduct of men in their transactions with each other and in their relations to the State, we must say that it has had comparatively little direct force or influence *proprio vigore;* and so far as it has had any authority, it has been derived from the State and dependent upon the State for its continuance. It has really been efficacious in dealing with civil concerns only so far as it has recognised and enforced the actual customs of civil society. The great Churchmen who in the Middle Ages and later so frequently filled the great offices of State were quite as skilful in administering temporal as they were spiritual affairs, and in the performance of judicial duties they conferred the greatest benefit by applying to the enforcement of the customs of life, the order, system, and methods which they had learned in the Roman and Canon Law.

In considering the instances of the employment of writing in the making of laws, I have thus far referred to those only (excepting the Canon Law) occurring in early stages of social development, and only the most notable. There are, however, many others to be found before either legislation or the law of custom and precedent had reached what may be called the scientific stage, and some brief attention to these will be instructive. There were quite a number of statutes, or ordinances in the nature of statutes, enacted in England, some of

them prior even to the Great Charter, but of many
of them no permanent memorial has been preserved,
a fact indicating that they were not of permanent
importance. Such of them as have been preserved
will be found to be in the main not attempts to reduce the customary law to writing, or to directly affect
the ordinary transactions of men, but to bring
about some political object such as the correction
of the mode of judicial procedure, relief from royal
oppressions, or the defeat of the pretensions of the
Church. Among these was the Charter of the Forest
(1217), one of the chief measures designed to afford
relief against the abuses and oppressions of the
Forest laws; also what are called the Constitutions
of Clarendon (1164) from the name of the place
where they were enacted. They are thus described
by Bishop Stubbs in his *Constitutional History:*

The Constitutions of Clarendon are sixteen in number, and
purport to be, as the history of their production shows them
to have been, a report of the usages of Henry I. on the disputed points. They concern questions of advowsons and
presentation, churches in the king's gift, the trial of clerks,
the security to be taken of the excommunicated, the trial of
laymen for spiritual offences, the excommunication of tenants-
in-chief, the licence of the clergy to go abroad, ecclesiastical
appeals, which are not to go further than the archbishop without the consent of the king; questions of the title to ecclesiastical estates, the baronial duties of the prelates, the election
to bishoprics and abbacies, the right of the king to the goods
of felons deposited under the protection of the Church, and
the ordination of villeins.[1]

And he further describes them as being "a part of

[1] Stubbs, *Constitutional History*, vol. i., p. 502.

a great scheme of administrative reform, by which the debatable ground between the spiritual and temporal powers can be brought within the reach of common justice and the lawlessness arising from professional jealousies abolished."[1]

The Assize of Clarendon, sometimes called the Great Assize (1166), was an enactment of which the principal feature was an improvement of judicial procedure in the case of criminals, and is a part of the same scheme of reform attempted by Henry to which the Constitutions of Clarendon belong. The statute of Merton (1236) is noted as being that in which the assembled barons declared they would not have the laws of England changed.

The reign of Edward I., memorable in the history of English law, was quite prolific in legislation. The famous statute of Westminster (1275) was passed in the first session of his reign, but Edward's purposes were, in the main, reformatory and political in that sense. The reformation of abuses, the due execution of the existing law, the providing of more efficient methods of procedure; in other words, the framing of sufficient instrumentalities by which the existing customs could be better enforced, were the things he had in view, and these he sought to compass by the statute last mentioned. The famous statute *De Religiosis* (1279), which forbids the acquisition of land by the religious orders in such wise that the land should come into mortmain,[2] is another political and reformatory measure. So also the

---

[1] Stubbs, *Con. Hist.*, vol. i., p. 503.

[2] *Ibid.*, vol. ii., p. 117.

Statute of Westminster the Second, and the Statute of Winchester, both enacted in the same year (1285). The first contains the enactment commonly called *De Donis Conditionalibus*, and also a provision for the better correction of errors of law committed in the course of a trial, and which therefore did not appear by the record; which is the original warrant for our present bill of exceptions. The important statute commonly known as *Quia Emptores*, which saved to the chief lord of a fee the services and profits due to him as the feudal owner notwithstanding any grant by the tenant, thus destroying one of the former consequences of subinfeudation, was enacted at the third Parliament of Westminster (1290). The object of this was the political one of saving to the King and his chief lords the services and profits just mentioned. The statute of Carlisle (1309) was one of the many acts of legislation designed to restrain the power and influence of the clergy and the Pope. The statute of *Præmunire* (1355), declaring forfeiture and outlawry against those suing in foreign courts for matters cognisable in the King's Courts, was a feature of the struggle between the King and the Church. The Statute of Treasons (1352) for the first time defined the offence and punishment of treason.

To further trace the course of British legislation down to the period to which I shall next call particular attention, would involve a detail beyond the scope of these lectures. I may safely say that this subsequent legislation, however numerous the instances, was in point of purpose and effect, as in the cases

I have already considered, special and particular,
the object being sometimes to correct an abuse,
sometimes to institute a reform, sometimes to carry
a point for or against the King, the barons, the
Church, or the people.

Still less have I room to trace for the same period
the course of legislation on the continent subsequent
to the promulgation of the Barbarian Codes. I must,
nevertheless, briefly indicate the general character of
the legal systems which grew up subsequently to those
Codes and the extent to which they were influenced
by legislation, confining my attention, however,
mainly to France and Germany. As we have already seen, the provinces of the Roman Empire of
which the Barbarians became masters, were civilised States in which conduct was regulated by a
law customary, but substantially Roman. The
Barbarian Codes did not entirely, or in the main,
replace this law, but superinduced upon it the
customs of the Barbarians, as a personal law, binding
in favour of the Barbarians and as between themselves, but leaving the vanquished nations otherwise
to enjoy their own customs. The shifting of the
Barbarians from place to place, and the mingling of
them together, aggravated the confusion caused by
the simultaneous existence of personal and territorial law, and made it intolerable. Besides this,
the unsettled condition of the whole territory, the
incessant wars for the extension of empire or the
aggrandisement of dynasties, the rapid changes in
the boundaries of States and provinces, would have
made orderly legislation impossible, had there been

at this period any developed capacity for legislation. Charlemagne, indeed, and his immediate successors, made efforts to reduce this confusion into something like order through their decrees called Capitularies, but I think it is agreed by legal historians that their effect was inconsiderable, and the practice of issuing them was soon discontinued. Law seems to have been left to work out its own solutions, and the result was, at least in France, that, after the lapse of four centuries from the Barbarian conquest, the confusion of personal and territorial law gave way to the establishment of different territorial systems, called *Coutumes*, in different provinces. These systems were in their nature customary law, variously compounded of the Barbarian customs and the old Romanised law, the latter almost continually growing in comparative strength, as society became more civilised and given to industrial pursuits. This growing predominance of the Roman law received a fresh impetus from the revival of the scientific study of that law, after the discovery of the Pandects, at the University of Bologna. Students flocked thither from all countries, and the legal doctrines there acquired were disseminated throughout the nations of the continent. A cultivated jurisprudence was more and more demanded as civilisation advanced and industry and commerce became more pervading. This was furnished ready-made by the Roman law, and the administration of justice in all the Western States of Europe became more and more permeated with it.

Little resort was had to legislation in France until

the middle of the fifteenth century. Between that
time and the reign of Louis XIV., a number of royal
ordinances were adopted, the principal of which had
for their object to reduce the *Coutumes* to greater
uniformity and precision and to improve judicial
procedure. France under Louis XIV., had become
a thoroughly consolidated absolute monarchy. The
sovereign was ambitious alike of personal and
national aggrandisement. His legislative power was
unlimited, and a great opportunity for improvement
in internal administration was opened to him. Under
the guidance of the wisdom of Colbert, this opportunity was employed in various efforts to reform the
public administration. So far as the legal system
was concerned there were three principal evils. The
first was the lack of an orderly and uniform method
of procedure in civil and criminal cases. The second
was lack of uniformity in the law growing out of
the various differing *coutumes*. The third was the
uncertainty and confusion in the law itself, the consequence of the different sources from which much
of it had been borrowed, and the want of harmony
and capacity in the courts which administered it.
The method of improvement adopted by Louis
XIV. appears to have been to select branches or
subjects of law, in which improvement was most
needed, or perhaps in which it was most practicable
at the time, and reduce them to writing. The most
important of the measures were: (1) An *Ordonnance*
for the reformation of the procedure of the courts
in civil cases. (2) An *Ordonnance* for the reformation
of the criminal procedure. The subjects embraced

by these two pieces of legislation are not substantive law, but instrumentalities, machinery, designed to carry such law into effect. They do not comprise rules for the regulation of conduct, but forms of proceedings designed to enforce such rules; and they are, as I may hereafter more particularly show, the proper subjects of written law. (3) The *Ordonnance du Commerce*, which was an attempted reduction of the commercial law into writing—in other words, a codification. (4) The *Ordonnance de la Marine*. This was a like attempted codification of the maritime law. In these two last mentioned pieces of legistion we find the beginning in France of those attempts for the reduction of the unwritten and customary law to writing which culminated later in the Code of Napoleon. It will be perceived that none of these *Ordonnances* of Louis XIV. were designed to remedy the confusion in French law arising from the differences in the provincial *coutumes*.

Louis XV. had the advantage of the advice and assistance of the Chancellor d'Aguesseau, a consummate lawyer, and under his inspiration a beginning was made in the task of bringing the law of the different parts of the kingdom into uniformity. This was done by the promulgation and execution of three separate *Ordonnances*, one relating to donations—*Ordonnance sur les donations*, which had for its object the reduction of the law in all parts of France upon this subject to uniformity, being an attempt in the way of codification. Another in relation to testaments—*Ordonnance sur les testaments*, which recognised and preserved the two different systems of law on this subject then prevailing in the Northern and Southern parts respectively of the kingdom; and the other relating to trusts—*Ordonnance sur les substitutions fidéi-commissaires*, designed to effect reforms in the constitution and administration of trusts. This legislation under Louis XIV. and Louis XV. was, to a considerable extent, embodied by the framers of the Code Napoleon in their work.[1]

In Germany, the course of development of law subsequent to the Barbarian Codes was somewhat different. The barbarous tribes, as they became by degrees more civilised, required, as we have seen, for the ordinary transactions of life a law more refined than the rude customs by which they were originally governed. Their civilisation was promoted by their contact with the Roman peoples, and hence arose a tendency in favour of the adoption of the Roman law. This tendency was greatly strengthened by the establishment of the Holy Roman Empire. The close connection of that Empire with Rome and the Church and its pretence to be the successor of the Empire of the Cæsars dictated the sanction of the Roman law. But what more, perhaps, than all else led to the general adoption of that law was the circumstance that the administrators and teachers of the law, bred in the universities, everywhere participated in the revived study of the Roman law consequent upon the discovery of the copy of the Pandects, and exerted a steady influence in favour of its general introduction as the governing law in all private transactions. Never-

[1] Lee, *Historical Jurisprudence*, ch. xv., sec. iii.

theless, the old customs were retained by the different provinces as they became consolidated into larger States, and the reconciliation of these with the Roman law was the continual task of judicial administration. I suppose it would be true to say that the Roman law came to be adopted except where it was in conflict with settled local customs, and there the latter prevailed. Prior to the general movement in the direction of codification initiated by the Code Napoleon there was little in the way of legislation touching the law of private transactions. Some important private efforts were made to set forth the law of particular States, but these had no other authority than that of text-books. Prof. Lee states that "according to the German opinion, the legislative authority of the rulers had little to do with the private law. That was a matter of custom and should be left to the local communities to develop as they wished."[1]

In Italy, the Ostrogoths maintained, for a time, some of their barbarian customs superinduced upon the basis of the Roman law, but the latter was never displaced, and upon the revival of the study of jurisprudence it resumed its sway as the sole guide for the regulation of conduct.

The Visigothic conquerors of Spain seem to have been ambitious of substituting their own law in the place of the Roman jurisprudence, but their successive declarations of the supremacy of their codes, and interdicts of Roman law, serve to show how difficult it is to supplant the law of a conquered

[1] *Historical Jurisprudence*, p. 409.

8

people without exterminating them, and also how ineffectual are all efforts to govern the conduct of a civilised people by the customs of barbarians. The Jesuits of Spain have been wont to insist that their law is Spanish, not Roman, but the contents of their written codes and their own law-books contradict this pretension.

LECTURE V

THIS rapid and glancing review of the most conspicuous instances of legislation in the ruder
periods preceding the present enlightened age, is
quite sufficient to enable us to answer the question
for what purpose and to what extent it was resorted
to throughout those periods. We have seen that it
was employed to compose differences between various
classes in society and to furnish machinery by
which the customary law might be more efficiently
administered, and from time to time to better adapt
that machinery to the changing and developing
wants of society, and that where it was aimed directly
at individual conduct it was for the purpose of securing better obedience to the customary law by public
punishment of the more flagrant violations of custom,
which is the office of the criminal law; in other
words, we find that at the first appearance of legislation its province and the province of Public Law
were nearly conterminous. The province of Private
Law is scarcely touched.

In the present enlightened age we find a much
greater resort to legislation; but the important
question is whether its purpose and nature have
been changed. This is easily answered. The whole
of the legislation of any American State, to take an

example, is contained in its easily accessible statute-books. We may know the general contents of all of them from an examination of those of one State. They will be found to embrace its fundamental Constitution creating the Executive, Legislative, and Judicial Departments, the organisation of the State into political districts, the creation of the the various State and local officers and the designation of their duties; provisions for the conduct of elections; a system for raising money to support State and local government by taxation and applying it in many different ways; provisions for creating and maintaining public highways, including railroads; for forming corporations, for preserving the public health, and for supervising many important public concerns, such as banking, insurance, etc., and a multitude of other public provisions including the whole of the law relating to the designating and punishment of crimes. Besides this, we find in the numerous volumes of statute-books vast masses of matter which, though in the form of laws, are not law in any proper sense. These consist in the making of provision for the maintenance of the public works of the State, for the building of asylums, hospitals, school-houses, and a great variety of other similar matters. This is but the record of the action of the State in relation to the *business* in which it is engaged. The State is a great public corporation which conducts a vast mass of business, and the written provisions for this, though in the form of laws, are not essentially different from the minutes of ordinary corporate bodies recording their action. But when we search for any matter relating to the regulation of the ordinary conduct of men in their transactions with each other—that is, to Private Law, we find exceedingly little, and we may say that it is substantially true that the whole vast body of legislation is confined to Public Law, and that its operation on Private Law is remote and indirect and aimed only to make the unwritten law of custom more easily and certainly enforced. If we make a similar examination of the Statutes at Large of Great Britain the result is the same; and the same also, if we examine the legislation of Rome in the classic era of jurisprudence.

There is one great seeming exception in the case of the various codifications of the customary law. We find in Roman Law the great volume of the Pandects; we find the Civil Code in France. There are Civil Codes in Germany. There is a reduction to writing of one or more chapters of Private Law in England; and there are Civil Codes in several American States. But the exception in these cases, when we consider its true nature, is more apparent than real. The law enacted in these Civil Codes was not *made* by the legislation enacting them. It existed, for the most part, as law before, and the enactment added no force to it. In the cases of Rome, France, and Germany the unification of different peoples and provinces into larger nations had made it necessary for the tribunals to enforce different customs for different places, an inconvenient task; but this difference was gradually disappearing in the closer relations brought about by the consolidation of nationalities, and the main purpose of the codification was to hasten the coming uniformity, which could be completely accomplished only by legislation. The motive to such codifications as have taken place in the United States and Great Britain was the supposed increased accessibility of the law by enabling it to be found in a single book, the same motive which led to the production of Digests. The creation of new law was but a small part of the object.

There are some smaller exceptions in which legislation is employed in shaping rules of private conduct. I refer to instances in which actual changes are made in Private Law in particular cases; but they are quite exceptional and occur in cases where the courts are in conflict, or where the customs as enforced by the courts have been gradually changing in the course of social progress, and conflicts in custom arise which the courts find it difficult to deal with. But these exceptional cases really fall within the province of Public Law, because it is the office of that law to furnish to the judicial tribunals a warrant for making those changes in decision which the changes in custom require, but which a regard for consistency prevents them from making. My conclusion is that so far as Private Law—the law which governs our conduct in our ordinary transactions with each other—is concerned, the influence of legislation—of written law—has been exceedingly small. The latter, in fact, constitutes what has been not inaptly styled "a mere fringe on the body of law."

I have now completed my survey of human life in

all ages and in all stages of social progress, for
the purpose of ascertaining the *causes* which have,
in point of fact, governed, and which still govern,
human conduct. This survey has embraced primitive
man, the savage member of a wandering horde; man
when he first adopts a fixed place of abode; man
when he first consciously organises a social state;
man when he has first acquired the art of writing
and when he first employs that art in the composition
of laws; man as the subject of a conqueror imposing
his dominion over realms not his own; man as the
member of a conquered nation accepting submissively
the rule of strangers; man in society where there is
no power to protect him save his own right arm;
man during the long period in which he seeks by the
establishment of judicial tribunals to supplant the
violence of self-help; man down to the period
when judicial tribunals and legislatures have been
established and perfected; man in the present enlightened age:—and the conclusion is clear that habit
and custom in each of these different conditions
furnish the rules which govern human conduct, and
that they still exert over enlightened man the same
imperious dominion that they did among the primeval hordes which peopled the world before the dawn
of civilisation, or that they now do among the barbarous tribes which inhabit the wilds of Patagonia
or Australia.

To the absolute generality of this conclusion an
exception is to be made for the influence of legislation; but the extent of this exception diminishes
to a point where we may, for all large and general

purposes, dismiss it from attention, when we consider that its principal function is to supplement and aid the operation of custom and that it can never supplant it, and also consider, what I may hereafter more fully show, that its own efficiency is dependent upon its conformity to habit and custom. What has governed the conduct of men from the beginning of time will continue to govern it to the end of time. Human nature is not likely to undergo a radical change, and, therefore, that to which we give the name of Law always has been, still is, and will forever continue to be Custom.

But while all Law is Custom, all Custom is not necessarily Law. Law differs from custom as a part differs from the whole. There is a large range of human conduct of which the law takes no notice, though it is under the control of custom quite as much as that part which the law assumes to regulate. A great part of this conduct falls under the control of moral rules which are enforced mainly by public opinion and form the subject of the science of morality, about which I shall have something to say hereafter. Other parts of it are such as are controlled by the usages of fashion or etiquette, and there is still another most important part lying beyond the immediate scope of my inquiries in which the individual alone is concerned, and which embraces what may be called his interior life. This is more especially within the sphere of religious thought and action.

This conception of law, identifying, as it does, all the rules which govern the conduct of men in their transactions with each other, including even the rules of morality, with custom and habit, will not, I suppose, be willingly accepted. Legal writers have at all times allowed much weight to custom, viewing it as one, but only one, of the *sources* of law, as if there were some governmental power standing above custom, the function of which was to pronounce judgment on the wisdom of custom, and select from it the rules it would enforce and reject the rest. *Ancient* customs they have indeed regarded as having the force of law, but this quality they impute, not to the custom, *qua* custom, but to its *antiquity*, whereas the conclusion at which I arrive erects *present existing* custom as the standard of law. This is not in harmony with the opinion of those who make law to be the positive command of the Sovereign power in a State, nor of those who, like the classical jurists of Rome, ascribe its origin to an incomprehensible something called the Law of Nature, and apparently not with the views of those who regard all morality as founded upon the command of God, directly or indirectly revealed. It will seem to all these to detract from the sublime dignity which they would ascribe to law and morality, and impair the reverence in which they should be held, to identify them with a thing seldom regarded as carrying with it any high obligation. We say of men, by way of derogation, that they do this or that, because they have got into the *habit* of doing it, or because they feel that *mere custom* requires it, and we are all inclined to regard it as evidence of a lofty character when men disregard custom, and act according to their own independent sentiments. Unvarying obedience to law we commend, but the followers of mere fashion, or custom, are regarded with a feeling akin to contempt. There are what we call, speaking in ordinary language, *bad* customs and habits (they are really practices contrary to custom), and we find it difficult to view anything as intrinsically lofty and good which so often appears in forms either indifferent or evil.

What is the reason of this hesitation and unwillingness? Is it that we assign too much of worth, dignity, and elevation to law and morality, or that our ordinary views of custom are too low? I am sure that the latter reason points towards the truth, and it suggests a closer inquiry into the real nature and meaning of custom. This question lies beyond the ordinary subjects of legal discussion, but it is one which the Philosophy of the Law should attempt to answer.

What then is wrapped up and concealed in the word *custom* which we so often employ, sometimes without assigning to it especial importance, and sometimes regarding it as importing something trivial or perhaps evil? We need but recall for a single moment the account we have given of it, in order to perceive that the ordinary views of it are inadequate and erroneous. That thing which has held imperious sway over the conduct of men of all races, whether savage or civilised, and in all times, can not be low, trivial, or evil. Where is the secret of its power? The simplest definition of custom is that it is the *uniformity of conduct* of all persons under like circumstances, but this suggests the question—"What is *conduct*, and what is its *cause?*" To answer this without indulging in speculation, but extending our attention to all known truths ascertained by observation, whether of the world of mind or of the external world, we must avail ourselves of the teachings of the science of Psychology. *Conduct* is some *physical movement* of the body, and is invariably preceded by some *thought* or *feeling* which is its *cause;* and this thought or feeling is produced by some operation of surrounding things—the environment—on the nervous constitution. Inasmuch as the constitutions of men in the same society are similar and the environments similar, the thoughts must be similar and the conduct consequently similar. Hence human conduct necessarily presents itself in the form of similarity—habits and customs. This is true, not only of man, but of other races of animals. The uniformity, however, is not absolute. There are multitudinous exceptions and variations. The original constitutions of men are not precisely alike, nor are the environments of men, even in the same locality and society, precisely alike. Their thoughts are to a certain extent different, and the acts consequent upon the thoughts in like manner different. These differences are, for the most part, exhibited in matters of small importance, and do not obstruct social harmony. But there are causes and occasions which disturb social peace. This is more easily to be perceived in the simplicity of primitive society. Some will have better weapons, more skill, and greater strength and enterprise than others. Some will desire the same things that others desire and to do things which others do not wish to do. Hence collisions arise, and some are irritated with the conduct of others, and exhibit that irritation by retaliation and revengeful punishment. If man lived in solitude, with no fellows, no such collisions would happen. They are possible only in society, and there they are inevitable. They necessarily tend to violence and strife, and unless in some manner restrained would cause perpetual private war. Our nature supplies the correction for this evil. Man seeks pleasure and shrinks from pain, and what he has once seen to take place he believes will happen under the like circumstances again. The child does not at first hesitate to thrust its hand into the fire, but does not make a second attempt. The savage, at first, may see no harm in taking the game another has caught, but when he receives punishment from the resentment of the other, or after he has received it many times and from many others, refrains from repeating the trespass. Things known to injure others thus come to be habitually avoided, and customs arise of carefully avoiding conduct giving offence to others. Again, as men act in nearly all cases according to custom, the expectation of all is that others will continue so to act, and any disappointment of this expectation causes offence if the act is of an injurious nature. Hence the tendency to follow custom and to enforce it upon others is intensified. Those who obey this tendency are safe. Those who act contrary to it are pursued and punished. The worst offenders are relegated to the criminal classes, but all incur disapproval.

The operation of the influences thus described is discernible in the earliest known displays of human action. When man made his first appearance upon earth, he did not wait until some lawgiver appeared to tell him how he must act. He asked no question concerning what he might and might not do. He was endowed with powers and desires which demanded activity, and he proceeded to act. The consequences of his first action began the formation of a guide for his future action, and every succeeding exercise of his powers was followed by consequences which he observed and from which he derived further instruction. He learned that he must not injure or assail the person of another. This teaching of experience was accepted by all, or nearly all, and the great right of personal security arose. He learned that he must not take the fruits of another man's labour, and under this lesson, taught to all, the great institution of private property came into being. His nature led him to unite himself to a woman and to cherish her and to care for their offspring, and the institution of the family arose. This little society was exposed to the depredations of strangers, and this danger prompted a unison of families into tribes in order to form a more perfect defence. He found a pleasure in plenty of possessions and, instead of consuming all the fruits of his labour, sought to save some. He learned to postpone present enjoyment to a future good, and wealth, with a division of employments, increase of population, and improved cultivation of the earth, succeeded to the precarious condition of savage life. He found his pleasures and his ambition centring more and more in the circle of his own fireside and extending to his kindred, and thus began the development of the Moral Sentiment, the original stimulus to the civilisation and refinement of the race. At the same time all these consequences of his activity were having a reflex influence upon himself, and became in turn the causes of the same things of which they were themselves the consequences. We know from physical and moral science that all the acts of man, including his thoughts, have lasting consequences affecting himself. They not only influence his future action, but enter into and modify his physical constitution, and this effect is transmitted to his offspring. A man is what his thoughts and acts make him to be, and his posterity inherit and reproduce his virtues and his vices. Every virtuous thought and act tend to make the man better, and are the parent of other acts more virtuous still. As every man knows to some extent, consciously or unconsciously, that every one of his acts will be followed by consequences agreeable or injurious to himself, and will be acquiesced in by others, or excite their displeasure, he is constantly considering conduct and consequences both in respect to himself and to others. This is the great study of life with all classes at the present time and has been such study in all times. It results in tracing out a sphere of conduct within which the individual can move and act with freedom and security, and beyond which he cannot pass without encroaching upon the like sphere of another and exciting resentment with its consequences. If society were absolutely stationary, the boundaries assigning to each his own arena of action would become distinct and permanent, but as it is experiencing continual change, new conditions, exciting new thoughts and producing new forms of conduct, are continually arising and introducing confusion into customs which become gradually cleared up through the action of the same natural causes. Barbarous society is thus continually engaged unconsciously in the work of accumulating a body of custom embracing the wisdom of long experience transmitted from generation to generation, and increased in the transmission. Progressive societies both unconsciously and consciously, through the works of jurists, legislators, and reformers, pursue the same study of conduct and consequence, selecting and adopting whatever conduces to well-being, eliminating and repressing whatever is hurtful. The unconscious conclusions of the savage, the loftiest conceptions and aspirations of the sage, controlling manners and conduct, affecting the physical constitution and passing as an inheritance to posterity, become forever imbedded in the life of the race and express themselves in its customs. Custom, therefore, is not the accidental, trivial, and meaningless thing which we sometimes think it to be. It is the imperishable record of the wisdom of the illimitable past reaching back to the infancy of the race, revised, corrected, enlarged, open to all alike, and read and understood by all. It was a happy expression of Lord Coke that the wisdom of the law was wiser than any man's wisdom. The work of the jurist to-day, the work of all the highest tribunals of enlightened Europe and America, is that same study of conduct and consequence which has been forever engaged in by the commonest of men. How poor the conclusions of the wisest of lawyers gathered from their own original reflections when compared with those garnered up in the actual customs of life! And how wretchedly poor in comparison are the written commands of the Sovereign State so far as they relate to conduct and manners, coloured and affected as they are with the ignorance, passion, and self-interest with which legislative bodies are filled! What higher or more dignified conception of the study of the law can there be than to make it the task of seeking out, discerning, applying, and extending the principles upon which those grand generalisations of conduct have proceeded which are the fruit of human experience extending through countless ages?

It may be wondered why the study of the law, which is the study of conduct and consequence, thus prosecuted from the infancy of time, should have left so many problems still unsolved, but it must be remembered that no human actions are exact repetitions, and each as it occurs presents its own differences, most of them indeed immaterial, and yet multitudes of them important. Life is an ever unfolding spectacle of new transactions and phases of conduct, which will forever demand the work of study and classification. Moreover, as the moral nature becomes more sensitive, men become inclined to act more and more upon motives of justice and benevolence to others. The impulse is first felt by the more cultivated and intelligent, and tends to spread in ever widening circles throughout society. The higher forms of conduct ripen into new customs, and men become dissatisfied with the standards which the existing law applies. When these standards fail to conform to the actual customs their validity is challenged, and by degrees they become discredited and overthrown in the courts. The occupation of judicial tribunals and lawyers lies not only in solving new problems which the advance of time presents, but in correcting the errors of the past, or rather what would be errors if persisted in—that is, in conforming the law to the actual custom of the present.

We have now reached what I conceive to be a just conception of the nature of Law in its largest sense; and this, not by starting from any *a priori* postulate, but from actual observation of the causes and rules by which human conduct ever has been and is, in fact, governed. The main elements of this conception may be thus summarised:

(1) Law *begins* as the product of the automatic action of society, and becomes in time a cause of the continued growth and perfection of society. Society cannot exist without it, or exist without producing it. *Ubi societas ibi lex.* Law, therefore, is self-created and self-existent. It is the *form* in which human conduct—that is, human life, presents itself under the necessary operation of the causes which govern

9

conduct. It is the fruit of the myriads of concurring judgments of all the members of society pronounced after a study of the consequences of conduct touching what conduct should be followed and what should be avoided.

(2) Inasmuch as conduct is necessarily controlled by previous thought, and such thought is determined by individual constitution, that is, character, and the environment, nothing can directly control conduct, which cannot control both character and environment. It is not, therefore, possible to *make law* by legislative action. Its utmost power is to offer a reward or threaten a punishment as a consequence of particular conduct, and thus furnish an additional *motive* to influence conduct. When such power is exerted to reinforce custom and prevent violations of it, it may be effectual, and rules or commands thus enacted are properly called laws; but if aimed against established custom they will be ineffectual. Law not only cannot be directly made by human action, but cannot be abrogated or changed by such action.

(3) This *thought*, which must necessarily precede all voluntary action, is employed in the study of the *consequences* of conduct, and so far as concerns conduct towards others (which is the only field of conduct regarded by the law), it considers how any contemplated conduct will fairly be received—whether with satisfaction or with displeasure, whether with acceptance or with opposition; that is, whether it will comply with or disappoint a fair expectation. If the contemplated conduct is in plain conformity

to custom, or the contrary, the judgment is instantaneous; if it is novel, hesitation arises and careful, perhaps prolonged, thought is given to it; but the thought is employed alone in considering the *consequences* of the conduct. This is the daily study of life with all men, and the study of the lawyer differs from it only in being pursued scientifically by an expert.

(4) Since conformity to custom is the *necessary* form which human conduct assumes in social dealings, it is the only *just* and *right* form. No other standard can be erected over it.

The *raison d'être* of law, the function it discharges in the social organism, has already in great part been indicated; but the importance of a clear comprehension of this justifies a little more extended treatment, for how can the work of legislation, which, in the modified sense already indicated, is the making of law, be well performed unless the function of all law be well understood?

In considering the function of law we are looking at it in its dynamical aspect as an operative force. Statistically regarded law is custom, when dynamically it is the force acting in harmony with custom and compelling obedience to it. What is the service which that force performs in the social organism, or rather what is the ultimate *good* at which it aims? Primarily we know that obedience to custom enforced by law is a necessary condition to the existence of society, but society is not in itself an ultimate good; it is but a part in the scheme which looks to the good of its members, to the good of the individuals who compose the race. Have we any means of knowing what the ultimate individual good is, so far as conduct is concerned?

Going back to fundamental principles we find happiness to be "our being's end and aim," but in what line of conduct is the greatest happiness to be found? We have seen that it is not in immediate enjoyment, but that we often find a larger aggregate of happiness in postponing present enjoyment for more distant and wider results. These more distant results we may find to be desirable only because they are useful in securing results more distant still. Is there any final result, or condition, which we may pronounce to be good in itself, and at which we may aim as being the ultimate good, the *summum bonum*? Mr. Herbert Spencer gives an answer to this question which seems to me to be more agreeable to reason than any other. He regards the solution to rest in the answer to the question whether life itself is a blessing. Whoever thinks it is not a blessing, can find no real happiness anywhere. He is a pessimist and must welcome annihilation, as bringing an end to present misery. But there are no real pessimists, at least among the sane. Life is a condition to which all cling, and for which most other things will be sacrificed. And if life itself is the supreme desire, the largest and completest life must be the nearest approach to pure happiness; not indeed that momentary pleasure which accompanies the activity of any particular desire or passion, but that greatest aggregate sum of pleasures which is the fruit of the activity of all the powers of life.

Of the conditions necessary to enable the individual to attain this object I name, without fear of contradiction, as the first, Liberty, the choicest of human blessings; and I define Liberty as being the permission or power to do what one pleases to do without any *external* restraint. Self-restraint we must continually exercise, and the practice of it is a means of the highest self-improvement; but if one may do all he wishes to do without fear of external punishment or sacrifice he may be said to enjoy perfect liberty. He is then his own master. He then perceives the inevitable connection between his conduct and its consequence, recognises the fact that the pleasure or the suffering he experiences are rewards or punishments gained or suffered by himself. He is then in a condition which he cannot otherwise enjoy, of working out that ultimate destiny which is in harmony with universal development and progress.

It is manifest, however, that no such unrestricted liberty can be enjoyed in society. The primeval savage found that others desired the possession of the thing which was within his grasp, that he sometimes wished the exclusive enjoyment of what others possessed, and that moral struggles were thus produced which aroused mutual resentments and consequent punishments, given and received. He learned to refrain from exciting the resentment of others, taught others to refrain in like manner, and custom thus fostered and enforced became the beginning of law. The direct and necessary tendency of this restraint was to trace out boundary lines of individual action within which each person might freely move without exciting the opposition of others. Here we find exhibited in its earliest and simplest form the function of the law. It is to distinguish and separate the things which each individual may do or enjoy from the things which he may not do or enjoy without invading the equal liberty of others; and when this is done the nearest approach to perfect liberty is reached. And if we look at the operation of the law under the complex conditions of modern enlightened life we reach the same result. If we scrutinise the proceedings in any judicial controversy we shall find that it turns upon the examination of some particular piece of conduct to determine whether it is within the rightful sphere of individual action. The study of the consequences of conduct prosecuted through countless ages has been animated by no other purpose and has had no other effect than to gather together and consolidate in the life of the race that vast body of knowledge which sometimes consciously, but more often unconsciously, instructs us what we may do without disappointing the fair expectations and provoking the opposition of others. The great German philosopher Kant, assuming to proceed by an *a priori* inquiry reached the same conclusion and made this his definition of law: "The sum total of the conditions under which the personal wishes of one man can be combined with the personal wishes of another man in accordance with a general law of freedom" and Savigny, after an inductive inquiry, more clearly expresses the same conclusion in his definition:

"The rule whereby the invisible border-line is fixed within which the being and the activity of each individual obtains a secure and free space."

But the boundary line of individual action marks out not only the limits beyond which other individuals must not pass, but also the limits which the state in its corporate capacity must not pass, and so in determining the true function of law we also determine the true province of legislation. Society has an organised power which is usefully exerted only for the purpose of assisting man in working out his destiny. This power operating externally protects society against its enemies; its function in its internal operation is to insure the enforcement of law, that is of custom, and, so long as it confines itself to its true province, to make still more clear those boundary lines of individual action the observance of which is the supreme guaranty of Liberty. Any law which has an effect beyond that of maintaining these lines, is by so much an encroachment upon just liberty, and as that liberty is the choicest of blessings so that encroachment is the worst of woes; and whether it is made by the decree of an absolute monarch or by the regular enactment of the legislature of a democratic government, is, alike in either case, what we denominate by the word *Tyranny*. But I will not here disparage the high office of legislation by pointing out the evil which flows from it whenever it departs from its just province and invades the domain of Liberty. Within its province it is capable of a work of great and increasing beneficence. It is, even more than the work of the judge, the *conscious* activity of society to improve its condition by improving its laws. In the order of succession this activity follows the work of the judge. Custom first operates unconsciously to produce law. In a further stage of social advancement, society becomes an organised power and consciously exerts itself to aid and perfect the development of law. Finally it comes to do what the judiciary from its inability to break suddenly from the past and from its limited capacity to continue political instrumentalities for the enforcement of custom is unable to do, not to *make* law, but to make rules relating to law, as well as the complex machinery which the practical administration of law by the state requires. Here is a task the proper performance of which taxes the highest capability of the intellect of man. It is here that the so-called great law-givers of the world have earned their glory. Moses and Solon tower above the great captains of their times. "The vain titles of the victories of Justinian are crumbled into dust, but the name of the legislator is inscribed upon a fair and everlasting monument." But I must reserve the subject of legislation for a separate and more particular treatment.

LECTURE VI.

OUR scrutiny into the causes which govern human conduct, while it has led us to the conclusion that custom is the principal one, at least so far as our relations with each other are affected, and the only one which the unwritten law regards, has incidentally informed us that the law, whether written or unwritten, does not attempt to enforce custom always and universally, and common observation equally apprises us that there is a part of the field of conduct of which the law for some reason takes no notice, and which is yet, in great part, though not wholly, under the control of custom. We cannot fully understand the nature and function of law, without including the whole field within the limits of our inquiry, and ascertaining what part of it lies beyond the scope of the law and the reasons which underlie the limitations which the law imposes upon its own activity. It is thus that some consideration of the subject of Morality becomes pertinent to our main inquiry. No one can become a thorough lawyer without an intelligent comprehension of the general subject of Ethics, nor, let me add, without a fixed and constant sense of the personal obligation to conform his own life to the rules which the study of Ethics reveals.

That part of conduct to which I now call attention as being controlled by custom, without the aid of law, is that which relates to what are usually regarded, whether properly or not, as the smaller affairs of life, the less important intercourse of men with each other in society, and which is subject to social rules. We have found that the rules which the law sanctions require our obedience to custom because otherwise there would be incessant strife and violence; that is to say, that obedience to so much of custom is a necessary condition to the existence of society. It would seem to follow, therefore, that if there be any part of social conduct which, though not involving the existence of society, yet affects in a material degree the comfort and enjoyment of it,—and there is a large field of such conduct,—it also ought to be under the dominion of custom. This we find by observation to be true. If I am invited to a dinner party, and accept the invitation, I am bound to keep the engagement, and this obligation, though I cannot be held answerable to the law for its violation, is enforced by sanctions sometimes more powerful than those of the law. All that the law can do to enforce its obligations is to annex to the violation of them undesirable *consequences;* but to the violation of some merely social obligations society sometimes attaches consequences much more feared. The offender seriously disappoints the expectations of his friend, excites his displeasure, and perhaps forfeits his friendship. The circle of his friends participate in the displeasure, withdraw their courtesies from him, and continued repetition of the offence would bring upon him social ostracism. There are numerous offences against social custom which are punished in like manner. A man must not appear shabbily dressed, or in a state of intoxi-cation, or set a bad example. Offences like these disappoint expectation and create in others irritation and resentment. The ordinary rules of etiquette and fashion obtaining in social circles have a similar foundation and sanction. Social customs like these are often spoken of depreciatingly as merely con-ventional, or capricious, or whimsical. They do indeed differ greatly in importance from those of which the law takes notice, and very different degrees of culpability are attached to the violation of them. Such obligations, however, are, in their *nature*, the same as those of the law, the difference being in the rigour with which they are enforced. Where vio-lations of custom are calculated to excite such irri-tation and displeasure as to provoke violence and perhaps bloodshed they are destructive of society, and the repression of them becomes necessary to social existence. Society must apply to this repres-sion its most effective compulsory force, and this in civilised States is furnished by organised and regular law; but those offences which simply impair the comfort and pleasure of society are left to be re-pressed by the spontaneous action of social opinion operating in the ways I have indicated. The func-tions also of this social discipline are the same with those of the law, namely, to secure to every one the free permission to do all he wishes to do without encroaching upon the like liberty in others. Conduct by one person which, though it does not injure another either in his person or property, yet offends his feelings, is an invasion of his personal sphere within which all wish to be secure from intrusion, and such security is necessary to the equal freedom of all. Social discipline and punishment begin, long before the law is reached, with all offences. Where the force of regular law is applied it is directed against those of greater magnitude, leaving the others, however, to be still enforced by custom. These two modes of discipline are alike also in this: the sanctions of each—that is, the forces which compel obedience—are *external*. They are not like the promptings of what we call conscience. I do not mean that conscience does not ordinarily enjoin obedience to law or social opinion,—undoubtedly it does; but it does not necessarily do so; indeed it sometimes enjoins disobedience. Some, while agreeing that we are bound to conform to custom so far as the law enjoins it, may not be inclined to concede the view that a like moral obligation exists to follow custom even when it is not enforced by legal sanctions. They have the feeling that it is best, so far as possible, for each one to determine what is right and to do that, rather than conform to a mere social standard. I will not stop here to inquire whether there is any such thing as *absolute right*, or in what it consists. I think it true that we all have a certain feeling that there is such a thing as right in itself, and however difficult it may be to define it, such difficulties do not detract from the dignity and importance of the sentiment. Those to whom

I refer perceive, what is indeed true, that the dictates of custom, whether enforced by law or not, are of a *conventional* nature, and they are therefore inclined to deem them of less weight, and especially is this the case when they find, as they occasionally, and perhaps often, must, that they are not in harmony with their views of what is intrinsically right. They feel some hesitancy in determining what conduct to pursue when custom points in one direction and conscience in another. That there is at times a real opposition here is doubtless true, and I am one of those who believe that the command of conscience in such cases should be obeyed; but it should be the true voice of conscience, and not what it is apt to be, that of ignorance, self-conceit, or obstinacy. What I wish to point out, in the first place, is that custom, however conventional, does in nearly every case dictate what is just, according to the common sense of justice. I start with the assumption, which every one must concede, that human society is the necessary product of the human constitution. If we consult our own consciousness we find that we are so made that we cannot live except in society, and observation teaches that man is nowhere to be found living in any other condition. Whatever is necessary in the scheme of the universe must be right, and society therefore is right and necessary, and what is necessary to society is, in itself, necessary and right. Now, if in coming into society each individual should deem himself obliged to pursue that conduct, and that alone, which he deemed to be intrinsically right in itself, and should act accordingly, he would find that he was continually disappointed in the conduct of others affecting himself, and that others were alike disappointed in his action affecting them, for it is certain that their notions of what was intrinsically right would not agree. Some would be better educated than others, and would reject the standards which others would adopt. Some would be misled by vanity, or other faults, much more than others. In short, there would be every variety of difference of opinion, and consequently, every variety of action. If these differences were impartially weighed they would generally be found not to be of much moment, but such is the effect of vanity and obstinacy that, in the eyes of the individuals, they are magnified and assume an undue importance. Disputes and collisions, with the consequent disappointments and irritations, would mark all social intercourse, and greatly impair that harmony essential to the happiness and benefit of society. Nothing but law would prevent bloodshed and violence, and such dissension as the law did not assume to restrain would widely prevail. It is therefore manifest that some rule other than the individual sense of right should be adopted for the government of conduct in that field not occupied by the law. The notion that each individual should be left to follow the dictates of his own conscience must be at once abandoned. What substitute can be found? It might be suggested that a few of the wisest and best might be selected to frame rules, but they would inevitably frame such rules as would accord with their individual notions, and to impose them upon others who did not happen to agree to them would be mere tyranny, and defensible only because it seemed to be necessary. Moreover, how could any human beings, however good and wise, frame rules which would serve to govern those infinitely numerous and varied acts which make up the ordinary intercourse of social life, and how could the rules be learned? This is manifestly impossible. If it were possible that a body of rules could be framed by the equal voice of all, which would represent the average beliefs and sentiments of all, with a certainty which all would admit, and it could be perfectly learned, it would seem to be an expedient as good as could be desired. What is needed is an ever-present guide informing us instantly how to act without stopping to think.

Inasmuch as every one of our acts is preceded and caused by a thought, a man's conduct is the unerring evidence of those thoughts. Customs, therefore, being common modes of action, are the unerring evidence of common thought and belief, and as they are the joint product of the thoughts of all, each one has his own share in forming them. In the enforcement of a rule thus formed no one can complain, for it is the only rule which can be framed which gives equal expression to the voice of each. It restrains only so far as all agree that restraint is necessary. It is the reign of liberty, for it gives to each individual the largest possible area in which he can move and act with unrestricted freedom. This discipline is the source of the courtesy, deference, politeness, and all the graces of social life. Moreover it has the same supreme excellence which belongs to the enforced rules of law. It is a growth beginning like the law far back in the early stages of civilisation, cultivated by the contributions of wisdom and experience, the final result of the combined efforts of society to select and retain what is beneficial, and reject what is hurtful. Manifestly rules thus framed must be superior to any which the wit of particular men could devise. They are not indeed perfect, and as they are the product of the average thought, must change as that thought changes—that is, as the moral sentiment expands and develops.

There still remains another division of the field of conduct which I have not as yet touched. It is one over which custom, whether alone or reinforced by law, asserts no jurisdiction. It is where man enjoys absolute freedom from external control. Inasmuch as custom dictates what we must do in that part of our conduct affecting the existence, good order, and comfort of society, if there be any part of conduct which does not involve the welfare of others, there interference should stop, and man be left absolutely free. I do not mean that he should be free in the sense of being no longer governed by a regard to the consequences of his conduct, but free so far as respects *external* control. The great law of causation, as supreme in the moral as in the physical world, here operates to attach to every action its inevitable consequences, and this supplies motives and influences conduct; but, aside from this, man is here free. This is the world of personal and individual life, not less interesting than that of social life. It covers conduct so unimportant or so trivial that it is not worth while for others to concern themselves with it, as what a man eats, or drinks, or wears, what occupations he follows, what amusements he enjoys, what society he prefers; these are his concern alone. It covers also conduct too lofty and serious to be graduated by an average which would destroy individuality and bring all men to a common level. A man must practise so much of justice, charity, sympathy, and benevolence, as others may fairly expect of him, but while he must not display less, others will not complain if he displays more. He *must* be a good citizen and neighbour; he *may* be a conspicuous blessing to his race.

What is the rule which here regulates our lives? In considering that part of our conduct which concerns others, I have sought to discover those rules only which *actually* regulate conduct, not those which *ought* to regulate it. Science asks primarily only what *is*, not what *ought* to be. So the question here is what, *in fact*, regulates our personal and individual life, not what *ought* to regulate it, although I imagine that the rule which will be found in fact to exist, is the best. If there be any rule, it must be one founded in the nature of man, and we cannot change it if we would; and necessarily—so, at least, we must admit—it must be the best possible rule.

In answering the question I must take a step further back than I have yet taken towards the origin and cause of all conduct. The all-pervading law of causation teaches us that for every act there is a *cause*, and the cause of every voluntary act is what

we call a *motive*. Conduct of necessity obeys the
strongest motive, and if we perfectly knew in the
case of any individual what his constitution—that is,
his character—was, and what the surrounding attractions and repulsions presenting themselves to his
mind were, we could with certainty predict his
action. I shall not attempt to solve any of the
puzzles presented by the speculations concerning
the freedom of the will, but that we do in fact act
in obedience to the strongest motive is a truth made
evident by all human experience. If we wish to
induce any one to do a particular act, we know of
no means to that end except the furnishing to him
of something which will create, or strengthen, in
him some *motive* to do it. Even custom has no
power by which it can *compel* a man actually to do
anything. It can, by creating the fear of legal
punishment or of adverse opinion, induce him to do,
or to refrain from doing; but this is simply supplying
a motive; and the most dreaded punishments of
the law or of social opinion are effective only so far
as they create an efficient motive. And all motives
are, at the last analysis, of the same nature with all
men. They all resolve themselves into the simple
desire to enjoy pleasure or happiness and to escape
pain. The debauchee who plunges into sensual excess,
and the lone ascetic who seeks to mortify every
appetite with the scourge, the youth struggling for
the Olympian wreath, or the martyr at the stake,
are alike animated by the same motive—to experience pleasure, or to avoid a greater pain. But how
different the consequences of the conduct of different

men who yet act, and who cannot help acting, from the same motive! One man thinking of nothing but the pleasures of the flowing bowl commits excess, and awakens from debauch to find himself an object of pity or contempt to his friends and of self-disgust. Another thinks of next morning's headache, observes moderation, and awakens after his sleep happy and ready for the duties of the coming day. What makes this difference between the preferences which have shaped conduct in these two instances? I apprehend that it is just this; that one thought only of the pleasure coming immediately from indulgence, while the other looked further to the more distant consequences of conduct, saw pain to be avoided and other pleasures to be enjoyed by moderation, and in order to gain what would be, on the whole, a greater sum of pleasure, postponed a present enjoyment to a future good, and practised *self-restraint*. He looked beyond the immediate to the more distant *consequences of conduct*, and governed his own action by a regard for them, and found therein a greater sum of pleasure.

We here reach a thought upon which we cannot dwell with too much attention. Here is the respect in which man stands above the brute creation. Some of the lower animals do indeed store food in harvest-time for subsistence in winter; but I know of no other instance in which they practise self-restraint,—if indeed they do so here, for perhaps they do not lay away food until immediate appetite is fully satisfied; and so much is necessary for the preservation of the species. The provident conduct stops there. It is also the respect in which some men stand in supremacy over others, and the supremacy is in the proportion in which they exercise self-restraint. It is also the prime respect in which civilisation rises above barbarism. The savage captures wild game sufficient to satisfy the immediate demands of his appetite, and then sinks to ignoble ease, or indulges his brute and warlike passions. The civilised man undergoes what with other purposes would be painful labour, and gathers a supply more than enough to sustain himself and his family, and employs the surplus in improving his habitation, procuring better clothing, providing means by which he may better enjoy his leisure, not only in making himself and his family happy, but in creating a scene of happiness about him. Man here acts in obedience to immutable laws. He is impelled by nature to seek happiness. He finds that conduct in one direction is the source of happiness, in another of misery. The consequences which he has seen to flow from a line of conduct he expects to repeat themselves if the conduct is repeated. Moreover, his disposition to obey these teachings is strengthened and advanced by growing and developing moral sentiment. He finds, at first, his happiness increased in the narrow circle of his family and home, then his regard and interest extend farther, and he finds increased happiness in the enjoyment of his friends and society. His sympathies become developed and enlarged, and elevate and enlarge his standard of conduct, and lead him to take within its range broader and broader circles, and to this result of the alternate action and reaction between the sympathetic and the intellectual nature there is no end until it is recognised that—

"All are but parts of one stupendous whole."

And the habits thus engendered of seeking the more remote and wider good tend to rob that pursuit even of the pain of self-restraint and convert it into a pleasure. An object repeatedly pursued for the sake of the pleasure it eventually brings becomes loved for its own sake, and the ultimate pleasure in the end is sunk in the present enjoyment of the means, and thus real happiness is found to consist in the well directed activity of our powers. How true this is in the pursuit of knowledge we all know. "If," says Malebranche, "I held truth captive in my hand I would let it fly, in order that I might again pursue and capture it." [1]

Does man in thus forbearing to gratify immediate desire and practising self-restraint in order to gain a more distant, but larger, good obey a rule? I conceive that he does. A rule is something obedience to which implies the pain of self-restraint, which is a real pain, at least until obedience to the rule has become so habitual and full of reward as to be transformed into a pleasure. If man simply yielded his conduct to the attractions of immediate enjoyment without regard to the ultimate consequences, pleasure would be the *end* of his conduct, but we could not properly declare it to be the *rule*. We should rather say that the man acted without rule. But

[1] Hamilton's *Lectures on Metaphysics*, Boston, Lecture I. p. 9.

all men, except the utterly bad (if there are such), find that, in order to gain the largest sum of that which they universally and constantly seek, namely, pleasure, they must scrutinise the consequences of conduct and follow that line of action which, on the whole, is calculated to procure for them the largest measure of happiness; and the more civilised and enlightened they are, the more they feel bound to make this scrutiny, and to follow the conclusions to which it leads, even though it compels some self-sacrifice, self-restraint, and pain. Here is a *rule*, and an actually existing rule which men, or the bulk of them, really observe not completely and in all instances, for they frequently violate it, but it is none the less a rule. The law and custom are frequently violated, but they nevertheless remain rules. This contemplation of the probable, or certain, consequences of our conduct is obviously the mere exercise of what is called our *reason*. It is the endeavour to know what will happen in the future by considering what has happened under like circumstances in the past, and the rule of which I speak is a feeling that we must act in a certain way in order to bring about or prevent, as the case may be, the most desired, or the most feared, consequences. And there is no other actual *rule* in this field of personal and private conduct. If the violations of it were more numerous than the compliances, and were all, or the bulk of them, prompted by the same cause, and that cause were one that *restrained conduct*, they would themselves constitute the rule. But no one will contend that this is the case. That man should habitually act so as to gain misery for himself is not easily thinkable. All the violations of this rule consist, not in restraint, but in licence. The only consideration which restrains conduct is the dictate of reason advising the sacrifice of immediate pleasure for a more distant and wider happiness. The violations of the rule are really but exceptions, however numerous.

The rule therefore which *in fact* governs in this sphere of personal and private conduct is that which impels us to obey the dictates of reason founded upon a scrutiny of the consequences of conduct. Ought it to be the rule? This is an audacious question which we are not permitted to ask unless we are vain enough to presume to sit in judgment upon the work of the great Author of all, and imagine that we can discover a better one.

What is the name given to this rule? Common speech frequently affords the most precise definitions of things which it is difficult to well describe, and it does so here. It is *conscience*, the inward monitor—*con* and *scire*, to know or to feel—a conviction within one's self as the product of one's own thought. And thus the universal feeling that man ought to follow the dictates of his conscience has a scientific basis.

While conscience informs us that we should, in general obey the law and custom, for the reason that they embody the results of the common thought of all and of the operation throughout the unlimited past of that same reason which gives our own consciences the light by which they are guided, and are thus the fruit of the experience of the race, which is wiser than any man's wisdom, still its own final command is supreme over both custom and the law. There may be cases in which a man may be justified in defying custom, and even the law—

> " What conscience dictates to be done,
>   Or warns me not to do,
> This teach me more than hell to shun,
>   That more than heaven pursue."

But we should be certain that the whisperings of vanity or the promptings of obstinacy are not mistaken for the true utterance of the inward monitor. The former are likely to be regarded by others with contempt, the latter points out the pathway which heroism treads, and may win the crown of martyrdom.

There is a certain feeling common to all which tends to make us think that conscience is a separate faculty bestowed upon man, a *moral sense* which instinctively and immediately informs him what is is right and what is wrong. We speak of the "voice within" and use other phrases importing the existence of such a moral faculty. For this view there is really no foundation. It can hardly be that there are two independent rules for conduct. If we have a moral sense which by its inherent power discerns and declares what is right it must be unerring. We should follow its dictates implicitly. We should never indulge a second thought. If what we call reason, or a regard for consequences, should be allowed to control our conduct, in opposition to this interior sense, we should be following a false light. But we have no *moral sense* other than conscience, and this is, in fact, only another name for the dictates of reason founded on a view of the consequences of conduct. Whenever a *question* concerning conduct arises, we instantly proceed to ponder upon the consequences. We may be sure that those causes controlling conduct, which are the only ones we are ever conscious of obeying, are the only ones we, in fact, ever obey or ought to obey.

The illusion, so to speak, by which we are led to imagine that conscience is a special faculty bestowed upon us arises, I apprehend, from the *instantaneous* action of reason in many cases. When we reflect that during the years of childhood we were daily taught that we *must* do certain things, and must *not* do certain other things, and that ever since we have been habitually practising upon precepts thus acquired and upon others formed by ourselves, we need not marvel at the rapidity with which we go through the mental acts necessary to direct our ordinary conduct. It is analogous to the like rapidity with which we exercise our bodily muscles. The action seems spontaneous and instinctive.

What I have been saying tends to explain the peculiar significance of the word *ought* which has been the subject of much discussion. That we have a *feeling* well enough described as the "sense of *ought*" I readily agree. It suggests to us an immediate pointing of our conduct in a certain direction. It gives no reason, but assumes to speak, as it were, from its own authority. This arises, I imagine, from the immediate recognition of the moral quality of actions which have been many times in our thoughts. As just mentioned, in childhood we were taught innumerable things, which we must, or must not, do, and since the period of childhood we have been teaching ourselves, with the aid of experience and reason, similar lessons, and thus we have been forming vast classifications of such things, and when in the course of our daily lives the temptation, the impulse, the occasion for doing any one of them arises, we do not go through any consideration of the consequences which may flow from the contemplated conduct; all questions concerning its propriety have already been met and answered by early instruction or self-discipline; the act contemplated is at once perceived as falling within a class, the distinguishing characteristic of which is that it *ought*, or *ought not*, to be done; *oughtness* or *ought-notness* is the quality of the class, and affects the mind immediately, in like manner as the qualities of physical objects, such as whiteness, or smoothness, or hardness. This *instantaneous* recognition of the quality of actions founded on early teaching or self-discipline is, I apprehend, the feeling akin to the voice of conscience, which is often called our moral sense, or the sense of *ought*, or *ought not*. The utility of such a guide we readily understand. Were it necessary for us in our ordinary conduct to be pondering upon possible consequences at every point, life would be the scene of constant perplexity. The conclusions of reason tested by countless experiences, arranged and classified, are like the digested wisdom of a body of adjudications in the law. The habits of our personal lives, like the customs of social life, become the repositories of the numberless conclusions of experience. They are really the conclusions of reason founded upon the consideration of conduct, but they so instantaneously inform us as to what is to be done that we are not conscious of any deliberation and seem to be commanded by some mysterious inward monitor.

The word *ought* has its correlative in *right*. I *ought* to do whatever it is *right* for me to do; but *right* is more properly descriptive of the intellectual conclusion of reason, while *ought* imports the sense of obligation to govern conduct in accordance with that conclusion.

The reality and significance of the divisions I have made of the field of conduct are well illustrated by a comparison of the meaning of the words *just* and *ought*. *Ought*, as we have seen, is the voice in which conscience speaks; but what is the precise significance of *just*? What is *justice*? There has been much uncertainty upon this point. To some it has seemed to import a sublime attribute, almost an emanation, as it were, of the Deity, recognisable by an innate moral sense. Some regard it scarcely more than a synonymous expression of what is right or ought to be done. But the attempt to form a conception of some absolute attribute which would properly be named justice is an abortive one. All we know is that certain acts are called just, and we feel them to be just. The difficulty is in saying what things, and what only, belong to that class. Certainly all right things are not properly called just. It is right to aid the distressed, to go to church, to cherish one's friends, but such acts do not possess the quality which justice denotes. If a man indulges to excess in intoxicating drinks, or engages in any other vice involving himself alone, we should say that his action was very wrong, but we would not call it unjust. *Do unto others as you would that others should do unto you*, would satisfy the sentiments of love and charity, but not that of justice. Justice, in its primary signification, comes into play only in respect to that part of the conduct of an individual in which others are concerned, but yet not all of that falls within its sphere. There are a multitude of minor customs and observances of life in which the word is not well employed. The disregard of common social obligations would not excite the sense of injustice. It is the matters of graver importance of which the law takes cognisance that fall within the field where justice has sway. It has relation to that body of rights which the law actually enforces, and which is called in the Roman Law by the word from which it is derived, *jus*. Hence the term *jurisprudence*, which is the science of legal justice— that is, of justice so far as it is enforced. And yet justice and law are equivalent words. We say sometimes, very properly, that a law is unjust, meaning that it is not what it ought to be, but there is no point of view from which we can criticise justice.

Justice considered as a sentiment is the sense of

what *ought to be done by one to another*, and this is, necessarily, what one might fairly expect from another—that is, what is customarily done, for no one would think it justice to require from one anything not in accordance with custom. The occasions which call justice into activity are those in which there are differences between men, assertions of rival claims, irritations, and premonitions of strife, or actual strife. It is then that the need is felt of something which will allay hostility and bring about peace. This can not be done by mere force. You may let contestants fight it out until one has conquered the other, but this will not allay the irritation; it may serve only to fan the flame and induce preparation for another struggle. Nor will it be of any avail to imprison the contestants. The quarrel will be taken up by families and friends; but if that one thing were done which all—excepting perhaps the contestants—will regard as the thing *fit to be done* under the circumstances, the strife would be ended. The contestants could not continue it, for they could retain no sympathy or aid, and would be denounced on all hands as disturbers of the peace. Now there is one thing in such cases which all would think fit to be done, and that is what all, in general, would *expect* to be done, and this, as I have reasoned out at length, is a compliance with custom. But if the custom be doubtful. what then? This is the case in very many disputes; it is what the contestants are quarrelling about. The thing to be done is to ascertain the custom and conform to it. This is precisely the thing for which courts were established, and hence they are called courts of justice. This strict limitation of the word *justice* to such matters as the law takes cognisance of must be enlarged to take in other cases in which the word *justice* is used in an analogous sense. There may be disputes of which the law takes no notice. One man may have impugned the character of another and a challenge has passed; the seconds attempt to bring about a reconciliation without success. Each is prejudiced in favour of his principal; the intervention of third parties is accepted, and they ascertain as nearly as possible which of the combatants has made the first departure from custom, and dictate the mutual withdrawals and reparations which, in their opinion, should compose the difference, and all say *justice* has been done.

The absolute supremacy of the rule of custom in determining the character of conduct is well shown by one of the common employments of the word *justice*. Suppose a law be enacted making it a misdemeanour for a man to enter upon the land of another after the other has, by notice in writing, forbidden him to enter, and the person forbidden goes upon the land to recover some cattle belonging to him who have strayed upon it and are doing mischief. He is prosecuted and fined. The law has been executed, but all would say that injustice has been done. Justice, therefore, is something which sits in judgment even on the law. But what kind of law is it which thus sometimes operates to inflict injustice instead of doing justice? Not that *unwritten* law which springs from custom, but that written enactment which a few men called legislators frame. How seldom do we find anything but satisfaction with the judgments of our courts enforcing the unwritten law of custom? Suppose the trespass upon land just mentioned had been left to be redressed by an ordinary suit to recover the damages occasioned by it. The judge would have instructed the jury that the plaintiff was entitled to a verdict for whatever actual damages he had suffered, and the jury would have accorded him six cents, and all would feel that justice has been done.

What is it that gives to the word *justice* its deep and august significance—its supremacy among the moral sentiments? I think a sufficient answer to this question is found in what I have said of the true nature of custom. When we reflect that the lives, peace, and comfort of men from the infancy of the race have been threatened and disturbed by the conduct of one individual exciting the resentment and passion of another and prompting retaliation and revenge, and that the only escape from the terrors and fears thus arising has come from the doing of that thing which all agree is fit to be done, and that to this thing the word *justice* is given, we can understand the power and solemnity with which the word is invested. It imports the end of strife and violence and the incoming of satisfaction and peace, and as it is the only thing which will bring this satisfaction and peace, its dictates are supreme and final, admitting of no appeal. Why does not the written law in all cases affect us with the same reverent regard? Why do we feel at liberty sometimes to denounce a regularly enacted statute as wrong, tyrannical, and unjust? It is because it is but the product of the will of one or a few men, and is liable to be affected by the ignorance, passion, and error to which their judgments are subject; but there is no ignorance, passion, or error in those conclusions of wisdom, tested by the experience of ages, which lie imbedded in the customs of life.

We here again encounter a certain feeling of disappointment in finding Justice, which we have been wont to regard as an attribute almost of Divinity, so closely identified with the mere following of custom. We would have it something lofty, eternal, and unchangeable, but we find it, or rather its standards, shifting as custom shifts. This phenomenon, in the view of some great minds, has tended to dethrone Justice from its lofty seat. It provoked the misanthropy of Pascal into some striking exaggerations. He says:

"In the just and the unjust we find hardly anything which does not change its character in changing its climate. Three degrees of elevation of the pole reverse the whole of jurisprudence! A meridian is decisive of truth, or a few years of possession! Fundamental laws change! Right has its epochs! A pleasant justice that, which a river or a mountain limits! Truth on this side the Pyrénées, error on the other!"

But he hinted at a profound truth when he said:

"Custom is a second nature which destroys the first. Why is not custom natural? I am greatly afraid that nature itself may be only a first custom, as custom is a second nature.[1]"

[1] Pascal, *Pensées*, partie i., art. vi.

But the change is not in justice itself, but in the things to which it relates. If we remember that thought is the product of the action of the environment on our organs of sense, and that the environments and the constitutions of men are everywhere different, thoughts must be different and customs different. This is what separates man into different national groupings, and unites man with man in the separate groupings. The genial philosophy of Herodotus, springing from his communion with men rather than from solitary contemplation, took a different view of custom. He is thus quoted by Sir William Hamilton:

" The whole conduct of Cambyses toward the Egyptian gods, sanctuaries, and priests, convinces me that this king was in the highest degree insane, for otherwise he would not have insulted the worship and holy things of the Egyptians. If any one should accord to all men the permission to make free choice of the best among all customs, undoubtedly each would choose his own. That this would certainly happen can be shown by many examples, and, among others, by the following: The King, Darius, once asked the Greeks who were resident in his court, at what price they could be induced to devour their dead parents. The Greeks answered, that to this no price could bribe them. Thereupon the king asked some Indians who were in the habit of eating their dead parents, what they would take not to eat but to burn them; and the Indians answered even as the Greeks had done." [1]

And Herodotus added that Pindar had justly entitled Custom as the Queen of the World.

In associating Custom with Justice, therefore, we do not dethrone the latter, but seat Custom beside

[1] Hamilton's *Lectures on Metaphysics*, lecture v., p. 60.

her. Justice is the felt necessity of doing that which secures order and peace. Custom furnishes the rule which answers to that necessity. The imperious necessity of justice is acknowledged even by those who hate it. The bad must fly to it as well as the good. The footpad plying his avocation on Hounslow Heath, who filed a bill in equity to compel his pal to give an account of the purses he had taken, had an impregnable case on grounds of justice as between himself and his confederate, though he had mistaken his forum. Fisher Ames, in a celebrated debate upon the treaty with Great Britain, arguing that the carrying out of that treaty was required by a regard for justice, well described the force of that obligation:

" If there could be a resurrection from the foot of the gallows, if the victims of justice could live again, collect together, and form a society, they would, however loath, soon find themselves obliged to make justice, that justice under which they fell, the fundamental law of their State." [1]

Justice is, therefore, not an absolute, but a relative virtue, finding its play in that field of our conduct which, according to the division I have employed, relates to our dealings and intercourse with each other in society, and enforcing in that field the things necessary to the existence of society. This existence is assured when, and only when, each receives from all the treatment he may fairly expect. Then men love to live together; otherwise they fly apart as if charged with resinous electricity. Justice may therefore be defined to be the principle which dic-

[1] Fisher Ames, vol. ii., p. 61.

tates that conduct between man and man which may fairly be expected by both, and as none may fairly expect from another what is not in accordance with custom, justice consists in the compliance with custom in all matters of difference between men. It is the right arm of Peace and the antithesis of Force. This accords with the definition of the Roman Law—*constans et perpetua voluntas suum cuique tribuendi.* To each his due; but as we can know the due of each only from the common feeling of what is due, and this is dependent upon custom, the identity of justice with conformity with custom is implied.

The comparative significations of *justice* and *right* here become apparent. I have heretofore said that conscience is the supreme and final arbiter over the whole field of conduct, while justice is concerned with that part of it only, which relates to our dealings with each other. The dictate of conscience is properly expressed by right, and this, therefore, is a larger term than justice. Right includes the just. Whatever custom pronounces to be just, conscience in general accepts and declares to be right; but in the field of purely private conduct justice has no concern, and what is here right, is not properly described as just, and although in all ordinary cases conscience declares the just to be right, there may be an exception. It is this possibility which gives rise to one of the difficult questions in casuistry, namely, whether it can be right under any circumstances to violate a promise upon which the promisee has acted.

What is the difference between the words *must* and *ought* ? They are sometimes used in senses which have no ethical significance. Either word may be employed in common speech to indicate the necessity of some particular instrumentality to some particular object. Thus I may say I ought to have, or I must have, a sharper knife to cut this meat, and there is no important distinction between the meanings of the words when thus used. But there is a difference when they are used in their ethical senses; there is a difference which the dictionaries do not explain, and which seems subtle and obscure. I think that the obscurity will be cleared up by stating that these words relate respectively to the two principal divisions of the field of conduct. Where the conduct in question consists of transactions in which the interests of more than one are concerned, *must* is more properly employed. Such conduct is governed in part by the law and in part by the other rules of custom, and the sanction or obligation attached to them is *external* to the individual. It is an external force over which he has no control, which he feels bound to obey without stopping to consider what the consequences may be. The law tells me I *must*, not that I *ought*, and I say to myself —I *must* do this, or I *must not* do that, because the law in the one case commands, and in the other case forbids. And it is the same with those obligations of custom which are not enforced by law. If I have accepted an invitation to dinner, but do not wish to go, I feel an external force pressing me to go, and I feel that I *must* go. The question of *con-*

sequences is not ordinarily in these cases to be considered. I must obey the law without regard to consequences, and social custom as well, although the obligation is not in the latter case usually so rigid.

But when we come to the field of private personal conduct the case is different. Here we feel no external authority speaking in the language of command. Here conscience has an exclusive jurisdiction, and its language is not "you *must*" or "you *must not*," but "you *ought*" or "you *ought not.*" Nor are consequences felt to be immaterial here; on the contrary, the decision is arrived at as the result of a survey of all the consequences. The difference between the words comes into strong relief when they stand, as they sometimes do, in opposition to each other. Although private and personal life is the immediate and principal sphere of the activity of conscience, yet conscience as the ultimate governor of our entire conduct has a supervisory jurisdiction over the commands of custom and even of law. In ordinary cases conscience tells me to obey both, for both are in general necessary, or contributory, to the highest good; but sometimes it calls a halt, and advises a wider survey of consequences, and possibly disobedience. We can, indeed, hardly imagine conscience as advising disobedience to the whole body of the unwritten law, but particular enactments may easily be imagined, and perhaps found, which conscience would say might well be disregarded, and to overthrow the existing rulers and substitute new ones is a right which in certain cases Americans cannot deny. In such cases, "I must" yields to "I ought." I am a military officer and am challenged to fight a duel. I feel that I *must* accept it, but conscience may interpose and change the feeling to "I ought not." The *external* authority of custom, even when not enforced by law, carries with it in most cases the superior power; "I must" is more likely to be obeyed than "I ought," but with the men of the highest mould the obligatory force of *ought* is equivalent to that of *must*, and the words are interchangeable. Alexander Hamilton gave a pathetic picture of the struggle between these rival sentiments when, having on many previous occasions borne his testimony against the practice of duelling, he said on the eve of his fatal meeting with Burr, and in the last words he ever wrote: "The ability to be in future useful, whether in resisting mischief or in effecting good, in those crises of our public affairs which seem likely to happen, would probably be inseparable from a conformity with public prejudice in this particular."[1]

[1] Hamilton's Works, vol. viii., p. 628.

LECTURE VII

HAVING completed the survey I designed of the whole field of human conduct with the view of ascertaining the causes which in point of fact control and regulate it, it may be well to set forth in the form of a summary the general conclusions which that survey seems to justify and the steps by which it is reached.

Conduct consists in some physical movement of the body, and it is of such movements only that the law takes direct notice, although in some exceptional cases where the nature of an act is qualified by the intention which prompts it, it may inquire as to that intention. Man has thoughts or feelings moved by the action of the external world upon his physical constitution which necessarily impel him to action, and inasmuch as the constitutions of men are similar, and the environments, in the same society, similar, the actions of men in the same society are similar, and conduct is consequently necessarily exhibited in the form of habits and customs.

Man learns by experience that all action is productive, in its consequences, of either pleasure or pain, and, by a natural law, he expects that the same conduct, when repeated, will produce the like consequences. The motive to all action is to enjoy pleasure or to avoid pain, and he can know what will afford him pleasure or relieve him from pain only by attention to the consequences of his conduct. The study of the consequences of conduct is therefore the first, as it is the last, in which man is forever in every waking moment engaged. From this study he learns that certain kinds of conduct—that is, certain actions,—produce pleasure, and that others produce pain. These he classifies and is moved in his conduct to repeat the former and avoid the latter. He learns, however, that while the immediate consequences of some acts are pleasurable, they yet result eventually in a greater aggregate of pain, while others which have consequences immediately painful produce eventually a larger sum of pleasure, and he learns to forego the immediate gratification of his natural desires and tendencies in the hope of securing a more distant but larger good, or of escaping a more distant but greater pain; that is, he *restrains* and governs his conduct according to his knowledge or judgment of its consequences. Here we have a *rule* of conduct. When man acts in pursuance of immediate natural impulse, he acts without rule; but when he follows a teaching or principle formed by a generalisation of the consequences of all conduct open to his observation, and restrains his impulses in accordance therewith, he obeys a rule.

The phenomena of the development of this fundamental law require us to divide the field of conduct into two parts by separating that which affects only the individual acting from that in which his action affects others. In the first, man has ever

been and still is free from *external* restraint. He still
acts according to rule, but that rule is furnished by
his judgment of the consequences of conduct in their
operation upon himself alone—that is, according to
his reason, or what we call conscience,—and a survey
of this field with an arrangement of the different
varieties of conduct according to their consequences
constitutes one branch of the science of ethics. The
other field, the social one, differs only in this, that
the individual finds that unless he regulates this part
of his conduct in accordance with the fair expectations of others, he will suffer punishment of some
sort from them, and this supplies an external restraint as a motive to induce him to shape his conduct
in accordance with such expectation. The reason
why he thus governs his conduct is that if he fails
to do so he is likely to suffer punishment or disappointment from those whose expectation he disappoints, and this compels him to take notice of
what that expectation is; he finds that others expect
him to act as he expects others to act in accordance
with custom, and custom thus becomes the law in
this field of conduct. The only means of enforcing
this law of custom in those states of society which
precede that in which it takes on an organised form
is what is called *self-help* aided by social sympathy
and other social influences. The individual takes
the law, so to speak, in his own hands, and by in-
flicting punishment on those who violate custom
creates the motive for yielding obedience to it.
This punishment may not be physical or violent.
It is apt to be so where the offence is flagrant, but

minor offences are punished by social disapproval manifested in various ways.

A marked change follows the adoption of organised government. This organisation exists from an early stage in a simple form for various social purposes, but its improvement is very largely superinduced by the felt necessity of doing away with the violence and mischief of self-help. The men of approved wisdom or other experts in the knowledge of customs are employed who declare what custom requires in cases of dispute, and by degrees society comes to use means for enforcing their decisions, and regular law comes into operation. But as this organised control was reached in order to supplant the violence of self-help, its action is correspondingly limited, and is exercised only in the case of those breaches or alleged breaches of custom which endanger the peace of society. The less important conduct is left to the regulation of custom by the methods before employed, the expression of social disapproval and social ostracism.

As civilisation advances, and population, industry, and wealth increase, the social organisation expands and advances, and the means for ascertaining and enforcing custom become more perfect until regular judicial tribunals are established, armed with the whole power of the State to directly enforce their decisions. The proceedings of these tribunals are embodied in permanent records, and their decisions act as authoritative declarations of binding custom— that is, they become precedents, and thereafter in cases of litigation where an apt precedent is found it is followed without further inquiry, and the precedents themselves are by the private work of jurists arranged in scientific form and go to make up the fabric of substantive law.

In the course of this social progress the more completely organised State becomes capable of surveying its own condition and wants, and of perceiving that justice would be better administered if better provision in the way of courts and judicial precedure were made, and if mischievous acts which have not as yet been publicly punished were declared and treated as crimes, and that the mechanism of government in all its parts might be improved by new devices. It forms its *will* in respect to such concerns, expresses it in writing, and solemnly declares it by means of enacted laws. This is the making of Public Law in which legislation found its first employment, and which is still its chief, if not its only function.

If we scrutinise the actual process which we employ to-day in ascertaining the law in any particular case, we find that if the point in question be public law, we turn to the statute-book; if it be private law, we turn to the body of precedents. The information we thus derive suffices for all cases of ordinary doubt, and the great body of human conduct appears as a spectacle of peace and order. There are exceptions to this, where wrongdoers intentionally, or the ignorant innocently, violate the established customs, and there are other exceptions where from the novelty of the transactions it becomes matter of doubt even with experts to what class the conduct in question belongs. Inasmuch as human affairs are never precise repetitions, and the complicated societies of civilisation are in a condition of constant change, there are, in point of absolute number, many of such cases, although they are few when compared with the whole volume of conduct. They constitute the subjects of litigation which engage the attention of courts, and if we follow the discussions there we find the difficulty to be that there is no known legal class of actions under which they can be clearly and at once brought, and the effort of the judge is to *find* the *best* rule by which the case may be determined. In this search the things considered are the ordinary ways in which the business, the intercourse, and the conduct of life are conducted, and whether the conduct in question is in harmony with them, or, if not, in what particular it is discordant. This is manifestly a study of the consequences of the conduct, and if among them there is found in that conduct any element which operates to defraud or deceive or invade the rights of person or property as they are settled by custom, or to betray trust and confidence, or in any way to disappoint fair expectation, the conduct is in violation of custom and is placed in the class of things condemned by the law. The final study of the highest court of appeal is, therefore, in the last analysis, that same study of conduct and consequence in which all men are engaged every day and which began when man first began to act.

Even where the question is one of the interpretation of written law, involving the meaning of words and the legislative intent, the things contended

about in argument and decision are the customary
employment of language,   the customary motives
of action, and the mischievous departures from
established custom, which the statute was probably
intended to remedy.

The final conclusion of the inquiry, what rule or
rules in point of fact governed human conduct, was
that, so far as social conduct is concerned, *custom* is
not simply *one* of the *sources* of law from which
selections may be made and converted into law by
the independent and arbitrary *fiat* of a legislature or
a court, but that law, with the narrow exception of
legislation, *is* custom, and, like custom, self-existing
and irrepealable.

The necessary operation and therefore the *function*
of law thus defined we found to be the marking out
of the largest area within which each individual
could freely move and act without invading the like
freedom in every other—that is, to insure the largest
possible liberty.

I shall have next to deal with the consequences
of the conclusions thus summarised.

The first which I note is that they involve the rejection of the commonly accepted theories of the
law. In speaking in the first of these lectures of the
great number and variety of definitions which have
been given of law, I observed that, however differing
from one another in expression and in the less important particulars, they might be arranged in one
or the other of two classes, one seeking to establish
law upon the basis of absolute Justice and Right,
and the other making it proceed from the arbitrary

command of the Sovereign State; one seeking to
enthrone over human conduct a rule of Order, and
the other a rule of Force; one fairly represented by
the theory of Natural Law, and the other by the
doctrines of Hobbes, Bentham, Austin, and others
that law is a command. I have some observations
to make concerning each class of these two opposite
tendencies.

Historically the doctrine of the Law of Nature
had its origin with the philosophic jurists of Rome,
or, at least, the first enunciation we have of it came
from them, and by Nature they intended the Author
of Nature, Jove or God. They declared that the
true and fundamental law was in the mind of the
Deity himself when he created the universe. Cicero
sets forth this view in his treatises *De Legibus* and
De Republica with great nobility of eloquence.
According to him, the fundamental law which commands and forbids is the right reason of Supreme
Jove. *Quam ob rem lex vera atque princeps apta ad
jubendum et vetandum ratio est recta summi Jovis.*[1]
This pagan view has been accepted by many Christian
jurists, of whom Blackstone is a good example.
He says:

" This law of nature being coeval with mankind, and dictated
by God himself, is of course superior in obligation to any
other. It is binding over all the globe, in all countries, and
at all times; no human laws are of any validity, if contrary
to this; and such of them as are valid derive all their force
and all their authority, mediately or immediately, from this
original." [2]

[1] De Leg., ii., 4.
[2] Bl., book i., p. 41.

Now, in the language of Lord Bacon, "I would rather believe all the fables of the Talmud and the Alcoran than that this universal frame is without a Mind"; but science is the orderly arrangement of things we can *know*, and not of things we cannot know, and I think there is no irreverence in dismissing from our attention those theories which rest upon our feeble imaginations of the Divine Nature; indeed, I think the term irreverence more properly belongs to the methods I am declaring insufficient.

"God hath not made" [I am quoting the language of Sir Thomas Browne] "a creature that can comprehend him; 't is a privilege of his own nature; 'I am that I am' was his own definition unto Moses; and 't was a short one to confound mortality, that durst question God, or ask him what he was."[1]

We must, indeed, in tracing the line of causation along which the facts of any science are to be arranged, come finally to some ultimate barrier beyond which we cannot pass; but we should not too soon conclude that the barrier has been reached. The rule of dramatic poetry, not to introduce a God upon the stage unless a crisis appears demanding the Divine intervention, should be the rule of philosophy also:

Nec deus intersit, nisi dignus vindice nodus inciderit.

But the prodigious space which the doctrine of the Law of Nature has filled in philosophical speculation as the foundation both of Ethics and Law is itself a phenomenon to be explained. It could hardly

[1] Sir Thomas Browne, *Religio Medici*, sec. xi.

have assumed such magnitude unless it were supported by some great underlying truth, and if the explanation should not afford a reconciliation between this theory of law and the views I have adopted, those views would be open to a doubt more serious than any I have as yet encountered.

We must turn to the historical origin of this doctrine, which, as I have said, first appeared among the philosophic jurists of Rome. While the territory of Rome was confined within its Italian limits, justice was administered in her courts according to the customs of the city, in which there was a large element of technicality. This did not prevent the doing of substantial justice, for these technicalities and peculiarities inhered in the customs and thus entered into the contemplations of individuals in their dealings with each other. But with the expansion of Roman dominion and the enlargement of commerce came a great influx of provincials and foreigners, and extensive dealings between them and the native citizens. In any litigations arising out of such dealings it would have been gross injustice to apply the peculiar civil law of the city. Any person, whether he be called judge, referee, arbitrator, or by whatever name, whose office it is to settle disputes between others, must of necessity base his decision upon what he deems the parties fairly, and therefore probably, expected from each other, and in this task, when the dispute is between citizens of different States having many different customs, he seeks to find customs and ways which are common to men without regard to their particular nation-

ality. According to the civil law of Rome, a contract
might not be valid unless some technical formula
were complied with, and consequently Roman citizens would not regard themselves as bound in the
absence of such compliance. But men, as men, of
whatever nation, if they communicate at all, have
means by which they may express terms and conditions and assent and dissent, and where they do
this they expect compliance with their consensual
engagements. A method of treatment in harmony
with these conditions was applied by the Prætor
Peregrinus of Rome in litigations between Roman
citizens and provincials or foreigners, and while the
Prætor Urbanus regarded the Twelve Tables and
the Prætorian edicts, he looked only to the conduct
of the parties, its character and consequences. Two
bodies of laws consequently grew up at the side of
each other, the *jus civile* limited to transactions
between Roman citizens, and the *jus gentium* as
wide in its application as the inhabited globe. The
superiority of the latter as a scientific system was
recognised by the Roman lawyers, and the domestic
jurisprudence became from time to time enriched by
borrowing from it many sound precepts. The philosophic jurists, among whom Cicero was a shining
example, when they came to inquire into the nature
of Law, could not find its real foundation in the narrow *jus civile;* but in the *jus gentium* they found
four characteristic features: (1) that it was not
enacted by any man or body of men, for the Prætor
Peregrinus did not, any more than the modern
judge, presume to *make law;* (2) that it could not

12

be repealed, and was therefore self-existent; (3) that its particular rules were reached by the processes of reason; (4) that it satisfied the universal sentiment of justice. Whence did it proceed, and from what source did it derive its authority? It seemed inscrutable, and the only answer they could give to the question was to ascribe the origin and authority of law to that same Divine Power to which they attributed the other mysterious phenomena of the universe, the movements of the heavenly bodies, the successions of the seasons, the storms and tides of the ocean. It was Nature or God. Had they studied the facts of consciousness, and learned that conduct was necessarily exhibited in the form of habit and custom, they would have seen that the origin of law rested in a self-governing principle of society; and if they had carefully scrutinised the methods of the judicial tribunals, they would have seen that it consisted in the study of conduct and its consequences with the view of determining what was in accordance with custom or fair expectation, and that such study was simply the exercise of our ordinary reasoning powers upon the subject of conduct; in this way they would have reached the enlightening conclusion that law was tantamount to custom. Any further inquiry would be how and why our natures were so made as to compel us to think and act in such a way—an inquiry which would have baffled them no more than it baffles us. But in the law of custom thus reached, they would have found all the characteristics which they perceived in what they denominated the Law of Nature. The Roman jurists have conferred upon posterity by their conception of the Law of Nature one great benefit, a clear apprehension of the fundamental difference between the written and the unwritten law.

The doctrine which has in modern times divided with that of the Law of Nature the opinions of juridical writers is that which defines Law as the command of the Sovereign power in a State. It was not at first the product of an original and independent inquiry into the nature of law, but was contrived to answer the supposed exigencies of political necessity. It is first to be found set forth in the writings of the celebrated Thomas Hobbes in the early part of the seventeenth century. He was a thorough royalist in his political views, and writing at the time of the struggles against the House of Stuart, his main purpose was not so much to set forth a new theory of the ordinary law, as to justify the exercise of a severe authority in repressing rebellion against civil government. He was a rigid as well as a profound thinker, and never shrank from any of the logical consequences of his main tenets. His view was that the condition of man before the organisation of society was a state of anarchy or war, in which every man's hand was against his fellow, and that the only way of escape from such miseries was to be found in organised society, and that society was the more effective and beneficial the more the corporate power became complete and absolute. His ideal, therefore, was that of an unlimited and unquestioned supreme public authority, preferably, though not necessarily, a monarchical one. In his view the authority of the State should be supreme everywhere. Whatever the State commanded was just, and because the State commanded it, and whatever it chose to enforce must be taken to be its command. His definition of law thus became "the *speech* of him who by right commands somewhat to be done or omitted."

Nor did Jeremy Bentham, the next distinguished supporter of the theory, find his way to its adoption by a scientific inquiry into the nature of law. He accepted it because it suited his particular views and purposes. He was primarily a moralist, and believed that he had discovered the Summum Bonum in what he called the principle of Utility, which he described by the maxim, "The greatest good to the greatest number." It did not occur to him that, in the order of nature, happiness could be secured by man only by his own efforts and discipline in attending to the consequences of conduct and selecting those forms which experience taught him would secure it. He thought that the pathway to happiness for all men could be found out by one, or a few wise ones, and man could be compelled to follow it and thus be made happy by law. He found a great obstacle in his way; this was the practice of society to conform to rules of conduct declared by the judges. He insisted that they really *made* the rules while pretending only to *find* them, and made them without authority, and he came to regard the unwritten law as a hateful usurpation, and he described the common method adopted by the judges in making use of legal fictions in order to make legal remedies effectual, as "a wilful falsehood having for its object the stealing of legislative power by and for hands which could not, or durst not, openly claim it." The theory of Hobbes exactly suited his purpose. If law was a command alone, the judges would be obliged to look for their law to the only power that could make an authoritative command, namely, the Sovereign State, and the great condition of public happiness would be supplied by the preparation of a code containing the most wisely selected rules, and its adoption by legislative enactment. John Austin, whose lectures *On the Province of Jurisprudence Determined* have exercised so wide an influence, was a disciple of Bentham and a believer in the doctrine of Utility. But he had not that abhorrence of the unwritten law which animated his master. He believed that ultimately a complete written code enacted by legislation would be the perfection of law, but he doubted whether this was immediately practicable. His diagnosis of the actual condition of the administration of law seemed to be that mankind had stupidly and unnecessarily, as if for the want of competent advice and leadership, fallen into the blunder of allowing blind custom, instead of reason, to regulate their conduct, as if reason were some special faculty which could reach forward and discover those true principles of law and government which ought everywhere to be adopted. The following language employed by him is indicative of his view:

"Many of the legal and moral rules which obtain in the most civilised communities rest upon brute custom and not upon manly reason. They have been taken from preceding generations without examination, and are deeply tinctured with the childish caprices and narrow views of barbarity. And yet they have been cherished and perpetuated through ages of advancing knowledge to the comparatively enlightened period in which it is our happiness to live."

Believing with Bentham that "the greatest good to the greatest number" was discernible by reason, and should be made the rule of conduct by positive law, he made law to consist wholly in command, and framed his well-known formula: "Every positive law is set by a sovereign person or by a sovereign body of persons (a legislature) to a member or members of the independent political society wherein that person or body is sovereign or supreme."

This theory and definition of law has an apparent partial foundation. It properly defines *legislation*— that is, law consciously enacted by men, although a qualification is needed even here; beyond this it seems to me entirely erroneous. Inasmuch as in the view I have taken substantially the whole private law which governs much the larger part of human conduct has arisen from and still stands upon custom, and is the necessary product of the life of society, and therefore incapable of being made at all, the opposition between this view and the theory of Austin is irreconcilable. Inasmuch as I have established, as I suppose, my own view, I might, perhaps, regard this opposition as a sufficient refutation of that theory, but a separate and distinct exposure of its errors and inconsistencies will furnish additional confirmation to the doctrine I have supported.

While the Austinian definition encounters difficulty as soon as we come to consider the unwritten law, Austin felt that his master, Bentham, had fallen into a gross error in condemning and stigmatising this branch of law as the product of a fraudulent usurpation.

He regarded the bulk of this law as a rational and legitimate system of rules. He felt that it must in some way find a place under his theory, and his contrivance was to assert that the judges *made* the law declared by them, and made it, not by any usurpation, as Bentham insisted, but rightfully, in virtue of an authority delegated to them by the Sovereign. Here, however, he was met by the hard fact that no one of the long line of illustrious judges who had occupied the English bench ever supposed for a moment that he was *making* law, either by virtue of a delegated authority or otherwise, and that all, or nearly all, would indignantly have repelled any imputation of doing it; but he treated their view with contempt, speaking of it thus: "The childish fiction employed by our judges, that judiciary or common law is not made by them, but is a miraculous something made by nobody, existing, I suppose, from eternity, and merely declared from time to time by the judges."[1]

But where does he find an authority in the judges to *make* law in the shape of commands, for certainly they are not themselves sovereign or a sovereign body?

His way of meeting this difficulty is by imputing

[1] Austin § 919

the action of the judges to the real sovereign. He
declares that an authority to command is delegated
by the sovereign to the judges and that they command by virtue of this delegation. Both these
assertions are pure assumptions. The closest scrutiny can find no such delegation, nor any command
in pursuance of it. Austin concedes that there is no
direct evidence of such delegation, but says that
there is something *equivalent* to it, namely, the
fact that the sovereign has the *power* to reject or
disapprove the commands of the judges, and by not
doing so *ratifies* them. But this is attempting to
prove one assumption by making another, or rather
two others. In the first place, under the familiar
doctrine that ratification is equivalent to an original
authority, it is an indispensable requisite that the
principal should *know* the act of the agent which he
intends to ratify; but the supposition that the
sovereign person, or sovereign legislature knows
all the decisions of the courts, or any considerable
part of them, is utterly unfounded. To assume it is
not merely to assume a thing which we do not know
to be true, but one which we know to be *untrue*. The
second assumption is that of a ratification by the
sovereign. What evidence is there of this? None
can be discovered. All we have is the *silence* of the
sovereign. There is indeed in the law of agency a
maxim that where a principal has knowledge of an
act of his agent and makes no objection to it, it
may be inferred that he ratifies it, and this is the
ground upon which Austin bases his assertion of
ratification.

Let us see to what this reasoning will lead. The theory, it will be borne in mind, is of the creation—the origin—of law. Now upon the doctrine that the sovereign, by his silence, ratifies the acts of his judges, he must ratify just what they do, their *real action*, and nothing else. But they make no commands at all concerning conduct; they declare no rule; they simply sit in judgment upon controversies between litigants in a particular case, and declare that one shall or shall not pay money or deliver property, or accord some special relief, to the other. It might be said by a supporter of Austin's theory that although this is all they do in *form*, yet in fact, inasmuch as they make their decisions upon grounds and for reasons generally stated by them, they *really* declare what must be regarded as law at least for all like cases. This is a concession that the sovereign ratifies *what they really do*, and this is to declare that by virtue of some already existing law certain relief shall or shall not be awarded. What they really do, therefore, is not to create law, but to declare that the law already exists. If what the judges did was to declare a law not before existing, the subjection by them of one of the parties to liability for an infraction of the law, in a transaction occurring before the existence of the law, would be an indefensible outrage. Any one who undertakes to support Austin's theory encounters here an ugly dilemma; the law by which the judge makes a decision either existed at the time of the transaction involved in the case, or it did not, and was *made* by the judge;

if it did exist, the judge did *not* make it, and the imagined ratification by the sovereign did not make it, there being no need of his interposition, express or implied. If it did *not* exist at the time of the transaction, then what the judge has done and the sovereign ratified is to compel a man to suffer for the violation of a law committed before the law was made. No theory of law can stand which involves such a consequence. Our courts act consistently, and the record of an action exhibits a perfectly logical process; but upon the Austinian theory it would present a revolting absurdity. Let me illustrate the operation of that theory. A plaintiff brings his action in a novel case, never before considered, alleging certain facts and claiming that by *existing law* he is entitled to recover from the defendant a thousand dollars for an injury inflicted upon him; the defendant appears and admits the facts alleged, but insists that by *existing law* he did only what he had good right to do. The learned judge finds that neither party is right in his claim, because, as he says, there is no existing law applicable to the case, none having been made; but he is clearly of the opinion that there ought to be one which would support the plaintiff's claim, and that it is his duty, as the delegate of the sovereign, to make it, which duty he proceeds to perform, but in a most amazing manner. He does not dismiss the suit and at the same time declare what in all future like cases the law shall be, but, regretting, perhaps, the indirect manner in which he must perform his duty and the individual suffering he must inflict, he condemns the defendant to do, what he declares there was no law requiring him to do, namely, to pay the thousand dollars.

And yet this definition of law, though it has been subjected recently to much criticism, is still perhaps more generally accepted in England and America than any other. Sir Henry Sumner Maine, whose writings have commanded so much attention, while he has pointed out some of its errors, has given to it his general approval and praise. He declares that "to Bentham, and even in a higher degree to Austin, the world is indebted for the only existing attempt to construct a system of jurisprudence by strict scientific process and to found it, not on *à priori* assumption, but on the observation, comparison, and analysis of the various legal conceptions."[1] He has partially seen the absurd consequences of Austin's doctrine of ratification, and says: "It is a better answer to this theory than Austin would perhaps have admitted, that it is founded on a mere artifice of speech, and that it assumes Courts of Justice to act in a way and from motives of which they are quite unconscious."[2] Such difficulties, though they moderate, do not by any means destroy, Prof. Maine's estimate of the correctness of the Austinian doctrine, and he thinks a more complete understanding of the fundamental element of that doctrine will conduce to a recognition of, at least, its theoretical soundness and of its value. This fundamental element he makes to be Austin's conception

[1] Maine, *Early History of Institutions*, p. 343.
[2] *Ibid.*, p. 364.

of Sovereignty, to which he invokes especial attention. He says:

"When, however, it has once been seen that in Austin's system the determination of Sovereignty ought to precede the determination of Law, when it is once understood that the Austinian conception of Sovereignty has been reached through mentally uniting all forms of government in a group by conceiving them as stripped of every attribute except coercive force, and when it is steadily borne in mind that the deductions from an abstract principle are never, from the nature of the case, completely exemplified in facts, not only, as it seems to me, do the chief difficulties felt by the student of Austin disappear, but some of the assertions made by him, at which the beginner is most apt to stumble, have rather the air of self-evident propositions.[1] "

Let me then give that close attention to this conception of sovereignty which Prof. Maine commends, and to his statement of it. He says that Austin's doctrine of Sovereignty

"is as follows: There is, in every independent political community—that is, in every political community not in the habit of obedience to a superior above itself—some single person or some combination of persons which has the power of compelling the other members of the community to do exactly as it pleases. This single person or group—this individual or this collegiate Sovereign (to employ Austin's phrase)—may be found in every independent political community as certainly as the centre of gravity in a mass of matter. . . . This Sovereign, this person or combination of persons, universally occurring in all independent political communities, has in all such communities one characteristic common to all the shapes Sovereignty may take, the possession of irresistible force, not necessarily exerted, but capable of being exerted.[2] "

[1] Maine, *Early History of Institutions*, p. 362.
[2] *Ibid.*, pp. 349–350.

And further, he says:

"The way in which Hobbes and he (Austin) bring such bodies of rules as the Common law under their system is by insisting on a maxim which is of vital importance to it—'Whatever the Sovereign permits he commands.' Until customs are enforced by Courts of Justice, they are merely 'positive morality,' rules enforced by opinion, but, as soon as Courts of Justice enforce them, they become commands of the Sovereign, conveyed through the Judges, who are his delegates or deputies.[1]"

But this explicit statement of Austin's conception of sovereignty serves only to emphasise its falsity. It is useful only as a foundation for the proposition that the law declared by the judges is really made by them as the agents of the sovereign who ratifies their action and is thus *adopted*. The doctrine of ratification necessarily assumes power in the principal to perform the act. I think I have sufficiently exposed already the error in this notion of law-making by the *assumed* ratification of a sovereign possessing an *assumed* absolute power, but I may show that Maine's own argument refutes his own proposition. Let me throw that argument into syllogistic form. This is the first premise in the syllogism: Whatever the sovereign permits he commands. The second premise is—He permits courts of justice to sit and decide controversies by law which they declare to be *already in existence*; and the consequence is inevitable: he *permits* the courts of justice to so sit and declare. The declaration of the judges is the declaration of the sovereign.

[1] Maine, *Early History of Institutions*, pp. 363-364.

He *commands* it for he *permits* it, and therefore the sovereign declares that the law is not *made*, but that it already *exists!* Bentham may insist, as he does, that this declaration by the judges is a "fraudulent pretence" to conceal their usurpation of legislative power; Austin may aver, as he does, that it is a "childish fiction," but it is the "fraudulent pretence," or the "childish fiction" of the sovereign himself. This is the severe logical consequence of Maine's defence of Austin's conception of sovereignty. It establishes, not his definition of law, but the contrary one.

LECTURE VIII.

THERE are many who, though not accepting the theories of Bentham and Austin, have yet a feeling that the distinction between *finding* and *making* the law in a *truly novel case* is but a fanciful one, and that what is really done by *declaring* the law in such a case, it being before unknown, is to *make* it; they admit the seeming injustice of holding persons responsible for a violation of law not existing at the time of the action in controversy, but think it is no greater than to hold them responsible for a violation of a law at the time *unknown*. Such doubts deserve respectful treatment. Upon the view that law is *custom*, the maxim that all are presumed to know the law is well founded and reasonable. Custom is the one thing that all may safely be presumed to know. It is—what is more and better than known—*felt*. There is no injustice, therefore, in a rule which subjects men to the obligation of existing custom. There will be some cases of real doubt, but in all such cases the act or conduct concerning which the doubt exists really belongs to *some* class. It is either something which accords with fair expectation, or does not so accord, and the point is decided by selected experts. As in a game of ball or other athletic game, things will be done on one side which will be disputed on the other, and the referee will be called upon to decide. His decision will be that the thing objected to was right or wrong according to *existing* rules, and no one will think that he *makes* the rule. The case may be an entirely novel one and difficult of determination, but the defeated party suffers no injustice because of this difficulty. Both sides had equal knowledge of the rules and the existence of difficulty was the same burden to each.

In the great game of society, as in the little one of ball, all the players are justly assumed to know the rules. What is really done in a novel case is the same thing that is done in every disputed case. The features of the transaction are subjected to scrutiny in order to determine to what class it belongs. The classes are not *made;* they *exist* in existing custom. There may be a difficulty in ascertaining the class growing out of the *novelty* of the case. Some features of the transaction suggest that it should be placed in one class, others that it should be placed in another. The case is in no manner different from that in which a new plant or animal is discovered bearing resemblances to more than one species. Careful observation is requisite in order to determine under which class it should be ranked and naturalists may differ about it; but the eventual classification is determined by the qualities which are really *found* in it, not by any qualities artificially imputed to it. So in the case of a novel transaction. The conduct drawn in question *is* either right or wrong according to its own qualities; that is to say that its true legal character is already fixed, and the task of the expert—that is, the judge—is to find these

true determining qualities, and when he finds these
he finds the class to which the transaction belongs,
and therefore finds the law. He would misconceive
his task if he should say that it was a new case and,
without a correct ascertainment of its determining
features, should arbitrarily declare it to belong to a
class under which its real qualities did *not* bring it.
Should he do this he would be *making* the law, and,
indeed, the judge can only *make* the law by making
a wrong declaration—that is, he can only make
erroneous law. If, without scrutiny, he should
arbitrarily assign the case to its right class, he would
correctly declare the law, but he would not make it.

Thus far I have accepted the proposition lying at
the basis of Austin's theory of sovereignty, that
which the sovereign permits he commands, as true;
but only for the sake of the argument, and in order to
show that the consequences deduced from it do not
follow; but is it true in fact? Is it true that in every
independent human society there is a sovereign
power so absolute as to justify the inference that
what it permits it commands? To make it sure that
I am stating the proposition fairly, I give it in the
language in which Prof. Maine sets forth the fundamental position of the Austinian doctrine, namely,
that "in every independent community of men
there resides the power of acting with irresistible
force on the several members of that community.
This may be accepted as actual fact."[1] Prof. Maine
here fully commits himself to the assertion of Austin,
that in every independent State there is in the

[1] Maine, *Early History of Institutions*, p. 357.

13

sovereign or sovereign body the power of doing what he, in another passage already cited, declares "exactly what he pleases." An assumption more prodigiously untrue could scarcely be imagined. What! A power in an earthly sovereign or sovereign body, to control the conduct of all the people in a nation "exactly as it pleases"? This would be a power to *make conduct*, to construct life, to create, if the sovereign so pleased, a new world! There is one Being alone to whom such a power can be assigned—one Being alone who can do "exactly as He pleases."

It is quite needless for me to expose by any minute inquiry into the history of societies the error of the assumption, inasmuch as Prof. Maine immediately proceeds, quite without knowing it, to refute both Austin and himself. He goes on to say:

"An assertion, however, which the great Analytical Jurists cannot be charged with making, but which some of their disciples go very near to hazarding, that the Sovereign person or group actually wields the stored-up force of society by an uncontrolled exercise of will, is *certainly never in accordance with fact*." [The italics are mine.] "A despot with a disturbed brain is the sole conceivable example of such Sovereignty. The vast mass of influences, which we may call, for shortness, moral, perpetually shapes, limits, or forbids the actual direction of the forces of society by its Sovereign.[1]"

Here we have it that while the sovereign actually possesses absolute, unlimited power, he never exercises it! How then, I beg to inquire, do we know

[1] Maine's *Early History of Institutions,* pp. 358–359.

he possesses it? The only evidence we have of the possession of any power by a sovereign person or body is the actual *exercise* of it by such person or body. But Prof. Maine again relieves us of the task of detailed refutation by the language of the citation just made. "The vast mass of influences which we may call, for shortness, moral, perpetually shapes, limits, or forbids the actual direction of the forces of society by its Sovereign." It is hardly worth while to debate what sort of a thing sovereignty is which is perpetually *shaped, limited,* and *forbidden* by a "vast mass of influences." If there is a "vast mass of influences" which limits and forbids the exercise of sovereign power by a monarch or a legislature, they are the real sovereign, and what other name is there for them than custom? Austin's conception is sovereignty, plus a variety of things which prevent it from being sovereign. It is indeed what Prof. Maine styles it, "the result of Abstraction," and he may add, an abstraction which deprives the word, and the theory in which it plays so essential a part, of any significance or importance. To assert complete sovereignty in order to construct a theory, and then to say that the assertion is not in fact true, is to commit *felo de se.* The wonder is that Prof. Maine, after dealing as he does with Austin's theory, still continues to regard it as of such high value as a contribution to jurisprudence. The theory possesses for him the great attraction of *simplicity,* and with an evident desire to find support for it in the quarter where a theory must find support or be dismissed—that is, in the world of real fact, he casts a glance over the history of political societies and the present condition of social government. He first describes the sort of rule which obtains, or has obtained, in a recent native Indian empire, that of Runjeet Singh, in the northwestern region of India, called the Punjab. Nowhere has there been a more absolute despot, and one might think the monarch a fitting example of a sovereign who could do "exactly as he pleased." Prof. Maine thus describes his empire:

"After passing through every conceivable phase of anarchy and dormant anarchy, it (the Punjab) fell under the tolerably consolidated dominion of a half-military, half-religious oligarchy, known as the Sikhs. The Sikhs themselves were afterwards reduced to subjection by a single chieftain belonging to their order, Runjeet Singh. At first sight, there could be no more perfect embodiment than Runjeet Singh of Sovereignty, as conceived by Austin. He was absolutely despotic. Except occasionally on his wild frontier, he kept the most perfect order. He could have commanded anything; the smallest disobedience to his commands would have been followed by death or mutilation, and this was perfectly well known to the enormous majority of his subjects. Yet I doubt whether once in all his life he issued a command which Austin would call a law. He took, as his revenue, a prodigious share of the produce of the soil. He harried villages which recalcitrated at his exactions, and he executed great numbers of men. He levied great armies; he had all material of power and exercised it in various ways. But he never made a law. The rules which regulated the life of his subjects were derived from their immemorial usages, and these rules were administered by domestic tribunals, in families or village-communities—that is, in groups no larger, or little larger, than those to which the application of Austin's principles cannot be effected, on his own admission, without absurdity.

" I do not for a moment assert that the existence of such a
state of political society falsifies Austin's theory, as a theory.
The great maxim by which objections to it are disposed of is,
as I have so often said before, 'What the Sovereign permits, he
commands.' The Sikh despot permitted heads of households
and village-elders to prescribe rules, therefore, these rules
were his commands and true laws.[1] . . . The theory remains
true in such a case, but the truth is only verbal." [2]

I cannot think this argument entirely creditable
to Maine's powers as a reasoner. What sort of truth
is that which is only *verbally* true? A theory which
is consistent with the facts is a true theory, provided it well explains the facts; but a theory which
is inconsistent with the facts is false, even as a theory;
and to say that it remains *verbally* true is to say
something unintelligible. That the instance given
by him renders the theory he endeavours to support
ridiculous, at least at first blush, he admits, for he
says: "An Eastern or Indian theorist in law, to
whom the assertion was made that Runjeet Singh
commanded these rules, would feel it stinging him
exactly in that sense of absurdity," etc. Nevertheless,
in Maine's opinion, it is not *really* ridiculous; and
all that is needed to reconcile it with sense and
truth is to carefully bear in mind the fundamental
assertion admitted to be untrue, "What the sovereign permits he commands." I cannot see why we
may not with as much logical propriety say, "Whatever the peasant permits he commands," and thus
prove the peasant to be the author of law. The
only objection to it is that we have no evidence that

[1] Maine's *Early History of Institutions*, p. 381.   [2] *Ibid.*, p. 382.

the peasant has the absolute power which the proposition tacitly assumes, but that is precisely the
same difficulty under which the assertion of Austin,
thus defended by Maine, labours. But the real
purpose for which Maine introduces this example
of the empire of Runjeet Singh is to show that
while with some of the races of men the system of
Austin would be out of place, in others it would find
substantial support, and if not now in fact true,
would eventually become true. He takes the
dominion of Singh as a type of "all Oriental communities in their native state."[1] Here we have
it that over the greatest part of the world despots
have ruled for ages, and to a less extent are still
ruling, each being of a character more nearly than
anywhere else possessing the attributes of Austin's
sovereign, namely, the power to "do exactly as he
pleases," and yet here more absolutely than anywhere else the law has consisted of immemorial
usage, the sovereign never pretending to make a law!

The early Aryan communities, the originals of all
the States of the Western world, are regarded by
Prof. Maine as representing all social government
not of the Oriental type. The early government of
these he finds to be the village council, but he also
finds that it does not make laws, saying:

"If the powers of this body must be described by modern
names, that which lies most in the background is legislative
power, that which is most distinctly conceived is judicial power.
The laws obeyed are regarded as having always existed, and
usages really new are confounded with the really old."[2]

---

[1] Maine's, *Early History of Institutions*, p. 382. [2] *Ibid.*, pp. 388–389.

a not unfair description of our own unwritten law. Up to this point, Prof. Maine finds no appearance of law in the shape of a direct command of the sovereign, either in the Eastern or Western world, but he observes the tendency very manifest in history, of one Aryan community, to aggrandise itself by the conquest of those adjoining it, to enlarge the area of its dominions to the magnitude of an extensive territorial empire, and then to proceed to "triturate" (to borrow his expressive phrase) the various local communities into a consolidated and centralised nation. The Roman Empire was the first great example of this movement, and the States of modern Europe are other instances of it.

From these generalisations Prof. Maine draws a remarkable conclusion, and, in my view, as erroneous as it is remarkable. It is that in the passage of these local communities into an extended and centralised empire the laws distinctly altered their character; that while before the passage they rested upon custom, and were obeyed almost blindly and instinctively, seeming to be parts of mere order, after the passage they were broken up and replaced by rules directly emanating from the sovereign, and the power behind them assumed the attitude and character of purely coercive Force; that the theory of Bentham and Austin, while wholly inapplicable to Oriental conditions and to the primitive social conditions of Europe, did represent those in Europe which came into existence after the change; that legislative activity has rapidly increased and is increasing, and that eventually Austin's formula that law is the command of the sovereign will be as true in fact as it is elegant in theory. I must give in his own language the auspicious future which he predicts for this theory:

"But, if the Analytical Jurists failed to see a great deal which can only be explained by the help of history, they saw a great deal which even in our day is imperfectly seen by those who, so to speak, let themselves drift with history. Sovereignty and Law, regarded as facts, had only gradually assumed a shape in which they answered to the conception of them formed by Hobbes, Bentham, and Austin, but the correspondence really did exist by their time, and was tending constantly to become more perfect. They were thus able to frame a juridical terminology which had for one virtue that it was rigidly consistent with itself, and for another that, if it did not completely express facts, the qualifications of its accuracy were never serious enough to deprive it of value, and tended, moreover, to become less and less important as time went on. No conception of law and society has ever removed such a mass of undoubted delusion. The force at the disposal of Sovereigns did in fact act largely through laws as understood by these Jurists, but it acted confusedly, hesitatingly, with many mistakes and vast omissions. They for the first time saw all that it was capable of effecting, if it was applied boldly and consistently. All that has followed is a testimony to their sagacity." [1]

Sagacious indeed must those minds have been—and in a miraculous way—who, seeking to describe law as it was, failed only because they accurately described law as it was to become, and rose from the ashes of scientific failure into a glory of prophecy of which they had not dreamed!

Where does Prof. Maine find the evidence which

[1] Maine's *Early History of Institutions*, pp. 396–397.

convinces him that the doctrine that law is the command of the sovereign, erroneous in the past to the point of absurdity as he admits, is destined to become truth in the future? What is there to reconcile him to a change so momentous? It is in the progressive change which he thinks is observable in the history of the advance of all *Aryan* nations, as they pass from small local communities into strong centralised States. As such States advance in population, wealth, and power he observes a corresponding activity in Legislation. He saw the classical Roman law give way to the Pandects and the Code of Justinian, and he saw the ancient laws of France dissolved by legislative enterprise into the Code Napoléon. He says: "The capital fact in the mechanism of the modern States is the energy of Legislatures."[1] He thought he saw coming down from the past a conflict between the notion of Order and the notion of Force in the law, and that Force was to emerge triumphant. He says:

"The word 'law' has come down to us in close association with two notions, the notion of *order* and the notion of *force*. The association is of considerable antiquity and is disclosed by a considerable variety of languages, and the problem has repeatedly suggested itself, which of the two notions thus linked together is entitled to precedence over the other, and which of them is first in point of mental conception? The answer before the Analytical Jurists wrote would, on the whole, have been that 'law,' before all things, implied order. . . . The Analytical Jurists, on the other hand, lay down unhesitatingly that the notion of force has priority over the notion of order."

[1] Maine's *Early History of Institutions*, p. 398.   [2] *Ibid.*, p. 371.

And the "force" thus spoken of is pure arbitrary force, that described by Austin as belonging to the sovereign who has the power of doing "exactly as he pleases."

Prof. Maine does not offer to us reasons tending to show that legislation *ought* to supersede unwritten law, though this is probably his view, but yields his acceptance of Austin's theory for the reason that he thinks that it is now in fact superseding it, and will do so completely in the future. It would have been gratifying if he had pointed out the particular facts evidencing the progress of this momentous change, beyond the brief references to the activity of legislation in the later Roman Empire and in the modern States and to the Justinian and Napoleonic Codes. I think it will be found upon a weighing of the evidence that the notion that legislation is occupying the field and discharging the functions of the unwritten law is quite unfounded, and that the great change taking place, according to Prof. Maine, by which the notion of Force is to become supreme over Order, is quite imaginary.

In the first place, in order to estimate the weight of the considerations alluded to by him, it is to no purpose to make reference to the general fact of *legislative activity* in modern times. Is that activity employed in making the substantive laws regulating conduct—that is, in asserting jurisdiction over the field hitherto occupied by the unwritten law? This is the true question. I have heretofore, in marking out the province of written law indicated that the directions in which its activity, according to its essential nature, was properly displayed was, not in overthrowing or displacing the unwritten law, not by acting in hostility to it, but in acknowledging the supremacy of custom and becoming its faithful handmaid and servant, and supplementing and aiding it by doing those things which custom could not do for itself. Now, if we turn to see in what the activity of legislation, which Prof. Maine calls "the capital fact in the mechanism of modern States," is really displayed, we find it to be in performing the function I pointed out as the appropriate province of legislation—the political organisation of the State in all its branches, the making provision for the election and appointment of multitudes of officials, for the establishment and maintenance of schools, poorhouses, prisons, and other public works, the whole provision for criminal law, the maintenance of a legislative and judicial system, provisions for the creation and control of corporations, banks, insurance companies, for supplying details necessary to secure certainty in the operation of the unwritten law, such as fixing days of grace, prescribing positive precautions to determine responsibility in cases of negligence, conforming the unwritten law to custom where custom had outgrown precedent, and in attending to the vast business involved in carrying out these objects. Taking the statute-books of any of the States of this country or of England, we shall find, as I have heretofore observed, that nearly all their contents consist of work of this character, which is not the making of law in any juristic sense. That part which does really deal with the government of conduct is, so far as it is valid and effective, so small that it may well be neglected in any inquiry concerning the main factor in our substantive law. It has been correctly described as "a mere fringe upon the body of the common law."

It may be thought at first sight that the examples of the great codifications such as those of Rome, France, Germany, and some American States, are genuine instances of the assertion of the supremacy of legislation over unwritten law. I reserve the subject of codification for subsequent treatment; but I may remark here that since all these codifications are, with certain exceptions not important to the present question, avowed re-enactments of existing law, they do not evidence any assumption of its functions but rather a confession that all that legislation can do in relation to it is to acknowledge and adopt it. What is law without legislation cannot be made *more* law by enactment.

There are better ways of ascertaining whether legislation has during the period of its modern activity been gaining a supremacy over the law of custom, than by a general reference to the fact of such activity. There have been many attempts to introduce new rules abrogating existing customs or inconsistent with them. This initiates an immediate conflict and the result of it furnishes a crucial test by which we may determine the comparative force of legislation and of the unwritten law of custom. I purpose giving some attention to this test by citing instances in which newly enacted law has come in conflict with deep-seated custom.

These instances have sometimes arisen from the want of forethought in the legislator, in not fully perceiving what the effect of an enactment would be, and sometimes from the positive determination to change existing law. The original Statute of Uses, if enforced according to its terms, would have nearly created a revolution in the long-established customs by which men bestowed their property for the benefit of relatives or others; but the courts over-ruled the language of Parliament and so limited the law that its only effect upon these customs was to cause the introduction of two or three additional words in a conveyance. The Statute of Limitations would have prevented the redress of frauds after the lapse of a certain number of years, but the courts, obeying the deep-seated motives in the minds of men created by custom, did not hesitate, in case of concealed fraud, to disobey its injunction. The British Parliament, in obedience to a notion that the practices of dealers in provisions in market-towns, called *engrossing*, *forestalling*, and *regrating*, to buy up commodities coming to market and resell them at retail, tended to burdensome enhancement of prices, began as early as 1552 with an attempt to break up such practices by legislation, and between that time and 1706 enacted some prohibitory stat-utes; but this came in contact with large general customs and the freedom of contract, and utterly failed of enforcement, and by the Act of 1772 they were all repealed in penitential shame. The multi-tude of laws prohibiting the sale of intoxicating drinks, being designed to restrict their use, come in contact not indeed with universal custom, but with very common and widespread practice. It has been found impossible to enforce these except in small rural communities, and but partially there.

But a more complete illustration of the actual limitations of the so-called sovereign power, and the unwisdom of any exercise of it to change an established custom, is to be found in the events which are happening in the days now flying. Some consideration of these events is very pertinent here, and justifies a somewhat detailed notice. There is no custom more universal than that of the building and maintenance of the ordinary public highways at the public expense and the using of them by every member of the community upon absolutely equal terms. An exception has been indulged in the case of railroads, the construction and maintenance of which in most countries have been committed to the hands of private persons, or corporations, operating under franchises granted by the State. They still remain, however, *public highways*, and the equal use of them on equal terms by the public—an equality possible only by concerted action and agreement among the naturally competing roads—has been, for the most part, a jealously guarded custom. But no vigilance has been found sufficient to prevent numerous departures from it. Powerful interests, acting sometimes upon the cupidity and sometimes upon the fears of the railway companies, have been able to obtain preferential rates, and when we consider how much the price of all commodities depends upon the cost of transportation, it is not surprising that numerous vast private fortunes should have been secured by these discriminating practices. At first, they were scarcely considered objectionable, and were, indeed, almost regarded as proofs of the superior enterprise and merit of those who secured the benefit of them. But the unerring wisdom of universal custom was never more manifest than here. The advantages thus gained by a favoured few enabled them to crush their rivals in the great fields of industry, and the shocking injustice became more and more manifest. To repress and abolish these mischievous departures from custom was a clear occasion for the employment of legislation, and it was used by the enactment of the Interstate Commerce law, which enjoined the preservation of equality in rates and made the practice of discrimination criminal. But it was not found easy to enforce the law. The prohibition was easily evaded by resorting to rebates and other devices, and the mischief continued. It was a condition of things by no means satisfactory to the great and powerful railroad companies. Discrimination was the unwilling resort of weak companies whose necessities demanded the occasional purchase of traffic at rates unreasonably low, or whose fears of the withdrawal of traffic by powerful interests compelled them to yield to unreasonable demands. But if one line of transportation ventured to cut a rate it was a necessity for all the rivals to follow. The force of this necessity is not fully comprehended by all; but the truth is that the cutting of a rate by a railroad company, however secretly done and incapable of detection and punishment at the hands of a prosecuting officer, becomes immediately known to other companies and their patrons, for the traffic will at once flow to the road of the rate-cutting company. The situation, then, is this for the manager of a railroad company: Unless he conforms to the cut his company loses the traffic, and with the loss of traffic would come the failure, first, to pay dividends, then to pay interest on fixed charges, then insolvency and a receiver. Were the road his own private property his plight would be comparatively endurable, for he would have to render no account of his failure; but what answer would be expected from a numerous body of stockholders on reporting to them that one of his rivals had disobeyed the law and the common agreement by cutting rates, and that, as he could not conscientiously follow the example, misfortune was the necessary result? It would be likely to be that, if he entertained such sentimental views of the transportation business, he ought to have informed the stockholders before he accepted his office and took their property and interests in charge. The mischiefs arising out of the practice of discrimination had become so unendurable that the competing roads combined in different parts of the country, to put an end to it. The method employed (I speak of the efforts made by the great lines east of Chicago) was by an agreement containing very drastic provisions for detecting and exposing any discriminating practice, and really making it more dangerous for the companies to depart from the agreement than to keep it. It contained stipulations that the rates should be reasonable but left it eventually optional to each company whether to conform to the agreed rates or not, exacting compliance, however, for a few days, so that, in cases of an intended rejection of the rates, notice might be given to the other companies of a probable competition. On its *face* this agreement was wise and beneficial, and I know of no good reason for distrusting the actual intention of its authors, but it was destined to challenge hostility. It so happened that, several years before, Congress had enacted a law designed, on its face, to repress contracts, conspiracies, and combinations *in restraint of trade.* The spectacle of great combinations of powerful interests, commonly called "trusts" had excited public interest and suspicion and a clamour that Congress should take measures to prevent them or deprive them of their supposed powers for mischief. As usual, each of the rival political parties sought to turn this clamour to its own advantage and claimed to be the best guardian of the public interests against the encroachments of combined wealth. The party in power, in order to make good its pretences, carried the above-mentioned statute through Congress. Legislation framed to secure partisan advantage is dangerously apt to be fraught with mischief; but in this instance it was shaped by prudent and cautious hands. It declared all contracts, combinations, and conspiracies in restraint of interstate trade or commerce to be illegal, and subjected them to penalties of fine and imprisonment, and authorised in a vague way a resort for prevention to the remedy of injunction. Thus framed, the act could have no operation except against practices properly embraced under the class of "contracts, combinations, and conspiracies—*in restraint* of interstate trade," and by the long and well-established law, these restraints had been confined to such as were *injurious* to trade; and whether any particular contract or combination was really injurious was, *in its nature*, a question of economic *fact*, although some practices had been held *necessarily* injurious to trade, and therefore, as a matter of law, to fall within the condemnation. The undiscriminating suspicion of the public was extended to all powerful combinations, and embraced the agreement above mentioned between the railroad companies, and the government, whose policy was represented by the anti-trust legislation, could not maintain its attitude of assumed hostility to "Trusts" without attacking the agreement. A bill was accordingly filed by the Attorney-General for an injunction against the execution of the agreement, which, having been dismissed by a Circuit Court was carried by appeal to the Supreme Court. Much subsequent confusion and difficulty might have been avoided had the court deliberately and with no preconceived hostility scrutinised that agreement with the view of determining its real purpose, and whether its probable effect would be, *in fact*, injurious to commerce. But no court, however exalted, is uninfluenced by strong popular sentiment, and this high tribunal failed to keep in mind the imperious necessity of uniformity in the rates of railroad transportation over parallel lines, and consequently failed to perceive the merit of the agreement. It was animated by an underlying suspicion that the effort nominally to secure uniform rates was really designed to secure *high* rates, and it seized upon the provision which involved a slight, temporary, and innocuous restraint upon competition as vitiating the whole agreement, thus declaring that any agreement containing any restraint whatever upon competition, whatever the purpose might be, was *per se* injurious to trade. It is safe to say that this doctrine was without precedent. I should as a lawyer, especially as I happened to be of counsel for the defeated parties, have hesitated to indulge in any criticism of this decision pertinent to the questions I am discussing had not members of the court itself exercised that privilege in the fullest manner and made it manifest, I think it safe to say, that the decision will not be followed by the tribunal which declared it. Inasmuch as the decision of the court was founded upon an interpretation of the statute, it must be taken that Congress enacted a law respecting railway companies which made any contract, *combination*, or *conspiracy* containing any ingredient, however small, in restraint of competition illegal and a crime in those engaged in it; and consequently that an agreement between railroad companies simply designed to secure *uniformity* in reasonable rates, though not compulsory upon the parties save for a few days, was a crime! Now, as all the managers of all the great railways of the country were parties to the condemned agreement, or to others like it, express or implied, it was brought to light that some hundreds of citizens of eminence had been violating the law and were liable to fine and imprisonment; yet no criminal prosecutions were set on foot, and the Attorney-General seemed to have exercised the supreme prerogative of pardon which the Constitution reserves to the chief magistrate. But what effect has the decision had upon the conduct of the presidents, directors, and managers of the railroad companies? None whatever. They have indeed abrogated their formal written agreements, but they still confer and fix uniform rates by concert—that is, they are in the daily practice of forming the combinations and conspiracies which the law condemns! And no attempt is made to bring any one of the criminals to justice! The artillery of the Attorney-General's office is as silent as if every gun were spiked. It was easy for the Government to pretend to execute the law, but when it found out what executing the law really involved it recoiled. And both the railroad officers who made, and make, themselves criminal, and the Government that fails to punish them, are right. Both yield to a necessity which is absolutely imperious. What creates the wrong is the statute; that is, with the interpretation the Supreme Court has placed upon it.

This illustration gives a clear notion of the anomalous conditions thrust upon society when the written law commands one thing and the universal custom another. The Government, by the Anti-Trust Act, as interpreted by the court, has declared the slightest

degree of restraint of competition in traffic arrangements concerted between parallel railroad lines to be
illegal and criminal. This is to make *competition*
and *difference* in rates the supreme policy, whereas
universal custom requires the *suppression of competition* in rates and the *preservation of uniformity!*
The result of this conflict is not open to doubt.
The *Written* Law is victorious upon paper and powerless elsewhere. The Attorney-General is sensible of
the feebleness of the command resting upon him
to enforce a law the enforcement of which would
send a hundred of the most eminent citizens to jail
and throw the industry of the country into confusion. Meanwhile, the interests of peace and order
are left to the protection of the nominal criminals!
The command of the Sovereign will prove impotent
against the unyielding force of custom. Uniformity
of rates in railway transportation, upon which the
safety of industrial enterprises so entirely depends,
will be preserved. It will be preserved to a certain
extent by informal consultation and concert between
competing lines, but this being without the aid of
Government enforcement will be subject to frequent
and vexatious violations. The most effective method
will be the acquisition by one interest of the control
of the management of all competing lines by the
acquisition of ownership, or of the control of ownership. One gigantic scheme in this direction has
been baffled by what is called the Northern Securities
decision, made in an action instituted by the Government to enforce the provisions of the same Anti-
Trust Act. But other efforts will be made, and

should they not prove effective, real ownership will be acquired by one or a few individuals; and the goal least expected by those who have insisted upon competitive and discriminating war will be reached. The practical difficulties of another resort, that is, government ownership, or fixing of uniform rates by government, will be made clear when all others shall have proved ineffectual. The deep-seated and far-reaching custom of society demanding uniform rates for the enjoyment of the benefits of all government franchises, will render abortive all legislative attempts which stand in its way.

A still more impressive illustration of the impotence of written law when brought into conflict with custom is to be found in our present national history. During the existence of slavery in the United States, the negroes in the slave States were regarded and treated as personal property absolutely destitute of every civil right, and the notion that they could participate in government through the privilege of voting was something not to be dreamed of. This condition was a deep-seated and universal custom. The abolition of slavery, as a consequence of the civil war, converted the whole race at a stroke from slaves to freemen—at least in theory. But they were freemen in little more than name. They were not indeed any longer bought and sold or claimed as property by their former masters, but the equality which belongs to freemen was everywhere denied them, and various devices were resorted to, such as compulsory apprenticeship, by which the race might be again reduced on a large scale to a condition of practical slavery. The General Government then proceeded upon the notion that if the privilege of the ballot were extended to the freedmen there would be a competition, as elsewhere under free suffrage, for their votes, and legislators would be chosen who would enact laws to enforce their rights. But the expected competition did not arise, and the legislative bodies of the several Southern States, still composed of white men only, proceeded to enact laws embodying various devices which would, and did, practically nullify the gift of the ballot. This provoked a more energetic determination by the General Government to enforce the right of the freedmen to the ballot and to a general equality with the whites before the law. A formidable mass of legislation was enacted in pursuance of this determination, crowned by an amendment of the Constitution itself, prohibiting all political discrimination of every form between citizens, based upon the distinctions of colour or race. The legislative devices by which the white men had been enabled to baffle the gift of political equality to the freedmen being thus rendered ineffective, they took the only course remaining to them and resorted to such forms of force and fraud as seemed best calculated to defeat the Constitutional and Congressional enactments. In some places terror was produced among the negroes by a general and noisy display of firearms previous to and at the time of the elections, by which the negroes were intimidated and abstained from voting through fear; in others, where they ventured to vote, the ballot was fraudulently tampered with so as to

render their votes ineffective. To such an extent
had this almost unconcealed practice of force and
fraud by whole communities proceeded as to alarm the
more moral elements of the communities guilty of it,
and excite the fear that all distinctions between right
and wrong would become obliterated and society
itself fall into anarchy. Not even this suggested a
withdrawal of their opposition to the Federal legislation, but only more ingenious contrivances by which
they might avoid the grosser practices of fraud and
violence and borrow the appearance of legality in
their effort to deprive the black race of political equality. To this end constitutional provisions defining and qualifying the right of suffrage have been
contrived and adopted in some States, and are likely
to be further extended, whereby, without open discrimination, the practical exclusion of the inferior
race from political power is secured. The validity of
these constitutional provisions has been challenged
at the bar of the Supreme Court, and it is not easy to
see how they can escape judicial condemnation, but
thus far that tribunal has avoided the questions thus
thrust upon it, and there is an apparent disposition among the judges to escape them altogether.
Should this disposition prevail, the whole of the
mighty Federal legislation contrived to give political
equality to the blacks will be practically annulled,
leaving behind, however, the great constitutions of
States, which should be models of openness, directness,
and dignity, deeply marked by the evidences of concealment and deceit. I do not discuss the question
whether political equality *ought* to be bestowed upon

a race to which social equality cannot be extended. Even tyranny may be beneficent in its aims, but never in its results, and the attempt to compel a community of men to do right by legislative command, when they do not think it to be right, is tyranny. It is Force in conflict with Order. Force will not gain its end, but will superinduce a mass of evil and suffering which was the last thing it desired or expected.

Many other instances might be given showing the impotence of legislation when put in conflict with custom, and refuting the notion that Law is now tending, or ever will tend, to become the creature of Force rather than of Order. Conduct will forever follow the great governing influences proceeding from the constitution of man and the environment in which he is placed. It will change as these influences change, and not otherwise.

In nothing is human vanity more largely displayed than in the love of a theory. The simple and beautiful forms in which consequences develop themselves when a sufficient cause is assumed, as in the problems of mathematics, furnish a pleasure which the mind desires to hold in its grasp, and it recoils from any scrutiny into facts from a secret fear that the possession will be endangered and turns back to revel in the delights of the theory. Bentham could not contemplate without indignation the fact that the world was governed by something different from enacted law. To talk about conduct following its own laws, and obeying custom, would have put him in a passion. To remind him that every human society, from the beginning, had followed custom, would have probably drawn the answer that he was well aware of the stupidity of mankind, that that was the very thing which angered him, that were it not for that his system would have been adopted long before! Austin was somewhat less dogmatic but almost equally fond of his theory. The conception of a sovereign power in the State which could "do exactly as it pleases" would be in his view effective in reaching, by means of legislation, a consistent and simple system of law. He did not, like his master, Bentham, reject "judge-made law" with abhorrence, but saw in it an approach to what law ought to be; and as he found it enforced by the sovereign power of the State, he fell into the error of thinking that this sovereign power had really *created* what it thus enforced. Not stopping to inquire whether the so-called sovereign power was in fact sovereign, he chose to assume it; and his maxim that "what the sovereign permits he commands" furnished a ready demonstration that all law actually enforced by the State was the command of the sovereign. Prof. Maine was, apparently, a thorough believer in Austin's theories when he began his inquiries. He soon learned that when the actual facts of the origin of law are studied the notion that they are in any sense the creation of the sovereign must be relinquished. Nowhere in the actual world could a sovereign power be found engaged in the creation of law except in the Roman Empire and in the great modern States, and even in those States the sovereign was only beginning to be the author of law. He caught, however, at the appearance of this tendency and predicted its increase until it should become perfect, and then, in his prophetic view, the Austinian theory would stand justified and established. Neither Bentham nor Austin sufficiently held in mind that the province of science was rigidly confined to the observation and orderly arrangement of facts, or that it was anything more than a process of reasoning from assumed premises; but this was no particular failing in them. It was the common fault of the time in which they wrote. How great the real ignorance of true science then was, even with the most highly educated, may be imagined from an expression of Macaulay, who, eulogising Bentham, says that he found "Jurisprudence a gibberish and left it a science"! Prof. Maine lived in the full blaze of the scientific achievements which have lighted the way for all seekers after the truth. He knew the rigid pathway by following which those successes had been won, and makes the apology for Austin which I have mentioned, saying that he "more than once reminds us that, though his principal writings are not more than forty years old [at that time], he wrote before men's ideas were leavened to the present depth by the sciences of experiment and observation."[1] But Prof. Maine is guilty of the neglect which he seeks to excuse. He has indeed explored the early institutions of society to learn the forms of conduct which they exhibit and the rules which actually govern the action of men, but this is a part only of the territory of fact which the inquirer must explore before he can reach a true notion of the origin of law. It is only the *external* field of observation. There is an internal

[1] Maine's *Early History of Institutions*, p. 373.

field quite as important, into which Prof. Maine never sought to enter any more than Bentham or Austin.   He never scrutinised the realm of consciousness to learn how conduct really originates, and what is its cause or why it is that the actions of men so persistently present themselves in the form of custom, and why departures from custom are so universally condemned and punished.   No adequate conception of law can be reached until this task has been faithfully prosecuted.

LECTURE IX

I NOW turn to another of the consequences of that view of the nature and function of law which I have adopted, namely, the limitations it places upon the province of Legislation. In reaching that view it became necessary for me to treat briefly of the nature of enacted law as distinguished from that which is the growth of custom and to consider at some length the principal uses for which it had been employed from the earliest times, and I have been obliged to say much more upon the same topic in criticising the theory that all law is the *command* of the sovereign power; but the importance of the subject demands that I should present in a connected view the real nature of legislation, the uses for which it may be employed, and the mischiefs likely to flow from ill-advised resorts to it—in other words, that I should mark out the Province of Legislation.

The popular estimate of the possibilities for good which may be realised through the enactment of law is, in my opinion, greatly exaggerated. Nothing is more attractive to the benevolent vanity of men than the notion that they can effect great improvements in society by the simple process of forbidding all wrong conduct, or conduct which they think is wrong, by law, and of enjoining all good conduct by the same means; as if men could not find out how to live until a book were placed in the hands of every individual, in which the things to be done and those not to be done were clearly set down. The man who, by his writings, has done most to cultivate and propagate this notion in recent times is Jeremy Bentham, of whom I have had frequent occasion to speak. Although educated for the bar, he never engaged in the practice of his profession. He was a student, and Ethics, particularly what might be called the Ethics of Government, was the main subject which engrossed his attention. Inasmuch as Governments exist for the sole purpose of securing happiness to the governed, he thought it their duty to deliberately set about the accomplishment of that purpose and to ascertain what conduct would promote and what obstruct happiness, and to make laws in writing enjoining the former and prohibiting the latter, and insuring a fair distribution of the total amount of the happiness thus achieved among the governed in proportion to their obedience to the law. It provoked the rather coarse, but expressive, sarcasm of Carlyle, who, as you know, did not revel in pictures of human happiness, or greatly love the common herd, that it was a scheme "for the distribution of an attainable amount of Pig-wash among a given multitude of Pigs." I do not adopt this characterisation of the work of a great and philanthropic man.

This theory seems on its face very simple. Its complexities and difficulties appear only when we come to look at the means by which it is to be carried into effect. These means Bentham carefully elaborated by making a detailed analysis of the nature of man, and a careful enumeration and classification of all the pleasures and pains he was capable of experiencing, of all his various passions and tendencies, and of the multitude of varying conditions of time and place affecting his conduct. From investigations like these he gathered the principles which should guide the action of the legislator in the enactment of Codes of law, both penal and civil. The statement and explanation of these principles, with which, it is to be borne in mind, the legislator is to make himself familiar, occupies a space which would amount to thousands of ordinary octavo pages, and is a profound and instructive compendium, presented in accurate and precise, though not attractive, language. With Codes framed upon the basis of these principles he would supersede all existing law and have them contain the only rules of conduct which judges should be permitted to enforce. Here, it will be perceived, is an *a priori* scheme for the creation of human happiness through the instrumentality of Government. Man is not to work out his own happiness by learning from the teachings of experience what is right and what is wrong and acting accordingly, but by studying a book; and Bentham makes provision for beginning the instruction of children by learning the book by heart, and repeating it as they would the melodies of Mother Goose. He says:

" In this manner before sixteen years of age, without hindrance to any other studies, the pupils in public schools would become more conversant with the laws of their country, than those lawyers at present are, whose hair has grown grey in the contentions of the bar." [1]

This scheme assumes that the legislator can know beforehand from the nature of man all the conduct he can by possibility exhibit, determine, and enjoin what is conducive to the greatest happiness of the greatest number, and forbid what is destructive of that happiness.

The world-wide difference between this theory of law and that which I have ventured to think the true one, is palpable at a glance. They are, indeed. opposites. The one views man as coming into existence with faculties which enable him to perceive the consequences of his own conduct, and to regulate it accordingly; so that when he finds that action of a certain character arouses the resentment, anger, and retaliation of others, he avoids it, learns that compliance with custom is expected both by himself and others, and that consequently when he complies with it he is safe, and thus makes compliance with custom his rule of action; that in this way a boundary line is marked out within which every man may act freely, but beyond which he must not go; that with this freedom of action he is left to work out his own happiness or misery by his own efforts; that society enforces this conformity to custom by punishing departures from it, and to this end constructs the machinery of government and enacts the laws which are adapted to the purpose, the whole scheme being the result of an Order altogether analagous to the

---

[1] Bentham, *Works*, vol. i., p. 158.

order which governs the movements of the physical world. The other is a scheme by which society is made to engage in the business of finding out what conduct on the part of its members will secure the greatest amount of happiness to all, and then compelling its adoption by Force. The one is founded on the belief that no part of the universe is outside of the domain of existing Law; that when the human race was brought into the world, as it was composed of beings who were to act, their actions would follow an already existing law, and not present a scene of anarchy. The other assumes that the race was, so to speak, dumped upon the earth without rule or compass, unable to properly govern itself until some philosophic moralist arose to turn his thoughts inward and discover that the chief end of man was happiness, and that the way to live was to form a government which should appoint a commission to frame a body of rules for attaining happiness, which rules the government would by force compel all men to obey. The one view of the function of government may be symbolised as that of a *policeman* who stands by and does nothing as long as no one in the crowd breaks the peace, acting on the assumption that right consists in minding one's own business, and wrong in trespassing upon others, and that every one knows perfectly well, without being told, what is right and what is wrong; the other as that of a *schoolmaster* with the whole of society for his pupils, all ignorant how to act until they had learned what the end of action was and the way to attain it. Bentham had a talent for apt illustration,

15

which he frequently employed to satirise the things he disliked, and he once said, speaking of the un-written law, that law was taught as a master teaches his dog, by waiting until he did something wrong and then beating him! He could not have described it more accurately. That is the way of nature through-out the universe. Why should not the master wait until the dog had done something wrong? Certainly he should not have punished him before. But per-haps Bentham intended that the master beat his dog for doing something the animal had no reason to think wrong. But this is not true, at least of good masters, such alone as Bentham can be supposed to have had in mind. If he had been asked how he knew that the dog was ignorant of wrongdoing, I cannot imagine what he would have said. Certainly he would not have intimated that a code of dog conduct ought to have been prepared in some language known to dogs and distributed among them. The way in which the dog had learned that the conduct for which he was punished was wrong was that when he was a puppy he was petted, caressed, fed, and otherwise made happy when he obeyed his master, and when he disobeyed him, at first gently scolded, then more sternly, afterwards slightly punished, and finally more severely, until he had learned to associate happiness with obedience and misery with disobedi-ence, and thus well knew that he had deserved the blows he received. The same is the case with the human being, child and man. The child is taught as the puppy was. Where the parental relation does not exist the discipline may be less gentle and affectionate, but it is the same in method. In the infancy of society, when one man encroached upon another he met sometimes with reproof, sometimes with retaliatory resentment, sometimes with violent punishment. It thus came about that certain things became associated with the prospect of suffering and others with that of reward, or, at least, of acquiescence; and as this instruction is one which goes on with every man every moment of his life, it is perfectly learned. This is the sort of knowledge that every man has of the law resting upon custom. There may be cases where the legally right and the legally wrong may not be known, but how few they are ! Every convicted criminal knows that it is idle to pretend that he did not know he was doing wrong, for no one would believe him. Of this mode of knowing the law Bentham apparently had no knowledge. He really seemed to think that the enactment and publication of the law was not only the best but the only way of bringing a knowledge of it to the bulk of the members of society.

Of course that knowledge which all have of what things are right and what wrong in the unwritten law does not often include a knowledge of the precise penal consequences which may follow the commission of a wrong, nor is it of any importance that it should. It is enough for a man to know that a thing is right and that he ought to do it, or that it is wrong and that he ought to abstain from it. The notion that the whole criminal class are entitled to have brought home to them the particular amount of the penalty which the law attaches to particular offenses, in order to enable them to weigh more exactly the chances they are contemplating, is wholly irrational. The absurdity—I can call it no less—of Bentham's view is that the true method of making law known is to first enact it in writing and then print and publish it. There is no objection to this, but its efficiency is based upon the assumption that the bulk of mankind do and will read the laws that are so published, whereas, in fact, it is safe to say that scarcely one man in a thousand does this.

But the consequences of misguided legislation should not blind us to its beneficent uses. It should make us only the more solicitous to learn what its true nature is, what its uses are. and the dangers against which caution should be exercised in the employment of that instrumentality; that is to say, to know the Province of Legislation and the limitations of its exercise. In what I have had to say heretofore concerning written law, it has been mainly in pursuance of my general purpose to explore the whole field of human conduct with the view of discovering all the causes which *in fact* restrain and regulate it; and so far three things have appeared to be true as matters of fact concerning legislation: (1) that it is an instrumentality first employed at a somewhat advanced state of social progress and after society has come to assume an organised form; (2) that the purposes for which it was at first and still is employed were political rather than juristic. to remove political evils, perfect the organisation of the state and thus to aid the unwritten law of custom and make it more effective, rather than to attempt to furnish a substitute for it; that its action, therefore, was confined to the province of Public Law; (3) that the only considerable exception to this was the instance of codification, an exception more apparent than real, the cases in which it was resorted to being mainly where several states or provinces having different customs had become united under one government, and the different customs were confused and needed unification.

Since legislation has for the period of three thousand years been confined to the province of public law, as above indicated, I might be warranted in drawing the conclusion that this was the only purpose to which it was adapted; but I shall be abundantly justified in this if, after considering its essential nature, it shall appear to be quite unfitted, and, indeed, incapable of taking a principal part in the regulation of the conduct of men in their private relations with each other.

I have remarked that Austin's definition of Law was a tolerable description of Legislation; but I think it would be a better definition to say that it is simply the formal written expression of the *will* of the Sovereign State. When society has become a conscious organism it has a *will*, and the act of expressing this, whether by the decree of an absolute monarch or by the voice of a legislative body, is what is commonly called *legislation*. All such expressions are called laws, but all of them are not really such in the sense in which I have regarded law. As I have already pointed out, the State is a great corporation having many things to do, such as the building of roads, and constructing a great variety of public works, appointing officers and marking out their duties. It can express its will in these particulars only by declaring it in writing, but such declarations are not in the strict sense laws, because they are not designed to regulate directly the conduct of men in their dealings with each other. Such acts are really nothing but expressions of the corporate will of the State in the transaction of its particular business.

Legislation does, however, in a large number of instances express the will of the State in relation to conduct, and its acts of this nature are without impropriety styled laws. For instance it confers upon individuals the power of acting under corporate forms and prescribes numerous rules to which such action must conform, thus laying the foundation for the law of corporations. It imposes upon the people generally many duties such as the payment of taxes, the rendering of military service, etc., and its acts of this nature affect conduct, but incidentally only, their chief object being to create efficient instrumentalities for enforcing and aiding the fundamental law of custom.

Between legislation, even when thus embracing the commands of the State aimed at conduct, and the unwritten law, the difference is, we might say, worldwide. The former is made by a single human person, or by a very few persons, and necessarily exhibits the imperfection and error which attaches to all such works. It is created by a breath of the human will and may be abrogated by another breath. The latter is self-existent, eternal, absolutely right and just for the purposes of social government, irrepealable and unchangeable. It may be justly called Divine; for, being identical with custom which is the form in which human nature necessarily develops conduct, it can have no other author than that of human nature itself.

These fundamental distinctions between the unwritten law of custom and the commands of the sovereign have been recognised in the thought of the world ever since legislation began. Universal custom in Athens made it the duty of relatives to bury the bodies of the dead; and when the tyrant Creon made a decree forbidding, under penalty of death, the burial of Polynices, and ordaining that he should be left a corpse for birds and dogs to eat, a ghastly sight of shame, his sister Antigone dared to disobey the decree; and when asked by the tyrant, "And thou didst indeed dare to transgress that law?" answered: "Yes, for it was not Zeus that had published that edict; not such are the laws set among men by the justice which dwells with the gods below; nor deemed I that thy decrees were of such force that a mortal could override the unwritten and unfailing statutes of Heaven. For their life is not of to-day or yesterday, but from all time, and no man knows when they were first put forth." And the voice of human feeling as expressed in dramatic poetry was the voice also of the philosophic jurists of antiquity. Cicero in his dialogue *De Legibus* makes the interlocutor thus define the fundamental unwritten law:

MARCUS: Therefore law is the discrimination of things just from things unjust; proceeding in obedience to that original and fundamental nature of all things in accordance with which the laws of men are framed which inflict punishment upon the wicked, and defend and keep guard over the righteous.

QUINTUS: I understand it very clearly, and I not only think that no other enactment should be regarded as law, but should not even be so called.

MARCUS: Would you not, then, call the Titian and Appuleian enactments laws?

QUINTUS: No, not even the Livian.

MARCUS: And you are right; especially for the reason that they may be annulled by a mere line of the Senate, while that law the force of which I have explained can neither be enacted nor repealed.[1]

Again, the law proceeding from legislation consists of a multitude of distinct propositions or commands having no necessary connection with each other, and all of them absolute and arbitrary. No reason is assigned for them. *Stat pro ratione voluntas.* A certain fact, or grouping of facts, is taken and erected into an ideal class, and it is declared that whenever such fact, or grouping of facts, occurs in conduct certain legal consequences will inevitably follow, whether just or unjust. Now such fact or grouping may, for aught the legislator knows, or can know, be accompanied by some other fact which will modify the character of the grouping and convert what otherwise would be just into injustice. Nevertheless, the law must have its course unaffected by such unforeseen circumstance, although the result will be to defeat the intention of the lawmaker and create

[1] Cicero, *De Legibus*, lib. ii., ch. v, vi.

injustice where he designed to prevent it. The unfitness of such law to govern the unknown conduct of the unknown future is manifest.

In the unwritten law of Custom such anomalies cannot occur, for in that law there are no absolute and arbitrary rules. There is, indeed, one absolute rule, but it is not arbitrary. It is that *custom* must be obeyed. This is not the expression of *will*, but the dictate of order. Whether any particular conduct does or does not conform to custom can be told only when it comes for the first time to be displayed, and, in cases of dispute, only by the judges who are the experts appointed by society for that purpose. The vast body of so-called rules of law found in our digests and treatises and mentioned in the reports of decided cases are but the results, and logical deductions from the results, of the cases thus decided, arranged and classified with regard to scientific order. None of them are absolute. They are all provisional and subject to modification.

Having pointed out the true measure of legislation and its wide difference from the unwritten law, I proceed to enumerate the principal uses which it is capable of serving and which are embraced within what may be called its province.

First: The State may, by an expression of its will, simply *do* something, in which case all that it has directly in view is accomplished by such expression: for instance, it may grant the public franchise of building and operating a railroad. This neither adds to nor changes existing law, and is not, therefore, in a narrow and precise sense, legislation, although after the road is constructed a variety of rights and duties relating to it will arise under existing law. But a simple grant by the State of something which it has the right to grant differs in no respect from the grant by a private person of something he has a right to grant.

Second: The State may *command* something to be done by others; for instance, it may command one of its officers to cause a prison, a courthouse, or other public building to be constructed. This does not make law in the proper sense of law. It affects the conduct of the person it commands, but in no other sense than that in which the conduct of a soldier is affected by the command of his superior officer. It is a *particular*, not a *general* command. This species of legislation is often employed in conjunction with that first above described, as when an act is passed creating a Banking Department. Certain offices are created, which is a thing done; besides this, the persons appointed to fill them are commanded to perform the various duties assigned to them in exercising a supervision over banking institutions, and the bank officers are required to make regular reports to the department, containing particular items of information concerning the operation and condition of the corporations under their management. Legislative commands thus made, requiring special things to be done, are part of the machinery of government, but a part very different from that relating to the rules which govern the ordinary conduct of men in relation to each other. It is properly described as *public* law, by way of distinction from *private* law.

Third: Another form in which the State may express its will is that of commands which do affect the conduct of all the members of society, as where a law is enacted defining and punishing a crime, a species of legislation also belonging to Public Law; and the State may enter the province of strictly private law and affect the conduct of its members in their ordinary relations with each other, as where it enacts a law for the registry of deeds and declares that a registered conveyance shall take precedence over one prior in date but not registered; or it might go further and define a contract, and declare what contracts should be valid and what invalid.

These forms in which the will of the State may be expressed indicate the purposes towards which its conscious action may be directed, and lead to the inquiry whether there are any, and what, useful rules of wisdom and prudence for guiding its action. Manifestly there are such; but before endeavouring to state them we should have a clear understanding of the *quality* of the power, for rules very largely depend upon that. If legislators, whether one alone or many in a body, possessed perfect intelligence and wisdom, the purest morality, the most sincere desire for the public good, and were without selfish interests and ambitions, there would be little need for laying down rules to guide their action. The most unlimited scope might safely be given to their authority. A moment's reflection informs us that this is not and cannot be the fact, although some reformers who are animated by the passion of making men good and happy by law are apt to think so. They fall into the

error of thinking that legislators must be animated
by the same elevated purposes of which they are
conscious. Bentham could never have believed in
his theory of the universal government of men by
legislation, based upon the principle of securing the
greatest happiness to the greatest number, unless he
had in his mind the notion that such was the character of the legislative power. Had any body of reformers set themselves about the task of elaborating
a detailed scheme of legislation upon his theory, the
chances are that he would have been foremost in
denouncing it, thus confessing that his theories of
legislation were unfounded, unless he, or some one
equally enlightened and just, were made the legislator. When we look at the sovereigns of history
the contrasts we find to the conceptions of the just
legislator are so broad as to be amusing. We may
find a Nero or an Antonine, a Peter the Great or a
Merovingian sluggard, a Louis the Fourth or a Louis
the Fourteenth, King Stork or King Log. And if
we turn to popular forms of government the spectacle of the fact when compared with the theory is
often only less amusing. The members of the
Legislatures of our own States are likely to be not the
wisest, but the smartest only. Instead of having the
public good at heart they often have only their own
personal interests or ambitions, or they have been
elected through the patronage and money of some
powerful pecuniary interest and are faithful alone
to that influence. Moreover, the pecuniary value
which may lie in some special legislation is often so
great that powerful private interests are found willing

to pay prodigious sums to secure it, and corruption and bribery are practised to a frightful extent; the forces of corruption become organised by some skilful leader, expressively called a *boss*, who acquires a control of legislation greater than that enjoyed by many sovereigns. It may be asked with a sigh of despair what use there is in laying down rules to guide the actions of such legislators. The answer is that the dark picture is not always the true one, and is perhaps rather the exception than the rule. The worst of men are not always bad; indeed, they prefer right conduct and will follow it where temptation is not too powerfully misleading. Many—sometimes a majority—are right-minded, and many measures of public importance contain in them no element furnishing temptation to desert duty. Besides this, the movement for important public measures usually springs up among public-spirited men outside of legislative halls, and is communicated and propagated by means of the press, and legislators are powerfully affected by the loud public voice. It is highly important that these disinterested influences should be instructed in the rules which ought to be the guide in legislation. I may endeavour to enumerate the more important of these rules.

All the things indicated by the first two of the forms in which I have said the *will* of the State may be expressed are obviously within the province of legislation. Where a thing can be done only by the State in its corporate capacity it must be done under an act expressing the corporate will that it should be done, as the making of a grant of land owned by the State, or the granting of a public franchise, or the construction of public works. And the whole political organisation of the State is essentially of this character; for, although in the early stages of social organisation some progress is made by mere custom, yet eventually the entire subject properly falls under legislative control, and where States are newly organised, as most of the American States, the whole work is accomplished by legislation from the beginning. This field of legislation is of vast extent, embracing the organisation of the General and State Governments with their executive, legislative, and judicial departments, the system of taxation, prisons, schools, courts, the dividing of the territory into counties, towns, etc., and the delegation to such divisions of the powers of local government, and a multitude of other subjects of like character, the whole composing the public machinery and equipment of the State. There is one quite distinct and very noticeable branch of law, one which is involved in the daily work of a lawyer more than any other, which belongs to this category; this is the law of judicial procedure, which embraces the various sorts of actions and proceedings which may be instituted in the courts to enforce private or public duties and the public discipline: writs, process, trials, judgments, executions, etc. Law of this description, being the machinery by which the ordinary law is administered, is apt to be regarded as part of that law; but it has no direct connection with conduct. Its rules are not rules of conduct, but are incidental to them and designed to make them effectual. They are sometimes, and quite accurately, distinguished from the law with which they are so closely associated, by putting them together with the law of evidence in a special class called adjective law, in contradistinction to the rules which really govern conduct, which are appropriately styled substantive law. The law of procedure cannot be created by general custom. It is the work of conscious contrivance, and belongs to the category of public machinery. As such it lies in the field of legislation; but the actual work of shaping and adapting it should, for obvious reasons, not be undertaken by the Legislature itself, but should be delegated to the body best capable of performing it. This is the judges whose duty it is to apply it. They understand what machinery is best fitted to facilitate their action and make it effective, and, the working of it being under their daily observation, they are able to correct and reshape it as occasion may require. It should be established, and from time to time improved by what are called Rules of Court, which are really legislation. The whole of this machinery of government assumes that the body of the people are living under a system of customary law which governs their conduct in their relations with each other. It does not purport to affect that law otherwise than by providing the instrumentalities and facilities by which it may be the better enjoyed and enforced. Of course in all this body of contrivance, with its multitude of officers, many commands are prescribed concerning the duties of the officers and of the members of the community in relation to the public establishment, and a vast quantity of legal obligation and, therefore, of law is created; but the nature of it is widely different from the law of custom which governs the private transactions of men.

LECTURE X

AT the conclusion of the last lecture I spoke of the first of the rules that ought to guide in legislation. I now continue the enumeration.

The next form of proper legislative activity consists of commands directly affecting conduct. I mean the Criminal Law. It is in a high degree important that this, and its true place in the body of law, should be well understood, inasmuch as many disorders and mischiefs spring up out of mistaken notions upon the subject. And in the first place, there should be a clear notion of what a *crime* is in the eye of the law. Wrong conduct, socially speaking, is simply a departure from custom. Custom being the only test of right and wrong in the law, there can be nothing which in the view of the law is wrong except a violation of custom. But all wrong conduct is not criminal—that is, it is not properly punishable by law. All crimes are violations of custom, but all violations of custom are not necessarily crimes. There are many departures from custom of which the law takes no notice, or should take no notice, but which it should leave to the jurisdiction of the moral forces of society. The line of division between those offences which are properly punishable by law and those the repression of which is wisely left to moral forces is the line of probable violence. The function of the criminal law is to preserve society from violence, for violence is war, and threatens the existence of society. It may be asked why all social offences should not be punished by some legal penalty. The answer is that legal penalties should be inflicted only where it is necessary. The punishments of the criminal law fall with very unequal weight upon the different victims. Little notice can be taken of relative ignorance, guilty intention, temptation, and provocation; whereas the discipline of the moral forces is tempered by a regard for all these circumstances, and is likely to be more effective. In the next place, and more conclusively, the moment the line of violent wrong is passed and offences of little magnitude are subjected to legal punishment, the hazard is incurred of including in the prohibition and subjecting to punishment conduct which very many, perhaps a majority, regard as right, and this is tyranny, an abuse of law more fruitful in mischief than many crimes. This line limiting the exercise of criminal prohibition is deeply stamped on legal history. I have already pointed out the fact that before the institution of judicial tribunals the only mode of punishing and repressing crime which involved the use of force was by the employment of self-help, the infliction by private hands of punishment upon an offender. The evils of this condition were the cause of the creation of such tribunals, the purpose of their creation being not to supplant the operation of the moral methods, but to obviate the necessity of a resort to private violence, and thus the punishment of graver crimes was transferred to the courts and became regulated by law. I have referred also to the fact that any breach of the King's Peace, which originally embraced a narrow territory surrounding his person or possessions, but was subsequently extended over the whole kingdom, was regarded as a crime, and that nothing was punishable as a crime which did not imply and carry with it such breach. From time to time with the progress of order and refinement, additions have been made to the list of criminal offences, but the *rationale* by which they are brought into that character is the supposed direct tendency of the offence to lead to a breach of the peace; and to this day any offence, however free from actual violence it may have been, is charged in the indictment to have been committed by "force and arms," and "against the Peace of our Lord the King," or, in this country, "against the Peace of the People of the State." There is no difference, apparently, between slander and libel except that the one is oral defamation while the other is written, and yet libel is an indictable offence while slander is not; and the reason commonly assigned for the distinction is that a written defamation is more likely to lead to violence and a breach of the peace. Language is employed in the ordinary definition of crime quite significant of that class of offences which the law regards as calling for punishment. They are called evils *in themselves* (*mala in se*)—that is, evils of which no account need, or can, be given other than that they are in fact *wrong*. Now, as there is no test of right and wrong in the law save custom, *mala in se* are simply palpable violations of custom, while the converse expression, *mala prohibita*, indicates acts which the law makes criminal without regard to custom.

This is all I need say concerning the original and still primary class of criminal offences; but the necessities of civilised, industrial society in modern times have required an extension of the province of penal law by the positive enactment of numerous commands and prohibitions not to be found in the law of custom. As communities become more populous, as towns and cities increase in number and size, and as industries become organised in establishments of great magnitude, the appliances of machinery for manufacturing, locomotion, and transportation become multiplied, and the degree of co-operation required among the members of society becomes prodigiously increased, and individuals touch one another in many different ways, and consequently the duties of each towards others become multiplied and increased. Customs of precaution and care become necessary and grow in importance. A failure by a single person to observe the duties thus prescribed may involve great injury to many others. Under such circumstances the law of negligence becomes of great importance and the need of special rules is felt. The operation of custom in fixing such rules is slow, and until they become established all that a court can do, in the trial of a case where a charge is made that one person has been guilty of negligence causing injury to another, is to leave it to a jury to say whether the accused person has used, in some cases, extreme, and in others. ordinary, care; but there is a tendency in the courts to insist more and more upon the adoption of special positive precautions which experience has shown to be necessary or useful in the prevention of accidents. Legislation performs a useful office here by seizing hold of these tendencies and converting growing customs into positive rules. The numerous laws specifying positive safeguards which railroads, steamboats, and other public conveyances and manufactories operated by machinery must supply belong to this province, as also the rules of navigation designed to prevent collisions at sea.

There is another frequent and proper occasion for the employment of penal legislation in preventing evils which arise from the competitive struggles of modern life in industrial pursuits. The employment of child labour is to be restricted, tenement building needs regulation in order to preserve health, and in these and other like directions positive injunctions and prohibitions must be made and enforced. This greatly increases the class of offences known as *mala prohibita*.

So much concerning the various employments of legislation in the field of criminal law, but here the liability to cause mischief, in the attempt to remove it, is very great and suggests a corresponding degree of prudence and caution. So far as offences consisting of those clear departures from custom which the law denominates *mala in se* are concerned, the danger is not great. Such offences already stand in the popular mind as crimes which ought to be punished, and the employment of regulated force should take the place of irregular violence. However men may differ as to whether it is good or bad to do this thing or that, all are agreed that violence is wrong and must be prevented and the common complaint is that the State is less energetic in this work than it ought to be. The principal danger lies in the attempt often made to convert into crimes acts regarded by large numbers, perhaps a majority, as innocent—that is, to practise what is, in fact, tyranny. While all are ready to agree that tyranny is a very mischievous thing, there is not a right understanding equally general of what tyranny is. Some think that tyranny is a fault only of despots, and can not be committed under a republican form of government; they think that the maxim that the majority must govern justifies the majority in governing as it pleases, and requires the minority to acquiesce with cheerfulness in legislation of any character, as if what is called self-government were a scheme by which different parts of the community may alternately enjoy the privilege of tyrannising over each other. The principal evils of legal tyranny arise from the instrumentality which it employs, which is always *force*. What is called the tyranny of fashion, or custom (using this word in its common sense), does no great harm. No one is compelled to submit to it, and the penalty of being unpopular is not ordinarily very severe; but when *force* is called in to compel men to act in accordance with the opinions of others rather than their own, the worst mischief ensues. There is a great misapprehension as to the extent of these mischiefs and also as to the cause of them. When a law is made declaring conduct widely practised and widely regarded as innocent to be a crime, the evil consequences which arise upon attempts to enforce it are apt to be viewed as the consequences of the forbidden practice, and not of the attempt to suppress it; and it is believed that the true method of avoiding, or doing away with, these consequences is to press the efforts at enforcement with increased energy. But when a mistake has been made, its consequences can not be avoided by a more vigorous persistence in it. The best means of inculcating caution in this employment of criminal legislation is to have clearly in mind its evil consequences. The species of criminal legislation to which *sumptuary* laws belong furnishes an apt illustration of them. Take, for instance, the case of laws prohibiting the manufacture or sale of intoxicating drinks. The evils of drunkenness are so manifest that great numbers of excellent people are impressed with a conviction that some measures must be taken to repress them. The first efforts in this direction were a resort to what are called moral methods. The attempt was made to arouse a public sentiment so strong as to prevent men from indulgence, and discourage the sale of the mischievous article; but the results of such efforts are generally too slow and gradual to satisfy aroused and earnest minds. Besides the desire of doing good, the selfish determination is formed of carrying out a purpose, and the purpose comes to seem so important that no inquiry is made concerning the means except to consider what will be most effective. It suits the judgment of some and the temper of others to convert the practices they deem so mischievous into *crimes*, and they think that if nothing else will prevent indulgence in them, the fear of heavy punishment will at least be effective, and indeed many think that the force of law is so great that the mere enactment of a prohibition will accomplish the desired end, and all are inclined to believe that even if the laws are ineffective for the purpose for which they were enacted, they will at least do no harm. But men forget that their acts. whether in enacting and attempting to enforce written laws, or of whatever other nature, are subject to the great law of causality and will draw after them their inevitable consequences. The law when enacted will not execute itself. It requires the active interposition of man to put it in force. Evidence must be found and prosecutions set in motion, and as this is a task in which good men are commonly found to be unwilling, or too indolent, to voluntarily engage, others must be sought for who will undertake it. The spy and informer are hired, but their testimony is open to much impeachment, and is met by opposing testimony often false and perjured. The trials become scenes of perjury and subornation of perjury, and juries find abundant excuses for rendering verdicts of acquittal or persisting in disagreements, contrary to their oaths. The whole machinery of enforcement fails, or, if it succeeds at all, it is in particular places only, while in others the law is violated with impunity. Attempts are made to insure a more general and effective execution of the law by imposing the duty of detection upon the ordinary policemen, and giving them summary powers. This enables such officers to extend indulgence for a price, and makes their places positions of value which speedily fall into the hands of those who will not scruple to sell their indulgences, and bribery and corruption on a vast scale are the result. The necessity felt by the violators of the law to purchase protection carries the struggle for the control of the police establishment into politics, and mischiefs almost endless follow. An especially pernicious effect is that society becomes divided between the friends and the foes of the repressive law, and the opposing parties become animated with a hostility which prevents united action for purposes considered beneficial by both. Perhaps the worst of all is that the general regard and reverence for law are impaired, a consequence the mischief of which can scarcely be estimated.

If, at the expense of all these evils, the reformation sought by the law were really and fully effected, the benefit would not be worth the price paid for it, but it generally turns out in the end that the legislation is wholly ineffective and that the condemned practices, through successful bribery and by various devices, are carried on much to the same extent as before the enactment of the law.

What a spectacle is thus afforded of the impotence of man's conscious effort to overrule the silent and irresistible forces of nature! The object the law-maker seeks to gain by this legislation is to do away with, or greatly diminish, the indulgence in intoxicating drinks, for, although the sale only is prohibited, the real thing sought and expected is the prevention of the use. He wholly fails to gain the object in view; but objects not in view, and by no means desired, are brought about on the largest scale: vast and useless expenditure, perjury and subornation of perjury, violation of jurors' oaths, corrupt bribery of public officers, the local elections turned into a scramble for the possession of the offices controlling the public machinery for the punishment of offences in order that that machinery may be bought and sold for a price; law and its administration brought into public contempt, and many men otherwise esteemed as good citizens made insensible to the turpitude of perjury, bribery, and corruption; animosity created between different bodies of citizens, rendering them incapable of acting together for confessedly good objects!

The questions may be asked almost indignantly, whether society must endure the open maintenance of places where men are tempted to ruin themselves and their families by indulgence in drink and are led into the commission of the worst of crimes; whether gambling and vice must be permitted to go unrestrained; whether children are to be allowed to grow up in ignorance and idleness and become mischievous members of society; in short, whether society must content itself with waiting until mischievous practices ripen into manifest crime before it enforces its discipline, and refrain from all attempts to prevent the operation of causes known to be fruitful in the crimes it must eventually punish?

It may not be easy to give answers to such questions satisfactory to all, and the tasks of legislation are often undoubtedly difficult. Any detailed consideration of them is beyond my present purpose, which is only to indicate the general nature and function of criminal legislation and the general limits within which it should be confined; but I do not hesitate to say that any legislation which bears the characteristics of *tyranny*, as I have defined that term, is vicious in theory and has never yet succeeded, and never will succeed, in gaining its avowed end, or in having any other than an injurious effect; and I venture to add that if the zeal and labour which have been employed by what are called the better classes of society in efforts to enact and enforce laws repressive of liberty, had been expended in kindly and sympathetic efforts to change and elevate the thoughts and desires of those less fortunate than themselves, a benefit would have been reaped in the diminution of misery and crime which compulsory laws could never accomplish. Moral ends can never be gained except by moral means. All the advances in civilisation and morality which society has thus far made are due to the cultivation and development of those moral sympathies which find their activity in co-operation and mutual aid.

Crimes must be punished, and with requisite severity; but mistake in determining what constitutes crime should be avoided. We must obey the laws even when ill-advised, and must therefore regard as crimes what they declare to be crimes; but in the view of science, conduct can not be made criminal by a legislative declaration. In the true sense, crimes are those grave departures from custom which disappoint expectation, excite resentment, and produce revenge, and directly involve society in disorder and violence. The chief function and first work of organised and conscious society was to preserve internal peace and order by substituting the regular and formal punishment of such offences in the place of private chastisement and revenge. Murder, robbery, stealing, house-breaking, cheating, were from the first, and are still, universally regarded as crimes deserving punishment, and even admitted to be so by the offenders themselves. They are crimes because they are gross and palpable departures from custom rendering peaceful society impossible; but practices which by their nature do not directly and violently disturb society, whatever may be their ultimate tendency and effect, and which all engage in who desire to do so, cannot in a true sense be converted into crimes by a legislative declaration promoted by one part of society against the wishes of another. Crime, like law, can not be *made*, but must be *found*. Society is not an institution created by voluntary action for mutual improvement and discipline, but is a great fact springing from the nature of man as a social animal. It existed for countless ages before it acquired a conscious organism, and passed through many successive stages of progress in accordance with natural laws. Its nature was in no respect changed when man came to assume a conscious, but limited, control over it, and the success of man's administration of that control lies in his correct perception of those fundamental laws which it must necessarily follow, and shaping the exercise of his limited power to aid and not to supersede those laws.

The illustration I have taken from laws designed to prohibit acts which custom does not condemn suggests, however, a form of legislation not open to objection. Those features of the use of intoxicating drinks which are the sources of evil, such as drunkenness in public places, and disorderly resorts, are condemned by custom and directly lead to violence and crime. Laws designed to suppress these practices are in accordance with the true principles of legislation. Intoxication in public may therefore be punished, and the traffic may be restricted to a class of persons of approved responsibility. If the laws of this character we now have do not accomplish all that may be fairly expected from them, the fault lies in lack of proper execution arising mainly from the negligence and indifference of citizens themselves.

Thus much concerning the proper employment of legislation in what I regard as its special province, that of Public Law, and concerning the rules of wisdom and prudence which should be observed in contriving and shaping it. The general rule of wisdom which embraces all these precautions is this : that it should be kept constantly in mind by the legislator that the function of the law resting upon custom, the function of legislation and the function, indeed, of all Government are the same, namely, to mark out the sphere in which the individual may freely act in society without encroaching upon the like freedom in others; that this sphere is primarily marked out by the unconscious operation of custom with a wisdom far beyond that of the wit of the wisest; that the function of conscious government, whether in the form of legislation or otherwise, is subsidiary to it, and that all legislation should observe this subordination and never attempt to subvert or supersede that which it is designed to aid.

This brings me to the consideration of the remaining branch of legislative activity possible under the third above mentioned form of expressing the public will, namely, that in which it acts upon the Private Law. Of course those who believe with Bentham that nothing is entitled to the name of law except a direct command of the sovereign power, and that all law declared and enforced by the mere authority of a judge is a fraudulent usurpation of the office of the Legislature, must reject the limitations I have laid down and assert that the whole field of Private Law belongs to the province of legislation. And so also must those reject them who, like Austin and Maine, while not regarding the action of the judiciary as a usurpation, and indeed while imputing it to the sovereign by saying that he commands it because he permits it, think that Order is yielding to Force, and that all the unwritten Private Law is destined to become the direct written command of the sovereign. According to these jurists, the whole law should be transformed into written codes, either now or at no distant period. While I must regard these opinions as refuted by what I have already said, there is a form of codification which may, even in the opinions of those who do not accept the doctrine that law is a command, be practicable and expedient, and I have therefore reserved that subject for a later and more particular discussion. What I have now to say relates to those other employments of legislation in Private Law which are consistent with my own view of the respective provinces of Public and Private Law. One instance in which legislation may be made productive of advantage is in removing uncertainty and confusion. We have seen that no method is in general provided, or needed, in order to make custom known. The term itself imports that it is known to all. Otherwise it would not be custom. But cases of doubt do arise. Practices which are in reality departures from custom may become so frequent as to appear to be customs, whereas they are only bad practices. These are cases which occasion law-suits. Some one insists that a certain act is sanctioned by custom; another insists that it is a bad practice only. An expert—that is, a judge—is appealed to, and his determination establishes what is custom. But another judge in another locality may reach a different conclusion, and doubt and uncertainty arise. All such uncertainty, which is really the result of a difference of opinion among experts, may be removed by an appeal to a higher tribunal the decisions of which the lower ones are bound to follow. and uncertainty of this sort is best left to this method of correction.

But there is another species of uncertainty in the customary law. Sometimes it comes from the fact that different but neighbouring communities belonging to the same State were of different origin and history and had different customs which were adhered to in the different localities after they had become united under one nationality. This was the condition in England after the Anglo-Saxon conquest. As these communities become more closely united and blended together there is a tendency towards a reduction of such differences to uniformity, and eventually uniformity would be brought about; but the movement would be slow, and meanwhile much confusion would exist, and consequent uncertainty in the determination of rights. The approach to uniformity may be usefully assisted and accelerated by legislation. For example, the extent of the authority possessed by the owners of personal property to bequeath it by testament appears to have been at one time a matter of much doubt. By some it was thought that the most ancient custom common to the whole island of Great Britain permitted the owner to bequeath one third only, reserving the other two thirds for the wife and children. Others insisted that different customs existed among the different principal communities; but there was a general inclination, following the natural desires of owners, towards the complete authority of the latter. This tendency was recognised, and by several statutes passed in the reigns of William and Mary, William III., and George I. the rule permitting the owner to bequeath the whole was established successively in York, Wales, and London, bringing the last of those provinces into harmony with the rest of England.

This tendency in countries whose populations are made up of people once living under separate governments, and having different customs and laws, towards a unification of law, beginning first spontaneously and then taken up and consummated by legislation, is found in the history of many nations, and was, as I suppose, the main original cause of the Code Napoléon and of the recent codification in the German Empire.

Again, in the ordinary transactions of life, in consequence of negligence, ignorance, or fraud, disputes arise between individuals concerning past transactions with each other. One man alleges that another owes him money or service, in consequence of a contract, which the other denies. One may have forgotten or never clearly understood what had taken place between them, or fraudulently intended to enforce a claim in his own favour or to escape an obligation. Such disputes would have been avoided if the parties had exercised the prudence of expressing their transaction or promise in writing, and the practice became common of employing writing in the more important affairs. A court could not, however, without making law, declare that this, and not that, contract should be reduced to writing. The legislation commonly known as the Statute of Frauds,[1] by which certain classes of contracts were required to be in writing, was enacted to supply this want.

Again, society in most fully civilised nations is in a condition of incessant change, which means that

[1] 29 Charles II.

customs are subject to incessant change and that the law resting upon custom must change in accordance with it. New arts, new industries, new discoveries are continually arising, involving changes in populations, employments, and all other incidents of life. These and the diffusion of education create new aspirations and hopes which endeavour to realise themselves. In early society, prior to the organisation of legal tribunals, the final and complete establishment of a change in custom encountered no other obstacle than the tendency of some part of the community to hold on to the existing custom. This opposition, however, would gradually disappear, but the process was so slow as to be nearly imperceptible, and consequently to be free from great attending inconvenience. The establishment of courts, however, although designed to remove uncertainties and confusion in customs, and although having for the most part this effect, in one particular became the cause of those very evils. In order that they might produce certainty, it was necessary to treat their decisions as authorities and binding declarations of the existing law. The judges could not well say that their own decisions or those of their predecessors were not the law, and this obligation tended to make the process of change difficult. There would, indeed, begin to be a tendency not to follow precedent except in cases precisely similar, and the departures would extend wider and wider until the precedent had become so undermined that even the courts would disregard it. Thus a protracted period of uncertainty would arise, the abbreviation of which would be a great advantage. In such cases the Legislature, observing the tendency to change and perceiving that in the end it would be brought about, could most usefully terminate the existing uncertainty by making the change an accomplished fact. The existing law concerning the rights of married women is in large measure the fruit of legislation of this character. The ancient doctrine that during coverture the person and existence of the wife were merged in her husband, that her personal property, choses in action, and the income of her realty belonged to him, was firmly established in the law down to a period not very distant and involved many harsh consequences. Advancing civilisation and refinement many years ago began to exhibit themselves in the better treatment of women. The courts of equity, always the first to catch the growing spirit of humanity and justice, favoured this progress by extending a larger measure of protection to them than was allowed in courts of law, and finally the Legislature, foreseeing the results at which the tendencies of society were aiming, by numerous statutory enactments, gave married women the right to appeal to courts of law, and preserved for them after marriage substantially the rights of unmarried women.

Another occasion for legislative action such as I am now describing is found where incongruities have arisen in consequence of unharmonious action between the laws as enacted and customs sanctioned as lawful by the courts. The celebrated English Statute of Wills is illustrative here. There was in

England, at least after the Norman conquest, very little power to dispose directly of real property by will, but after the invention of the doctrine of *Uses* the expedient was resorted to of a conveyance of land to one person for the use of such other persons as the grantor might name, and he might name them in his will, and in this manner a gift of land to take effect upon the death of the owner might be made. The practice was recognised by the courts and devises of land by such means became very common. But the system of Uses gave rise to practices of a different character deemed mischievous, and in order to put an end to these Parliament by the celebrated Statute of Uses [1] destroyed, or sought to destroy, Uses themselves by directing that the use should be converted into possession. This made, or seemed to make, the contrivance by which devises of land became possible ineffectual, which was not the intention of Parliament, and therefore a few years later the Statute of Wills was enacted by which full power was given to the owners of real property to devise it directly without resort to any contrivance.

Another occasion for legislation, and the last of which I shall speak, is where conflicts arise between different bodies or classes in respect to their rights against each other, and attempts are made by one or the other class to establish their pretences in practice, and resistance is met with. The conflicts so menacing at the present day between labourers and the employers of labour are of this character. Protracted as they are through long periods, practices

[1] 27 Hen. VIII., c. 10.

grow up under which the parties become organised, as it were, in hostile camps, and the public peace becomes endangered; the passions become inflamed and whole communities are divided against each other; great difficulty arises in the execution of the ordinary law, and what may and what may not be lawfully done becomes itself clouded with doubt and uncertainty. It would be extremely difficult at present to devise any law the execution of which would compose the strife now going on. It seems necessary in such cases that the conflict should continue until, by the attrition between the parties, some reconciling custom begins to take form, and to foreshadow the promise of peace. Then the time will have arrived for wise legislation to put the growing tendencies into enacted law. It will be remembered that in an earlier lecture I pointed out that the Laws of Solon for Athens and the XII. Tables of the Roman Law were legislation of this character. The social conditions such as I have mentioned are extraordinary political exigencies, and whenever these arise they furnish occasion for the interposition of the legislative power. Inasmuch as in these internal conflicts neither party will yield to the other without a trial of strength they would proceed, unless arrested, to internecine war in which the vanquished would be obliged to submit. The office of legislation is to permit this war to be carried through to its result, but without violence. The doctrine that the majority must rule has a rightful sway here, for violence can be avoided only by permitting the stronger party to prevail without resort to actual force, and the stronger party is made manifest by the control of the Legislature. Such legislation, imposing, as it does, the thoughts and beliefs of one part of society upon another, is tyrannical in its nature, but in such cases, as violence can not be otherwise avoided, tyranny is necessary.

LECTURE XI

THE subject of codification, thus far reserved, belongs under the general head of legislation, and should be treated before departing from that topic. Codification in the view of many distinguished jurists, both in the past and at the present time, is the method by which the improvement and perfection of the body of our law is to be sought. This is quite inconsistent with the theory of the law which I have endeavoured to support, and makes it incumbent on me that I should state the grounds and reasons which seem to me to show it to be erroneous. In the first place, it is important that we should clearly understand what the advocates of codification mean by it. It will be remembered that I have attached much importance to the distinction between Public and Private Law, assigning to the former all those branches of law in which society as a whole is directly concerned, and which embrace the methods and instrumentalities by which society performs its various particular functions, and to the latter that body of rules which relate particularly to the transactions of individuals as between themselves; and that I have regarded Public Law as falling within the proper province of legislation, and Private Law as being, in general, irreducible to writing, and therefore not properly the subject of legislation. This distinction is not regarded as fundamental by the strictest advocates of codification. They proceed upon the view that every *law* is a command, and for that reason is most properly expressed in writing, and consequently, that a codification embraces and means the whole body of the law reduced to a concise, harmonious, and orderly form and made obligatory by a written enactment. In their view, indeed, the orderly arrangement of the law requires a disposition under leading titles, and the French Codification and that proposed by the late Mr. David Dudley Field, of New York, embrace a scheme of separate codes, one for each of the principal departments of Public Law, and another for Private Law. Now, that part of the law which, in accordance with my views, is necessarily, or properly, expressed in writing, that is, Public Law, tends to become, from the operation of numerous additions, amendments, and repeals, complex, voluminous, confused, and often inconsistent, and requires from time to time to be revised, reduced in volume, and simplified. This work is frequently performed, and our numerous revisions of statutory law are instances of it, and if the term codification were limited to such a work, I should make no objection to it. But what is generally intended by the believers in codification is the statement in writing not only of Public Law, but of all the rules of Private Law also, so that whether we wish to know what the political divisions of a State, or what the duties of public officers are, or what conduct is to be punished as criminal, or what contracts are to be enforced, or, in general, what rights may be asserted by one man against another, we must be guided by the statute-book.

The reason upon which codification as thus understood was supported by its original and illustrious champion, Jeremy Bentham, was derived mainly from his belief in the efficacy of legislation. I have heretofore observed that in his view, the conduct most conducive to general happiness, that is, of the greatest good to the greatest number, could be ascertained beforehand by intelligent men, and could therefore be stated in writing and enacted as law, and he seemed to think that if it were once so enacted the vast change for the better which it would everywhere produce would make society not only satisfied, but delighted with it, but that if all were not satisfied with it they should be compelled to accept it and govern their conduct accordingly. He was a courageous as well as a skilled logician, and never flinched from any true deduction from his theory. To any suggestion that upon his doctrine the task of the Judge would be made simply that of interpreting words, his answer would be that this was just what he meant; that there was nothing he so much detested as judge-made law, and that he would abrogate it, root and branch, by a declaration that there should be no enforceable rules outside of the code. To any suggestion that such *a priori* rules must often, through ignorance, carelessness, or negligence, be so framed as not to be applicable to the unknown transactions of the future and thus occasion injustice and inconvenience, he would say that such evils would be far less than those arising from the uncertainty, expense, and trouble incident to unwritten law, and, besides, that they would be temporary only, and could be remedied for the future by legislative amendments. If he were reminded that his proposal seemed contrary to the experience of mankind, of which experience the common law was the fruit, he would have answered that the common law was the fruit of a fraudulent usurpation of legislative power by the Judges! He would not hesitate to tear down the majestic fabric which the slow processes of nature, operating through ages, had reared, and replace it with the wretched invention of some committee in a legislature.

Lest I be thought guilty of exaggeration, I must borrow from his own language contained in the remarkable communications which he seriously addressed to the People of the United States, to the Autocrat of all the Russias, and to James Madison, President of the United States, imploring them to accept and to endeavour to establish in their respective nations the complete codes of law which he would undertake to construct for them. In his letter first above mentioned, that addressed to the People of the United States, he said:

Yes, my friends, if you love one another—if you love each one of you his own security—shut your ports against our *common law*, as you would shut them against the plague. Leave us to be ruled—us who love to be thus ruled—leave us to be ruled by that tissue of imposture; leave us to be ruled by our gang of self-appointed ———; by our lawyer-ridden, by our priest-ridden ———; leave us to be ruled by those ——— who never cease to call upon us to rally around our

————, ————— that poisoned and poisonous ————— by the *name* of which they have made us slaves.

No: never, never let slip out of your mind this lesson— *wheresoever common law is harboured, security is excluded.*[1]

It is manifest how he intended the blanks to be filled. And in his above mentioned letter to President Madison he said:

Yes, Sir, so long as there remains any the smallest scrap of *unwritten law* unextirpated, it suffices to taint with its own corruption,—its own inbred and incurable corruption,— whatsoever portion of *statute* law has ever been, or can ever be, applied to it.[2]

Yet he could not be insensible to the spectacle of judicial wisdom which characterised the action of the English courts, and he added in the same letter from which the last citation is taken:

All this while, incapable as, in respect of its *form*, it is of serving, in any tolerable degree, in its present state, in the character of a *rule of action* and *guide to* human *conduct*, nothing could be much farther from the truth, than if, in speaking of the *matter* of which English common law is composed, a man were to represent it as being of no use. Confused, indeterminate, inadequate, ill-adapted, and inconsistent as, to a vast extent, the provision or no-provision would be found to be, that has been made by it for the various cases that have happened to present themselves for decision; yet, in the character of a *repository* for such cases, it affords, for the manufactory of real law, a stock of materials which is beyond all price. Traverse the whole continent of Europe,— ransack all the libraries belonging to the jurisprudential systems of the several political states,—add the contents all together,—you would not be able to compose a collection of cases equal in variety, in amplitude, in clearness of state-

[1] *Bentham's Works*, vol. iv., p. 504.
[2] *Ibid.*, p. 460.

ment—in a word, all points taken together, in instructiveness —to that which may be seen to be afforded by the collection of English *Reports of adjudged cases*, on adding to them the *abridgments* and *treatises*, by which a sort of order, such as it is, has been given to their contents.

Yet among those who admired Bentham and accepted his doctrine we find names illustrious in law and philosophy such as Sir Samuel Romilly, John Austin, James Mill, John Stuart Mill, and many others. It seems strange that such powerful minds should not have perceived the error of a system so opposed to the universal practice of mankind; but it should be remembered that in Bentham's day the truth of the supremacy of the great law of causality as well in the moral as in the physical world, although generally admitted, was not carried out to its consequences. The law of Evolution so dominating in its influence upon recent thought, had not been stated. Psychology, Biology, and Sociology, now assuming the attitude of sciences, were wholly undeveloped, and the facts with which those sciences are concerned had been but little studied. The truth that society, like every other phenomenon in nature, was a condition resulting from the operation of causes reaching back into periods infinitely remote, was not understood. Had it been more clearly seen that human conduct, the great feature of society, was necessarily customary because determined by thought, or feeling, which being determined by original constitution and external environment, both similar, must also be customary, it would have been seen that the actual rules which conduct must follow are to be found in custom and cannot be formed or changed *per saltum* by an act of legislation; and that the conscious function of man in the making of law was the by no means humble one of discovering the tendencies toward which custom was aiming and assisting in their operation.

There are still numerous believers in the theory of codification. They cherish an admiration for Bentham and his doctrines. They accept his definition of law as a *command*, but, less courageous than he, they recoil before the *reductio ad absurdum* which that definition really involves. Nor do they have the boldness to assert that it is possible to draw from the theory of Utility, or any other theory, a body of *à priori* rules which, if enacted by a legislature, could be made to operate with effect and advantage. They are inclined to admit that the actual body of our present law, formed by the continuous declarations of judicial tribunals, and learned by the study of reported precedents, is an altogether excellent instrumentality, in general, for the government of conduct. They admit that in an ignorant and rude condition of society no satisfactory code could be constructed, but they insist that there is a point in the life of every civilised State at which all important legal principles have been discovered and are really known, and that when that point is reached laws can and ought to be stated in writing, and that by doing this a prodigious amount of existing evil and inconvenience in the form of doubt and uncertainty in the administration of the law, and labour and expense in acquiring a knowledge of it, will be done away with. That I may fairly represent the views of this class of believers in codification, I gather a summary of them from the *Introduction to the Civil Code*, reported to the Legislature of the State of New York by the Commission constituted under the Constitution of 1848, and which is understood to have been prepared by the late Mr. David Dudley Field. The propositions embraced in this Report are substantially these:

First: Whatever is clearly *known*, can be clearly *stated in writing*, and therefore, all that is clearly known of law can be clearly stated in writing;

Second: A Code therefore is practicable, for a Code is but the simple and orderly statement in writing of all we know of the law;

Third: It is true that we cannot foresee what the law would be for new cases, that is, for new groupings of fact arising in the future, but we are not obliged to lay it down for such cases, and should not attempt to lay it down in a Code.

Fourth: The benefits which would be derived from a codification of the law would be very great in number and variety; the law would be rendered much more clear and certain, and instead of necessitating a search through a library of books, could be found in a single volume, and the ordinary layman could obtain that knowledge of its rules to which every one is entitled who is bound by them.

This reasoning, if such it may be called, contains nearly every form of error. The first proposition is a mere truism. Who has ever doubted the possibility or expediency of reducing our knowledge of the law, as of everything else, to writing? It completely justifies, were justification needed, the very thing we have been doing ever since law came to be thought of, by our digests and treatises which are reductions of all we know of the law to writing, but it justifies nothing more. The second proposition would be true if *stating* law in writing and *enacting* law in writing were the same thing, but things more different from each other could scarcely be imagined. *Stating* law is the scientific work of putting into orderly form those customary rules of conduct which men in society have come to observe, and requires scientific knowledge in any one undertaking the task. *Enacting* law is the giving of a *command* such as a superior gives to an inferior, and does not absolutely require any knowledge at all in him who gives it, and such commands are in fact often given by those who have no, or little, knowledge or whose knowledge is of a kind not at all desirable. *Stating* a rule of the common unwritten law is putting into words a rule by which all conduct of the kind described may, so far as the past enables us to determine, be governed consistently with the sense of justice, but which future experience may require to be restricted, amended, or enlarged. *Enacting* a rule of the common law is *making* an absolute rule by which all such conduct *must* be governed, regardless of the sense of justice. I may thus illustrate the difference:— when the rule was first declared that a contract insuring a ship was not valid unless the assured, in applying for the policy, had disclosed all knowledge he possessed, material to the risk, it amounted to this only—that in cases *like the one decided*, such disclosure was necessary; that is, that under certain known conditions, disclosure was requisite. The decision carried our knowledge thus far and no farther, and if the law thus decided were to be precisely *stated*, the statement would be that under the circumstances of the given case a disclosure by the assured of knowledge material to the risk must be made. Now, if we were to enact the law which had thus been made known and confine the enactment strictly to our knowledge, the written rule would correspond exactly to the judicial declaration and be, that under such circumstances as the given case presented disclosure of knowledge was requisite. It is quite obvious that such an enactment alone would conform to the codification described in the proposition we are dealing with. It would be codifying the law so far as it was known to us; but while it is all that the defence of codification which I am considering professes to demand, it is not what it really demands. It would really enact unconditionally that the applicant for marine insurance must disclose whatever knowledge he has material to the risk. Such an enacted rule would govern cases not only similar to that in which the decision was made, that is, cases of a certain known character, but all cases of whatever character, whether known or unknown. The difference will appear if we suppose a case to arise after the enactment, in which an action is brought on a marine policy and it appears that the assured had, at the time of applying for it, knowledge material to the risk which he did not disclose, but it also appears that the underwriter, at the time, possessed the same knowledge. Common sense and reason tell us that in such a case the rule requiring disclosure has no just application; common sense and reason no longer govern the case. A rule has been enacted in writing requiring disclosure and the policy must be declared void on account of concealment. Codification, therefore, however limited or disguised, cannot, if it is made to have any effect at all, be confined to what is *known* of the law. Instead of declaring rules applicable only to known cases, and those like them, it declares rules applicable to all cases, known or unknown, described in the law. Mr. Field in the Introduction above mentioned, denies this : He says:

"This Code (his proposed Civil Code) is undoubtedly the most important and difficult of all; and of this it is true that it cannot provide for all possible cases which the future may disclose. It does not profess to provide for them. All that it professes is to give the general rules upon the subjects to which it relates which are now known and recognised."

But Mr. Field, if he was fully aware of what he was saying, could scarcely have been sincere. Where, I beg to inquire, is any such profession as above mentioned set forth in his code, or in any proposed codification? If that be what he really intended by codification, he certainly could not have objected to have the intention clearly expressed. He could not have objected to begin it with an article framed in his own language as follows: "This code is intended to give the general rules on the subjects to which it

18

relates which are now known and recognised." But as this would have utterly destroyed his code, *qua* code, by converting it into a ridiculous digest, he either did not mean that his code should have the limited operation he asserts for it, or he intended to conceal his meaning while he was urging its adoption. This notion that the operation of a rule may be restricted by making it more general, seems highly absurd. Every one must see that the more general an enacted rule is, the more of future unknown cases it will cover. Suppose a general rule were enacted that promises made upon consideration were binding. This, if it is made to mean anything, means that all such promises are binding, and the rule would cover a multitude of invalid promises, such as those made by infants or insane persons, or fraudulent promises, and promises against public policy Every case of a promise made on consideration, present or future, known or unknown, would be absolutely governed by such an enactment, and it would excite a smile of derision in any court called upon to interpret the rule to suggest that it did not *profess* to cover future and unknown cases.

There are some so-called practical minds who, while admitting the force of the reasons I have given for rejecting the theory of Codification, still think that there is a tendency towards it at present which cannot be resisted, and that this affords some proof that the system possesses real advantages, and they seem inclined to yield to this evidence. Their view seems to be that, though it is theoretically impossible to make law by legislation, under which questions

arising upon future novel transactions or new groupings of facts, can be correctly adjudicated, yet the
evil and inconvenience arising from this are exaggerated, and that the transactions of the past
which have fallen under judicial decision have
presented a variety and complexity sufficient to
produce a full development of legal principles, and
that the transactions of the future will be, in the
main, simply repetitions of those which have already
been considered—not indeed repetitions in all details,
but in all material features, and that if the law, as
at present developed and ascertained, were enacted
in writing, there would not be very many instances
in which it would fail to dispose correctly of disputes
as they arise, and that the evil and inconvenience
which would occasionally result from its ill-adapta-
tion to new groupings of fact would be outweighed by
the benefit which would be derived from the greatly
increased certainty and ease of acquisition which, as
they suppose are the distinguishing advantage of
codified law.

To think that an unscientific method may, on the
whole, be preferable to a scientific one, is a notion to
which not much indulgence should be extended
within the walls of a university; but in the endeavour
to secure the adoption of scientific truth the arguments of those who are called practical men should not
be altogether dismissed, even though they should be,
as they often are, merely superficial or ignorant men.
The view suggested is that while rules of law enacted
by legislation in a code might be of inferior *quality* as
instruments for the government of conduct, they

would tend to diminish the element of *uncertainty* in the law, and be of great advantage in this way, but I apprehend that this apology for codification has quite as little foundation as any other. What is the nature of that *uncertainty* which, to some extent, attaches to unwritten law? As to cases which have happened in the past and have been adjudicated upon, there is no uncertainty. The precedents make everything plain, but when a case arises different in some respect from any preceding one, uncertainty may arise. One person thinks that the new element of fact which makes the case a novel one is not material and that the rule already established should govern; another thinks it material and that it should constitute an exception, or matter for a new subclassification. Take for example, the case of marine insurance as we may suppose the law upon that subject to have grown up. An underwriter insures a ship against the perils of the sea, and she is lost or damaged by such perils. There is no uncertainty here. Contracts of insurance have long been customary. The event having occurred against which the insurance was made, the insured expects to be made good and the underwriter equally expects to indemnify him. Another case of such insurance occurs and a similar loss, but the underwriter now learns for the first time that the ship was unseaworthy at the beginning of the voyage. Let it be supposed that the ship owner himself did not know that she was unseaworthy. He demands his indemnity and perceives no sufficient reason why he should not have it. It is the universal custom for men to perform their contracts, and in the case of marine insurance, in particular, multitudes of instances had occurred in which losses were promptly paid; in other words, his expectation of payment, his feeling that he ought to be paid, his sense of justice—all different expressions of the same thing, are founded upon this custom. If we employed the language of logic we should say that he assigned the case to the class of binding contracts. But the underwriter takes a different view. He says "No intelligent and honest man sends an unseaworthy ship to sea. The universal custom is the other way. There may be exceptions, but they are very few. All ship owners have their ships examined and put in complete condition to meet the perils they are likely to encounter, and if any one fails to do this he is grossly negligent. I had a right to rely on this custom; I did rely upon it and supposed I was insuring a seaworthy ship." The ship owner replies, "No rule has ever as yet been laid down to the effect that an applicant for insurance warrants that his ship is seaworthy. You are endeavouring to incorporate into the contract a stipulation which is not to be found there. I did not deceive you. You could have examined the ship as easily as I could, and if you failed to do so the fault is your own. I know very well that ship owners are in the habit of examining their ships before sending them to sea. I examined this one, but did not happen to discover the defect." The case is made the subject of litigation, the reasons of the contending parties are subjected to close examination, and the final decision is that there was in the contract an implied warranty that the ship was seaworthy, and consequently that the assured was not entitled to recover for his loss. Here was an uncertainty arising from a reasonable doubt concerning the category in which a particular case should be placed. It was terminated by the decision; but doubts of the like character continually arose in the development of the same branch of the law, as cases presenting novel features disclosed themselves. When a ship owner, having a ship at sea uninsured or not fully insured, and having received intelligence that she had encountered severe weather which might have damaged or destroyed her, effected an insurance upon her without disclosing his knowledge, and a loss having occurred, made a claim for indemnity, it was a matter of uncertainty whether the law should allow it. The decision resolved that and added a new rule to the law of insurance, and when a similar claim was made upon a policy effected under like circumstances, and with a like failure to disclose, but with the new feature that the underwriter actually knew, from other sources, all the information which the assured failed to disclose, still another uncertainty arose, which was in turn removed by judicial decision, and another rule was added to the same branch of law. In this way, the whole law of insurance has been built up, and what is true of insurance is true of every other branch of the unwritten law.

If we consult the books of reports, the digests, and treatises, with the view of discovering how much of the uncertainty in the unwritten law is assignable to the same cause, namely, transactions presenting novel features, we shall find that nearly all is of this character, and that it should arise from this source, and exist to such a large degree, will excite no wonder when we again reflect upon what our analysis has informed us to be the true nature of the science. It is the examination of the features of transactions and assigning them to the jural classes in which they belong, or creating new classifications when this is needed; and as the law applicable to any case can not be known until this operation has been performed, it can not be known for any new case until such case has come to light and has been subjected to judicial decision. So far, therefore, as the future discloses to us new groupings of fact, the law must necessarily be uncertain, and inasmuch as the world and life are forever developing and displaying new features, this uncertainty will forever continue, and as it is according to the order of nature it can not be wrong or regrettable. To contend with such uncertainty, to dispel it by the exertion of our highest powers, is part of the discipline of life and the glorious arena for the display of those faculties which our profession calls into exercise. The work may be difficult, but difficulty is necessary to progress. "Progress is the child of struggle, and struggle is the child of difficulty."

Such being the nature of the uncertainty of the unwritten law, it is manifest that codification, however defined or modified, can do nothing to remove it. It can be cleared up only in the way pointed out by patiently scrutinising the features of each novel grouping of facts, as it presents itself, and determining the classification to which it belongs, but codification, at the start, refuses to adopt this method, and assumes to be able to classify transactions before they come into being, and, therefore, before they can be known.

There is a sort of unconscious belief with the practical minds of whose views I am speaking, that though enacted rules of law may not well suit many transactions in the future, yet that, being enacted, men will conform their conduct to them, and that thus uncertainty may be diminished.

But this supposes that we now have a fully developed and accomplished world, and that hereafter we are not to be confronted with novel transactions to any considerable extent. There is nothing to justify such an expectation. If we were to compare different periods in the past with the view of ascertaining in which one there was more of novelty in the conjunctures challenging judicial inquiry and doubt, I apprehend that the last century would be pre-eminent.

I have been speaking of one particular source of uncertainty in the law, that arising from our inability to foreknow an ever-changing future. But there is another even greater. Uncertainty arises whenever, from any cause, men come to differ in their opinions about the law. Now of all the causes creating uncertainty in opinions and beliefs the imperfection of language is perhaps the greatest. The most learned men have been employed unceasingly ever since the existence of the Christian Church in interpreting the Bible, and yet all Christendom is split up into sectarian divisions, based upon conflicting interpretations. Desolating wars have been waged as a consequence of such uncertainty.

Our own people have been divided into political parties, one of which interprets the language of the Constitution in one way, and the other in another. It would require many volumes to contain the record of the numberless conflicts in the Courts of England and the United States concerning the interpretation of a single statute—the Statute of Frauds—though it was framed by one of the greatest lawyers that have ever lived. Writing is the art of communicating thought by means of visible signs, every different thought having a different sign or signs. The number of signs is infinite, and to know them well and the exact signification of each is one of the rarest of accomplishments. The great majority even of educated men express their thoughts in language of every variety of uncertainty. Writers, however skilful, may not completely express the thought intended to be communicated, or may use an inappropriate word, and thus convey a thought different from the one intended, and those of only ordinary skill fall into numerous errors. A written rule of law tainted by any one of these defects is certain to raise doubts concerning its meaning. When interpreted literally, it may import something which does not accord with the sense of justice, and whenever the ordinary sense of justice indicates one thing and the written law another, the question at once arises not only with laymen but with lawyers, whether the law can really mean what it seems plainly to declare, and the effort is made to extract from the written language, by a species of violent interpretation, a meaning accordant with the sense of justice. For instance, the Statute of Limitations, as originally framed, declared, in substance, that actions of a certain description could not be maintained unless brought within six years after the cause of action had accrued. A base fraud has been committed by a man, and by another fraud he has succeeded in concealing it from his victim for more than six years. An action at law is brought after the expiration of this period, to recover damages for the fraud, and the wrong-doer triumphantly pleads the statute. Nothing can be clearer than that by the language of the statute the action is barred, and at the same time it is certain that the legislator never intended such a result. The opposite sides upon this question are confidently maintained by the counsel of the parties respectively, one insisting upon the very words of the statute, the other upon the intention of the legislator, and the law is uncertain until it is determined by a judicial decision. It may be thought strange that any one should doubt, upon such clear language, that the action was barred, but I remember that the very question was made at the Law School in this University, while I was a student, in a moot court case, and that the distinguished head of the school at that time, who had no superior as a common law judge, decided that the suit could be maintained, declaring with some humour, "Fraud is said to vitiate contracts; well it vitiates the applicability of the Statute of Limitations!" And so it will ever be; whenever the written law plainly contradicts the precepts of justice so inwoven into our nature as to seem instinctive, a doubt will be made whether the legislator really intended what he seems to have declared, and all the arts of reason and sophistry combined will be employed to put an interpretation upon his language consistent with justice. The Koran was a codification of Mahometan law, and if codification could anywhere succeed it would be in the stationary society of Islam; but the learned doctors who administered that law found it pregnant with the same uncertainties, and removed them in much the same way. Says Gibbon:

"From the Atlantic to the Ganges the Koran is acknowledged as the fundamental code, not only of theology, but of civil and criminal jurisprudence; and the laws which regulate the actions and the property of mankind are guarded by the infallible and immutable sanction of the will of God. This religious servitude is attended with some practical disadvantage; the illiterate legislator had been often misled by his own prejudices and those of his country; and the institutions of the Arabian desert may be ill-adapted to the wealth and numbers of Ispahan and Constantinople. On these occasions the Cadhi respectfully places on his head the holy volume and substitutes a dexterous interpretation more apposite to the principles of equity and the manners and policy of the times." [1]

The extent of the uncertainty thus necessarily incident to statutory law is vastly greater than is commonly supposed. The believers in codification are deluded by the notion that there is by means of language a capability, not only of making all things known by any persons clearly intelligible to others, but of making things clearly known which are in their nature uncertain. But upon any just com-

[1] Gibbon, vol. vi, p. 283

parison it will be found that the sum of the un-certainties arising from statutory law is many times greater in proportion to its extent than that met with in the administration of unwritten law. Such means of comparison as are open to us exhibit a significant result. I have caused an examination to be made of the comparative numbers of controversies arising respectively on written and unwritten law in a single year (1903), in three jurisdictions, namely those of England, New York, and Massachusetts. In England, out of four hundred and eighty adjudged cases, two hundred and fifteen arose upon common law and two hundred and sixty-five on statutes. In New York, out of seventeen hundred and eighty-eight decided cases, nine hundred and two arose upon common law and eight hundred and eighty-six upon written law. In Massachusetts, out of three hundred and forty-three cases two hundred and nineteen arose upon common law and one hundred and twenty-four upon statutes. Now when we con-sider that the field of conduct and consequent numbers of transactions subject to the control of the unwritten law are many times larger than those governed by written law, if the same degree of uncertainty obtained in each, there should be, *ceteris paribus*, a number of litigations springing out of un-certainty in the unwritten law many times greater than the number arising upon statutory law. There is not a day in which in the intercourse of active men transactions sometimes very numerous are not entered into which contain the possibilities of dispute concerning the common law, while the transactions

which turn upon the language of statutes are confined to a comparatively few subjects and few persons,
and yet the actual amount of statutory litigation as
appears from the comparison I have given, does not
fall largely below that of common law litigation.

Whoever has followed with attention the line of
reasoning I have thus far pursued, will, at some
point, ask how it happens, if all attempts to subject
the main government of conduct to the operation of
written law be, as I have endeavoured to show, unscientific, inexpedient, and, indeed, in a certain sense
wholly impracticable, that some of the most cultivated nations of ancient and modern times have
persistently acted upon a contrary policy, and made
general codes covering every province of the law the
basis of their jurisprudence. This inquiry is indeed
most pertinent; for if it be true that such nations have
subjected the whole matter of private law to written
enactment and still maintained a judicial administration which will stand without disadvantage in
comparison with our own, the foregoing reasonings
should receive further scrutiny, or at all events,
circumstances should be pointed out which might
explain this apparent incongruity between the
teachings of theory and experience.

The first observation to be made upon this possible
objection is, that it assumes what is not true. It
is not true that any nation, ancient or modern, has
successfully undertaken to subject the whole body
of private law to statutory forms; and it is true that,
so far as any such attempt has been made, it has, in
every instance, been attended by the confusion and

mischief which have been pointed out as the inevitable consequences of such a policy. I must therefore take some pains to expose this error by a reference to the actual experience of other nations.

Attention should be called, at the outset, to the exceedingly loose reasoning which marks most of the common arguments by which the expediency of codification is sought to be supported by the teachings of actual experience. The examples of Rome, of France, of Prussia, or of Louisiana, are frequently cited as proofs that codes of private law should everywhere be adopted. Such arguments can have no force unless coupled with proof of two things: *first*, that the judicial administration of private law in the countries referred to has actually been under the control of written codes; and *second*, that such judicial administration is superior to our own. But such proof is not even attempted. It would be impossible to make it; the argument, however, tacitly and falsely assumes the fact.

The example first to be considered is that of Rome. This is the one most frequently urged, we will not say by the few learned, temperate, and prudent advocates of codification, for there are such, but by those who imagine that most of the difficulties we meet in the administration of law come from the circumstance that it is not expressed in writing. They seem to have a notion that the jurisprudence of Rome, until the time of Justinian, was in a state of utter confusion and uncertainty, and that by the composition of a code embracing all departments of the law, that Emperor succeeded in bringing order out of chaos, and established a system which, in its actual operation, secured to the people over which it was extended the blessings, not theretofore enjoyed, of a scientific, certain, and easy administration of justice. Mr. Field, himself, in his defence of the policy of codification contained in the introduction to his proposed *Civil Code*, makes, as his first argument, an appeal to the example of Rome. He says:

"It [the feasibility of a complete codification of the law] was fully proven by what had been done in respect to the law of other countries. The law of Rome in the time of Justinian was, to say the least, as difficult of reduction into a Code as is our own law at the present day. Yet it was thus reduced, though, no doubt to the disgust and dismay of many a lawyer of that period. The concurring judgment of thirteen centuries since has, however, pronounced the Code of Justinian one of the noblest benefactions to the human race, as it was one of the greatest achievements of human genius." [1]

These sounding phrases would excite a smile from the civilians. The Code of Justinian is but a *revision* and consolidation of the imperial constitutions, which correspond with our *statutes*, and which, taken together, constituted what may be called the *statutory law* of the Empire, and which, for the most part, related to the organism of the State, the forms of its institutions, its officers and their duties, in other words, covering the same matter which our statute law covers, and which, as I have repeatedly said, is the appropriate province of written law. Instead of being one of the "highest achievements of human genius," it is a work certainly not superior to any one

[1] Field, *Introduction to Civil Code*, p. xv.

of a hundred similar ones which have been executed from time to time in our own States and in other nations, and instead of being properly described as "one of the noblest benefactions to the human race," it is something which very few individuals of the human race know or care, or need to know or care, anything about.[1]

The eulogy often expended upon the Roman law by its admirers, which Mr. Field has borrowed and applied with somewhat ludicrous effect to the Code, belongs to another part of the work of Justinian, the Digest, or Pandects, which consisted of a digest of the treatises of the most illustrious writers, selected from a preceding and purer age of Roman jurisprudence. This work covered the domain of *private* law, that which relates to the rights and obligations of men in their ordinary dealings with each other, and which I have so often insisted upon as being the appropriate and peculiar province of *unwritten* law. It was an attempt to gather together, to consecrate, and by consecrating to preserve those priceless contributions to jurisprudence which the blended thought and experience—the unwritten law—of a thousand years had

[1] " The Code contains the decrees of the Emperors, from Constantine to Justinian and has the least reputation of Justinian's works. In respect of Latinity, it is inferior to the Digest and Institutes; as regards style, it is bombastic and inflated. Its arrangement is not superior to that of the Pandects, while in respect of esoteric merit it is contradictory and sometimes even unintelligible. Professors fear to attempt its explanation; students shrink from it, while commentators only use it to explain passages in the Digest."

Juridical Society Papers, vol. i., p. 487 by Patrick MacChombaich (Colquhoun.)

made, and which a declining age was no longer able to enlarge and was beginning to forget. The design was noble, although the execution was exceedingly imperfect; but it would be the gravest of errors to seize upon the glory which belongs to the authors of this system of law and transfer it to Tribonian and his colleagues who abridged it, or to their imperial master, who gave it his sanction.

In order to ascertain the true import of the lesson taught by the history of Roman law and the work of Justinian, we must consider with some precision what the sources of that law were, its condition when it engaged the attention of that Emperor, and his dealings with it. A very hasty sketch is all that my limits permit.

I have heretofore spoken of the law of the Twelve Tables, which was the work of a Commission styled the Decemviri, created about the year 450 B.C., designed to compose the dissensions between the plebeian and the patrician classes. Of this law, in its original form, fragments only remain; but it seems probable that its framers extended their work over a larger area than the points in dispute, and attempted to reduce to written forms the main body of the pre-existing law. The Twelve Tables, therefore, were, to some extent, in the nature of a general code, which attempted to provide for future cases. What must happen in every such case to the end of time, happened here. In the practical work of administering justice, the Twelve Tables were found to be an obstacle; the rigid letter of the law was constantly found not to be suited to the new and unforeseen cases, arising in endless succession. One of two things was necessary; either that the letter of the law should be departed from, or the right administration of justice be sacrificed. In such a contest there can be but one result. It is the letter of the law which must yield; and this was accomplished in Rome, as in like cases it has been accomplished everywhere else, by the arts of subtle *exposition*, and the invention and employment of fictions, and other devices by which the written law is apparently obeyed, but really evaded.

One agency by which this result was accomplished came through a peculiar incident of the action of the judicial tribunals. The Roman prætors, whose office most nearly resembled that of our judges, found continual occasion to supplement or evade the rigid and ill-adapted language of the Tables; and in order that the public might know beforehand the extent to which this discretionary power of the prætor would be carried, it became the custom for each of these magistrates before entering upon his judicial functions to draw up and promulgate what was styled an *edict*, in which the rules were laid down by which he avowed that he would be guided in his official action. This edict, however, not being strictly law, was itself interpreted and applied with as much latitude as it exhibited towards the rigid code it was designed to supplement; and as the prætor's term of office embraced a year only, the successive prætorian edicts effected those gradual and almost insensible changes in the administration of private law which constitute what is very properly termed its development or *growth*. Each prætor took the edict of his predecessor and adopted it so far as it had stood the test of actual experience, supplementing and amending it in those particulars in which it had proved defective. The Roman prætor, however, was not a master of the science which he affected to expound. He was not, as with us, selected from the class of experts in the law, wholly by reason of his supposed prominence among his fellows, and called upon to devote himself for successive years to judicial duties. He was an aspiring politician, passing through the various grades of official dignity on his way to the consulship, and discharging for a single year the duties of judicial office. It was impossible that the great function of administering justice in a civilised state could be performed by the unassisted labours of these fleeting officials. In the law, as in all other sciences or arts, society demands the genius and skill of experts; and in some form, direct or indirect, this demand must be supplied; and this introduces me to the *second* and principal agency by which the customary law in the Roman State was at the same time cultivated, developed, and applied to the actual business of life.

This was the class of *jurisconsults*—private citizens, whose highest ambition was satisfied by the employment of studying the science of jurisprudence and bestowing the benefit of their labours upon the public or their clients. To them the prætor resorted for aid in the composition of his annual edict, the private citizen for advice, and the principal officers of State, and the Emperors themselves, for guidance in the discharge of legislative and executive duties.   Never in any society, ancient or modern, was the office of the jurist more respectable, or more gloriously filled. The classic age of the jurisprudence of Rome, co-inciding with the period of her renown in arts and arms, and extending from the birth of Cicero to the reign of Alexander Severus, is full of illustrious names, whose lives were devoted to the task of developing the science of jurisprudence, and adapting it to the evershifting phases of human affairs.[1]

The development and growth of Roman juris-prudence, as thus sketched, continued until the reign of the Emperor Hadrian; and during this long period, the just boundary between the provinces of written and unwritten law was preserved.   The public administration of the State was regulated by the former, and the field of private rights and duties was

---

[1] Gibbon has sketched in a few master strokes this peculiar feature of Roman policy by which the *unwritten law* became supreme in the administration of private justice.   The shining paradox which closes the citation, compresses into a line what might be expanded into pages: "A more liberal art was cultivated, however, by the sages of Rome, who, in a stricter sense, may be considered as the authors of the civil law.   The alteration of the idiom and manners of the Romans rendered the style of the Twelve Tables less familiar to each rising generation, and the doubtful passages were imperfectly explained by the study of legal antiquarians.   To define the ambiguities, to circumscribe the latitude, to apply the principles, to extend the consequences, to reconcile the real or apparent contradictions, was a much nobler and more important task; and the province of legislation was silently invaded by the expounders of ancient statutes.   Their subtle interpretations concurred with the equity of the prætor to reform the tyranny of the darker ages; however strange or intricate the means, it was the aim of artificial jurisprudence to restore the simple dictates of nature and reason, and the skill of private citizens was usefully employed to undermine the public institutions of their country."   Gibbon's *Decline and Fall*, (Murray, 1862) vol. v. p. 273.

occupied by the latter. The Emperors had, indeed, long been invested with absolute power, but it was sparingly exercised in the province of private law, the great mass of which still remained substantially unwritten.

The Empire was now verging towards its fall. Rome began to feel more and more the arbitrary hand of her master. The decadence was marked by a corresponding decline in jurisprudence, and the extension of the province of legislation over the proper domain of the unwritten law was one of the principal features.[1] Whether this extension of legislative power over the domain of private law was the cause, or the consequence, or simply an accompaniment of the decline in the juristic literature, we will not undertake to pronounce; but upon either view the fact is significant.

It was indeed, impossible for the noble jurisprudence of Rome, which had its origin under the free influences of the Republic, to preserve its integrity amid the general decay of morals, arts, letters, and arms which marked the decline of the Empire, but two circumstances tended greatly to

[1] " Hadrian appears to have been the first who assumed without disguise the plentitude of absolute power. And this innovation, so agreeable to his active mind, was countenanced by the patience of the times and his long absence from the seat of government. The same policy was embraced by succeeding monarchs, and, according to the harsh metaphor of Tertullian, 'the gloomy and intricate forest of ancient laws was cleared away by the axe of royal mandates and *constitutions.*' During four centuries from Hadrian to Justinian, the public and private jurisprudence was moulded by the will of the sovereign, and few institutions, either human or divine, were permitted to stand on their former basis." Milman's *Gibbon*, vol. iv., p. 313.

hasten the march of its degeneracy. In the first place the changes in human affairs were continually rendering much of the works of the classic jurists obsolete, and requiring new adaptations and changes of the law. In the next place, before the art of printing was known, the cost of the materials of writing was so great that the works of a past age could not be perpetuated and multiplied at a price which would enable any but the very rich to possess them. They gradually disappeared and perished under the decay of time, except so much of them as were preserved in the treatises and commentaries of succeeding jurists; and the genuineness of these fragments was the subject of frequent, and sometimes insoluble, dispute.[1]

Such was the condition in which Justinian found the Roman law. It may be briefly summed up as follows:

First. The *statutory law* was embodied in the earlier collections known as the Gregorian, the Hermogenian, and Theodosian Codes, and in the subsequent Constitutions of the later Emperors, and was encumbered with the superfluities and con-

[1] The books of jurisprudence were interesting to few, and entertaining to none; their value was connected with present use, and they sunk forever as soon as that use was superseded by the innovations of fashion, superior merit, or public authority. In the age of peace and learning, between Cicero and the last of the Antonines, many losses had been already sustained, and some luminaries of the school or forum were known only to the curious by tradition and report. Three hundred and sixty years of disorder and decay had accelerated the progress of oblivion; and it may fairly be presumed that, of the writings which Justinian is accused of neglecting, many were no longer to be found in the libraries of the East."—Milman's *Gibbon*, vol. v., p. 286.

tradictions which necessarily result from successive enactments relating to the same subjects through a long period of time. It required a thorough *revision*.

Second: The unwritten law, the authoritative sources of which for a thousand years had been the writings of private jurisconsults, was in still greater confusion. The works of the universally recognised masters of the science had first become in part superseded, and finally lost. Their successors were an ignoble multitude "of Syrians, Greeks, and Africans, who flocked to the Imperial court to study Latin as a foreign tongue and jurisprudence as a lucrative profession." There was a want of that instrumentality, indispensable in the administration of unwritten law, namely, *universally recognised authorities* to which appeal could be made.

LECTURE XII

WE are now in a situation to understand and appreciate the nature of Justinian's work. It embraced three principal features: (1) To reduce to one compact and consolidated body the whole mass of statutory law, and republish it, so that it should completely supersede the former Codes and the subsequent imperial Constitutions; (2) To make an *authorised digest* of the whole mass of the juristic literature, embracing, as it did, the entire province of the unwritten private law of the Empire, the prætorian edicts, and the writings of all subsequent jurists; (3) The composition of a treatise or manual for the instruction of students and magistrates in the elementary principles of this legal system.

The *first* part of this scheme was carried out by the execution and publication as law of what is called "The Code," which is confined, for the most part, to the proper province of written law, the law relating to the public administration of the Empire, and fills somewhat the same place in the Roman law of this period as is occupied by the Revised Statutes in the legal system of New York. We may dismiss this from further notice as being a work of comparatively little interest to succeeding ages, and throwing no light upon the main question with which we are dealing.[1]

The *third* part of Justinian's work was accomplished by the composition of what is called "The Institutes," and this also merits little attention here. It was in no respect a Code of law, but a manual for the instruction of students in a knowledge of the law.

It is the *second* part of this imperial scheme which especially demands our attention; for it is this which is really intended when the work of Justinian is appealed to as supporting an argument in favour of codification. It consisted in a digested abridgment of all that was supposed to be true and of present utility in the treatises of the Roman jurists. Rejecting the feeble and degenerate productions of the later lawyers, he went back to the time of the

[1] "In general it may be said that the Codex consists, to a much greater extent than the Digest, of *public* law in all its departments; that is the law which prescribes and regulates the organism of the State, with all State institutions, whether civil or ecclesiastical. Here belongs all that relates to forms of government, modes of administration, duties of public officers, and the like. Under public law is included also *criminal* law, the law of crime and punishment—a crime being a wrong action viewed as affecting the rights, not of individuals, but of society, as a violation of public peace and order, as an offence against the State. On the other hand, *private* law is occupied with the rights of individuals, with the modes by which individuals may acquire such rights or transfer them to others, and the ways in which individuals may obtain personal redress when these rights are impaired by fraud or violence. Now, the fact which I wish to emphasise is this: that the Digest is composed of private law in a far larger proportion than the Codex. This is a fact which gives to the Digest something of the superior interest and importance which belongs to it. It is mainly by reason of the private law which it embodies that the Corpus Juris has exerted its immense influence on jurisprudence and justice in Modern Europe." —Hadley's *Introduction to Roman Law*, p. 14.

perfecting of the Perpetual Edict by Salvius Julianus, and selected some forty treatises composed within the century succeeding that work. These were condensed, digested, and arranged in fifty books, and the completed work was published and declared as authoritative law.

But the important thing to be here observed is that this work bore little resemblance to ordinary written law, or to a Code, in the sense in which we are considering that term. It did not speak, as a statute speaks, in the shape of simple rules or commands. Composed from scientific treatises, it preserved many of the features of a scientific treatise. It was a statement of the principles of the science of the law in the language of the authors whose works were selected, accompanied with argument, explanation, and illustration, and naming the jurists whose language was adopted. The stamp of imperial recognition added no new element to the authority of the writers whose works were thus abridged. They possessed the authority of law before. The effect of the codification was simply to make the Digest the only book in which these precepts could be sought. The law in this form had, in large measure, the attributes of *unwritten* law. It was still a law of *principles* more than a law of *words*. It was plastic, susceptible of such interpretation and application as would suit the infinite variety of aspects exhibited by human affairs.

It was, indeed, no part of the design of Justinian to change in any respect the essential nature of Roman jurisprudence as a system of unwritten law.

The idea of a Code in the modern sense, as a legislative republication of the whole system of law in
the imperative form of a statute, was not present
to the minds of Justinian and his advisers. That
idea is of modern origin altogether.[1] His scheme
was in strict accordance with the historical development of Roman law. It recognised the fact that
private, as distinguished from public law, was the
product of the learning and labours of the jurisconsults; that after a degeneracy of three centuries
the age no longer produced any of those great examples of original and independent genius which
had illumined the golden era of jurisprudence; and
that it was no longer possible to find among the living
oracles of the law any voices which commanded that
reverence and obedience which are at all times
absolutely essential to the administration of private
justice between man and man. He sought to correct
this evil: and his method was to gather together the
authentic remains of the earlier and better jurists,
to attach to them selections from later writers which
were necessary to accommodate them to the practical
needs of the present time, and to add to the whole
work his imperial declaration that it alone should be
appealed to as authoritative.

One would imagine on reading some of the high
sounding eulogies of the Justinian codification, such
as that of Mr. Field which I have quoted, that it was
the same sort of treatment of Roman law as that
which they advocate of our own law, and that it conferred upon Roman society a vast and permanent

[1] Austin's *Jurisprudence* (Campbell's Ed.), vol. ii., p. 920.

benefit. Both these notions are erroneous. That
the first is so, is manifest from the sketch I have
given; and that the second is equally the case appears
from the fate which legal historians inform us the
work of Justinian met with. The whole scheme,
Code, Pandects, and Institutes proved, so far as
respected their practical efficiency for governing the
affairs of the Empire, an utter failure. Scarcely
had they been completed before necessities for
amendment revealed themselves. Change succeeded
change, and the whole system seems, in a comparatively short period, to have become either superseded or ignored.[1] No support, therefore, can be

---

[1] " But the Emperor was unable to fix his own inconstancy; and,
while he boasted of renewing the exchange of Diomede, of transmuting
brass into gold, he discovered the necessity of purifying his gold from
the mixture of baser alloy. Six years had not elapsed from the publication of the Code before he condemned the imperfect attempt by a
new and more accurate edition of the same work, which he enriched
with two hundred of his own laws, and fifty decisions of the darkest
and most intricate points of jurisprudence. Every year, or, according
to Procopius, each day, of his long reign was marked by some legal
innovation."—Gibbon's *Decline and Fall*, vol. v., p. 287.

" The great law-book of Justinian seems to have gained no very wide
currency among those for whom it was intended, It was, to a great
extent, superseded in practice by paraphrases and abridgments of the
whole or of particular parts. An inquirer two or three centuries later,
looking at the fate of this Justinian legislation, might have said that
it was a splendid and elaborate failure. In the reign of Leo the Isaur-
ian (717–741) the books of the Corpus Juris were hardly used at all in
their original form; and even the paraphrases and abridgments
founded on it were so ill-adapted to the existing state of the law, that
this Emperor thought it necessary to issue a compendious Code of his
own. This was the state of things in the Eastern Empire. In Western
Europe the Corpus Juris had never found currency, except in Italy;
and here in some parts and cities of the peninsula it still enjoyed an
obscure and precarious influence."—Hadley's *Introduction to Roman
Law*, p. 24.

drawn from this experience in favour of any con- version of our unwritten law into statutory forms. The true greatness and glory of the Roman law does not proceed in any degree from codification. It has become attached to that word by accident. The great classical jurists who reduced that law to scientific form had passed away before the time of Justinian, and afterwards their names and their works were alike overwhelmed in the avalanche of barbarism which swept over Europe. The discovery of the Pandects coinciding with the general awaken- ing from the ignorance of the Dark Ages revealed to the rising modern world the treasures it contained, and the merit of these has thus come to be connected with the imperfect instrument which preserved them, but the real merit of the Pandects belongs not to the compilers of that very imperfect work, but to the original authors of perhaps the most consistent sys- tem of unwritten law which the world has yet seen.

The principal modern states whose example may be appealed to by the advocates of codification are France and Prussia. Indeed, it may be said that a code, in the modern sense of that word, was for the first time adopted in Prussia. The measure was initiated in 1751 by Frederick the Great. It was at first styled the *Gesetzbuch*, but was afterwards de- veloped into what is now called the *Landrecht*. Concerning this code two observations are to be made: (1) It had its origin in one of those political emergencies which, as I have heretofore explained, justify and require a resort to statutory law. A number of originally independent states had become consolidated into a political unity and subjected to the dominion of the House of Brandenburg. Each state had its own customs and consequently its own laws, and the great increase of intercourse between the citizens of the different states was attended with mischievous confusion and conflict which would eventually pass away by the prevalence of some common customs over the conflicting ones. In such cases the approach to unification may be greatly assisted and hastened by making the customs tending to prevail, compulsory. This can be done with great advantage by statutory law. Such law will be attended with difficulties in the enforcement of it, but the confusion and difficulty will be less than those which it supersedes. (2) The merits of this work, other than those of hastening a desirable consolidation of discordant social elements are to be estimated by its actual results; and upon this point there can scarcely be a question. It became loaded with declaratory laws passed to explain its obscurities, correct its errors, and supply its deficiencies.

The example of France is frequently appealed to, and by Mr. Field himself, as a proof of the success and utility of a general reduction of private unwritten law to statutory forms. But none of the strictly scientific supporters of codification have ventured to employ so unfortunate an illustration. As in the case of Frederick, the leading motive with the Emperor Napoleon was political and dynastic. France was composed of states originally independent of each other, and still maintaining their several and discordant legal systems. It was a sound dictate of public policy as well as the ambition of the Emperor to consolidate these different elements into one harmonious state. But looking to what the Code Napoleon may have accomplished in the way of establishing a system of law certain, easy to be learned, and easy to be administered, it must be pronounced a failure. In neither of these respects will it bear comparison with the system of our common law. Upon this point the testimony, not of an enemy, but of a distinguished supporter of the theory of codification may be invoked:

"It is well known, for instance, that the set of French Codes, which in time became the most comprehensive and self-dependent of all, have been completely overridden by the interpretations of successive and voluminous commentators, as well as by the constantly accruing decisions of the Court of Cassation. In France, as was intimated before, in treating of another subject, there can be no reliance, in any given case, as to whether a judge will defer to the authority of his predecessors, or will rather recognise the current weight attached to an eminent commentator, or will extemporise an entirely novel view of the law. The greatest possible uncertainty and vacillation that have ever been charged against English law are little more than insignificant aberrations when compared with what a French advocate has to prepare himself for when called upon to advise a client."[1]

And John Austin may be called as a witness still more distinguished, who, although a thorough believer in the feasibility and expediency of codification, confesses his inability to find anywhere in human experience a successful example of it. He says:

"In France the Code is buried under a heap of subsequent

[1] *An English Code*, Sheldon Amos, M.A., &c., &c., p. 125.

enactments, and of judiciary law subsequently introduced
by the tribunals. In Prussia the mass of new laws and
authoritative interpretations which have been introduced
subsequently to the promulgation of the Code is many times
the size of the Code itself." [1]

A brief reference must be made to the example of
Louisiana where, as is well known, a Code professing
to embrace the principal subjects of private law has
been for many years in force. The following observations are to be made concerning this piece of
codification:

1. There was a political necessity for an extension
of the province of legislation over the field of private
law, arising from the circumstance that Spanish,
French, and American law in many cases competed
with each other for supremacy.

2. The code actually adopted was substantially
borrowed from the Code Napoleon, and is, so far,
subject to the same criticism as has been visited upon
that work by the advocates of codification.

3. The defects so strikingly characteristic of
French jurisprudence would have been repeated here,
but for the practical good sense which has been
exhibited by the Bench and Bar of that state.
Largely imbued with the principles and methods of
the English Common Law, they have looked to that
body of jurisprudence, so far as the code permitted
them, as containing the real sources of the law, and
have fully adopted its maxim of *stare decisis*.
Nothing is more observable than the extent to which
the English and American reports and text books

[1] *Lectures on Jurisprudence*, Campbell's Ed., vol. ii., p. 125.

are cited as authoritative in that state. It would seem that the courts, except when there is some provision of the code directly in point, and except in those cases where the Civil Law, which lies at the basis of the legal system of Louisiana, notoriously differs from the Common Law, seek the rule in any given case in the same quarters from which it is sought by us, and then inquire, if occasion arises, whether there is anything in the code inconsistent with the rule thus found.

4. But a most impressive testimony against the expediency of codification is found in the deliberate criticism upon this code pronounced by one of the most distinguished of the judges who have administered its provisions. It contains *definitions* of the principal technical terms which it employs; and it must be admitted that no code can otherwise well be constructed. Full, complete, and accurate *definitions* are insisted upon by the scientific advocates of codification as the first requirement for such work. Austin declares that the paucity of such definitions is the most glaring deficiency in the French Code. Now the very existence of these definitions in the Louisiana Code was found to be one of the greatest difficulties in administering it. Says Mr. Justice Yost in giving the opinion of the Court in Egerton *vs.* The Third Municipality of New Orleans:[1] "Definitions are at best unsafe guides in the administration of justice, and their frequent recurrence in the Louisiana Code is the greatest defect in that body of laws."

20   [1] 1 La. Ann. 437.

The extent to which this difficulty is lost sight of by the advocates of codification is indeed marvellous. It would seem as if the ordinary experience of every lawyer would be enough to convince him of the hopelessness of any attempt to contrive definitions of terms which would answer the unknown exigencies of the future. How can that be defined the boundaries of which are not known and cannot even be imagined? It must turn out that the new phases and aspects of human affairs as they arise will continually prove contrary to all expectation, and will be found, on the one hand, to have been caught up and carried by an ill advised definition into a class to which they do not belong, or that no definition has been framed to suit them and they are thus left wholly unprovided for. The great jurists of Rome, unquestionably the most complete masters in the accurate use of language, after a thousand years of effort, gave up the task in that maxim of despair, *Omnis definitio in jure civili periculosa*[1]; yet it is still argued that the whole system of private law can be successfully embodied in written language, although accurate and infallible definition is an essential requisite at every step of the process!

Of the so-called codes recently compiled for the British possessions in India, I need only say:

1. That the utter confusion existing in those countries in respect even to native law, without mentioning the competition between that and British law, rendered a resort to statutory enactments a necessity ;

[1] Dig. 50. 17. 202.

2. Mr. Sheldon Amos, already referred to, in his plea in behalf of an English Code, deprecates any resort to the example of the Indian Codes for light in relation to the problem of codifying the laws of civilised nations: [1]

California adopted some years since, substantially the same *Civil Code* as that which has been so often pressed for adoption upon the Legislature of New York. So far as the experiment affords any instruction, it is of the same character as that derived from the other examples already commented upon, and justifies the following observations:

1. Even less than in the State of Louisiana do either the bench or bar look to it for the true sources of the law. These are still sought for the most part, as elsewhere in communities inheriting the traditions and methods of the common law, in the reported decisions of that and other States, and in authoritative text-books; and the code seems to be brought into consideration only, or chiefly, when a question arises whether its provisions have changed the law.

2. The volume of litigation, so far as may be inferred from the number of reported controversies, has certainly not been diminished. There is no evidence whatever that it has had any sensible effect in lessening the magnitude of libraries requisite for obtaining an adequate knowledge of the law, or diminishing the labour of professional study. In short, no one practical advantage can be pointed out as having been gained by this experiment in legislation.

[1] *An English Code*, pp. 36 *et seq.*

3. But the mischiefs which are inseparable from the scheme have already manifested themselves in notable ways. The Legislature has been unceasingly assailed with projects for amendment. Some of these have been well-founded, and others, doubtless, without merit. It is a misfortune to live under erroneous law. It is scarcely worse to live under laws liable to annual change. The worst result, however has attracted the attention of the learned Professor Pomeroy, so well known to our profession by his numerous treatises. The courts are obliged, where it is found that the code has changed the pre-existing law, to follow the code, although against their will. The departures may be so slight at first as not to prompt a resort to the Legislature for amendment; but they tend gradually to become wider and deeper and this result has proceeded so far in California as to threaten a wide divergence from the law as settled in other states. Professor Pomeroy became alarmed at these symptoms and called public attention to them in a series of articles published in a leading law journal. He suggested a remedy which, in my opinion, is likely to be adopted sooner or later wherever a codified law is administered. We all know that when the courts of common law in the infancy of legislation came to be called upon to interpret statutes, they soon displayed their wisdom by hitting upon the now familiar rule that statutes in derogation of the common law are to be *strictly construed*. The effect of this was to establish the doctrine that if any particular case did not clearly fall within the statute, the common law

was still in existence as to such case, and the doubt would be thus disposed of. When at a later period statutory revisions came up for interpretation, a similar course was adopted by the rule that it was to be presumed that the revisers did not intend to change the pre-existing law, but simply to re-enact it in a more suitable form, unless it appeared from the revision that there was a positive intent to make a change. These rules Professor Pomeroy advised should be adopted by the concurrent action of all the courts in the interpretation of the California Code.

Such advice would have made Bentham turn in his grave, but who of his disciples could object? Austin has distinctly declared that the sole purpose of codification was to reduce to writing what was *now known* of law, and that while the novel and unknown cases of the future could not be governed by the code, the unwritten law could not govern them because, *ex hypothesi*, all that was in the code. The consequence he admitted to be that there was *no* law in existence for such cases, but he insisted that the same thing was true both of a code and the common law; that in either case the decision must be left to the *arbitrium* of the judge. [1] I have already quoted Mr. Field's assertion to the same effect, and I may add that if he did not think that there was no existing law for the decision of future novel cases, he intended to make it so, for he introduced into his proposed code a clause to the effect that the rule that statutes in derogation of the common law should have no application to the code! Now if it be

Austin, Lecture XXXIX, §§ 951, 952.

true, as these distinguished codifiers assert, that all that is intended by codification is to reduce to writing only such parts of the law *as are known*, what objection can there be to a statement of that truth in the code itself?

They would say, probably, that this would do neither good nor harm, that it would not *create* law where none existed. If to this the answer were made that the judges would not think so, and that if the code itself were made to declare that it intended only to reduce the law to writing so far as known precedents made it possible, they would experience no difficulty in *finding* a law by which to decide any future case on the facts being presented, even if it was up to that time unknown. "Yes," they would say, "but their decision would proceed, not from *law*, but from their mere *arbitrium;* they would *make* the law by which they gave judgment." As I have fallen into the form of dialogue, I must pursue it a little further.

Ques. Do you mean to say that the judge in such a case follows no *rule*, but he decides according to his mere pleasure and under no responsibility, for if you do, you mean that he might freely govern his decision by tossing a coin and not be held accountable therefor.

Ans. Oh, we do not mean that. The Judge is undoubtedly bound to make his decision according to all those considerations of human experience, sound sense, custom, right reason, conscience, equity, and justice which lawyers apply to such cases.

Ques. Then there are certain things which exist

in the absence of all law and these things you indicate by the words human experience, sound sense, right reason, conscience, equity, and justice; now are these *existing* things really different things, or one thing expressed by the union of all these different words?

Ans. You are pushing us into rather more exact definitions of words than is usual.

Ques. Do you mean that you cannot define more precisely the language you employ?

Ans. No, we do not mean that exactly; the terms we have employed may be said to indicate the various *sources* of law.

Ques. The judge then finds in those sources of law a rule by which he may decide the case, and when he finds it he is bound to apply it. Is that what you mean, and is this process the exercise by the judge of what you call his *arbitrium?*

Ans. That is quite true.

Ques. Now, when any future similar case comes before the judge is he not bound to apply the same rule?

Ans. Certainly he is.

Ques. And why?

Ans. For the reason that the rule has now become, by his decision, the law.

Ques. Was anything added to or taken from the rule by the judge when he applied it in the decision of the case, or was he under any greater or other obligation to apply it in the decision of the second case, than in that of the first?

Ans. We admit that there was nothing added to or taken from the rule and that the obligation of the judge was the same.

Ques. Have you not then, gentlemen, admitted that there is always in existence a *rule* by which every controversy as it arises must be decided, and is this not entirely contrary to your theory that there is no law for the decision of future unknown cases, and that the judge *makes* the law for them by an exercise of pure *arbitrium?*

Ans. We prefer to leave that question to be answered by others.

It will be perceived that this short dialogue really brings out the principal conclusion which it has been my object in these lectures to establish. It would manifestly, be impossible to distinguish and assign to reason, sound sense, experience, conscience, etc., the several shares which they take in the process of finding the rule of decision. One thing only is done, —called by whatever name,—and that is to consider the consequences of conduct with the view of finding what conduct is on the whole, most productive of the equal happiness of all in society, and inasmuch as the first lesson which man in society learned was that the greater degree of social happiness was produced by a conformity to custom, the real process becomes an inquiry as to what is the custom. When this is found, it is declared and enforced, and it is there-fore the rule for the regulation of conduct which is enforced by society, and this is the precise definition of law. The one fundamental truth at the bottom of all and which more than anything else is to be continually kept in mind is that human conduct regulates itself by enforcing custom; and therefore that law, being nothing but enforced custom, is self-existent, and cannot be made by legislation however legislation may by the subordinate and subsidiary action I have heretofore described aid and improve it.

But even the advantages which Austin thinks are possible under a system of codified law can, in his own opinion, be secured only when the task is executed by the most competent and skilful hands ; and he confesses himself unable to point to an example among all the efforts in that direction which have as yet been made. I have quoted his condemning the Prussian and French Codes. The only other example of an attempt at General Codification is that of Mr. Field which has been adopted in some of our States. I have called attention to the grave censure of this by the learned Prof. Pomeroy and to this I may add the more thorough condemnation of Mr. Amos. He says:

" The New York Civil Code may be described rather as a Codification of Text books on the English Common Law, than as a Codification of English Common Law itself. Apart from occasional scraps of terminology and arrangement borrowed from Justinian's Institutes, and the Code Napoleon, the whole Work reproduces, in an utterly undigested form, the notions and the very phraseology in which the English Law is clothed in the most hastily compiled Text books. There is scarcely a symptom of a single ambiguous Term having been submitted to the crucible of logical criticism, or of a complex notion having been reduced to its component elements with a view to its being introduced afresh, under a simpler guise, into the body of the new Code.[1] "

The same writer, after pointing out many fatal

[1] *An English Code*, p. 99.

defects in this attempt at codification, thus concludes his review:

"The above faults and shortcomings in the New York Code have been pointed out simply in order to guard the English public and the Legal Profession against the temptation to construct, under a sudden impulse, a worthless Code. The Code here criticised may not be worthless for New York, though such an one would be far worse than no Code at all for this country. The peculiar state of society in a new and undeveloped country makes the kind of demand very different there from what it is here. Accessibility and verbal simplicity in the law may be of far greater importance to a restlessly energetic and commercial community, than precision and accuracy of expression. In England, on the contrary— with its antiquated institutions, so fondly cherished by the mass of the community; with its constitutional system so repulsive of change, and so jealously as well as tenderly watched; with its conservative sentiment which is strong in politics, and all but omnipotent at the Bar; a Code which in every line of it violates a familiar principle, or introduces a novel terminology, and yet is consistent in doing neither, would never hold up its head for so much as the first hour's debate upon its acceptance in the House of Commons.[1]"

And yet this was the work of one of the ablest lawyers constructed after long study aided by the widest experience.

And finally, Austin himself while insisting that a code is the true pathway to an improved condition of the law, admits that the question whether it would be wise to endeavour to frame and adopt a code for any particular nation is open to doubt. He says:

"But taking the question in concrete, or with a view to the expediency of codification in this or that community, a doubt may arise. For here we must contrast the existing law—

[1] *Ibid.*, p. 107.

not with the *beau idéal* of possible codes—but with that particular code which an attempt to codify would then and there engender. And that particular and practical question, as Herr von Savigny has rightly judged, will turn mainly on the answer that must be given to another: namely, Are there men, then and there, competent to the difficult task of successful codification, of producing a code, which, on the whole, would more than compensate the evil that must necessarily attend the change? [1] "

Well may the advocates of codification shrink from a task which sheer presumption only would assume when the nature of it is fully understood; for, disguise it as they may, the task is to frame rules which the unknown conduct of the future will follow and obey. This necessarily supposes that the legislator can compel the members of society to act with uniformity in obedience to his dictates, in other words, that there is or can be a human sovereign able to do, as Austin and Maine say, "exactly as he pleases." The attempt, whenever made, will prove as futile and miserable as the effort of the scenic artist to mimic the thunder of Jove.

> *Demens qui nimbos et non imitabile fulmen*
> . . . *simularet.*

I dismiss the topic of codification with the conviction that so far as it is a scheme for the conversion of the unwritten into written law because of a supposed superiority of the latter, it is entirely inconsistent with the fundamental principles of law. The peculiar condition which has sometimes obtained and may hereafter obtain, where different political societies with different original customs are struggling

[1] *Ibid.*, Lecture XXXIX, §. 968.

for unity may justify a limited reduction of conflicting usages by a codifying statute. But when any such attempt is made the true nature of law will re-assert itself. A judiciary law will grow up around the code and will eventually replace the written enactment and the law actually administered will be that which conforms to the customs of men.

Naturam expelles furca, tamen usque recurret.

Even under these political conditions, however, general codification is not necessary. Time will, itself, under the ordinary operation of social tendencies, bring about the desired uniformity. The consolidation of different states under one nationality produces a greatly increased intercourse between populations once foreign to each other, and a consequent tendency towards the assimilation of customs. In the progress of time, the differences will by slow steps disappear through the triumph of one custom over another. The English nation affords an example of this process. Its original elements were drawn from both Anglo-Saxon, Danish, and Norman sources, and multitudes of different and inconsistent customs and laws were consequently to be found in the same nation; but through the instrumentality of greatly increased intercourse between the different elements and the consequent tendency to the adoption of the same customs, and by the steady and constant influence of the King's Court in favour of general uniformity, nearly all these original differences have passed away with the aid of but little in the way of legislation. Some of the customs, however, were so deeply seated in large local provinces that none of these influences tending to uniformity were powerful enough to change them, and they still remain and are enforced as local customs. Of these the custom of gavelkind in Kent is perhaps the most conspicuous.

The conditions in France were different. There the separate provinces united under the kingdom were much larger and had been under the dominion of different established governments. The differing customs were established in territories sharply separated from each other by recognised boundaries, and the process of natural reduction to uniformity was thus rendered difficult, slow, and indeed almost impossible. Many successive efforts in the way of legislation had been made to abrogate the differences. I have heretofore alluded to the more important of these. The Revolution with its ideas of universal freedom and equality was a prodigious impulse towards uniformity, and presented an opportunity which the bold genius of Napoleon was quick to embrace, and thereby to establish the renown of a lawgiver. The Code Napoleon is an avowed attempt to reduce the law, whatever local differences may be exhibited, to a uniform system of written rules; but in one important particular it did not conform to the doctrine of Bentham, nor to some of the examples framed by his followers, especially that of Mr. Field. Bentham would not allow an appeal to any authority save the written rule. He would compel a decision under some precept of the code, however inapplicable it might be, or if this could not be, he would have a case undecided and *anarchy* rather than judge-made

law. Mr. Field would allow the existence and binding force of the common law in a case not provided
for by the code, of course leaving the question
whether it was provided for or not as a theme of
contention fruitful in uncertainty. The French codifiers were wiser. They did not act upon the arrogant
notion, that they could foreknow the future, and say
what groupings of fact would arise, and how they
should be disposed of; and they recognised the fact
that if cases should arise as to which the code was
silent, there was an existing law by which they
should be governed. The Fourth Section of the
Preliminary Chapter declared "A judge who refuses
to render judgment under pretence that the law is
silent, obscure or insufficient, may be prosecuted as
being guilty of denying justice."

If the view I have supported be correct that Law
is self-created and self-existent and can neither be
made nor abrogated however it may be, in some
degree, incidentally shaped, enlarged, and modified
by legislation, we should expect a vast body of gloss
and comment under the name of interpretation,
gathered and gathering around the Code Napoleon,
and indicating the methods by which the resistless
force of conduct under the guidance of custom is
reconciled with the code, and represented perhaps as
being in pursuance of its commands. The clause I
have just quoted enables this course to be taken
without judicial embarrassment, but it would have
been taken all the same if the clause had not been
adopted. The fact is strikingly in accordance with
this expectation. It would be a bold assertion to

declare that the volume of literature devoted to the law in France has in any measure diminished in consequence of the code, and if the learned author I have heretofore quoted is a candid expert the main source of uncertainty in legal administration in France is that often much vaunted enactment.

It is thus that written law always is and always must be treated. Our own Federal Constitution is an admirable specimen of written law. Its framers, well knowing the folly of attempts to foresee the future, confined themselves to large general enactments under which any of the policies which experience in the actual course of human events should advise might be adopted. If it had been pointed out to them that under the instrument they had framed with a jealous care to limit the central power, banks could be chartered, railroads constructed, seceding States reduced to subjection by war, the privileges of the mail service denied to lotteries in which many of the States themselves participated, and the President of the United States exercise authority to permanently rule over populations of millions inhabiting territories in distant seas, it would have commanded the assent of but a feeble minority; but had they lived to the present time all or most of these successive extensions of Federal power might have been acquiesced in by them as authorised by their own language.

LECTURE XIII

THE doctrine which so closely identifies Law with custom suggests some important questions bearing upon the subjects both of legal and of social progress and improvement. Law, Custom, Conduct, Life —different names for almost the same thing—true names for different aspects of the same thing—are so inseparably blended together that one cannot even be thought of without the other. No improvement can be effected in one without improving the other, and no retrogression can take place in one without a corresponding decline in the other. Law we have found to be based upon and to be dependent upon Custom, and therefore we cannot materially change Law without changing Custom, and to change Custom, is, as we have found, a thing beyond our power, that is beyond our direct and immediate power. Society cannot, at will, change its customs, indeed it cannot will to change them. This seems, at first blush, to hold out but feeble encouragement to efforts for social improvement, and yet we know that improvement does take place and we cannot help thinking that the numerous forms of activity having improvement for their object do bring it about or aid in bringing it about. The things which it is important for us to know are how far this improve-

ment depends upon causes beyond our control, and
to what extent and in what way our conscious efforts
may aid it.

Under the great process of Evolution, man began
to advance—to go no further back—from his savage
condition to higher physical, moral, and intellectual
levels; and this was not by virtue of his own conscious
effort, but because of the nature of his original
constitution and the environment in which he was
placed.   The progress thus begun has been carried
forward by designed effort, and it is that effort, and
the rules which should govern it, which most deserve
our attention.

The first great fact to be kept in mind is that man
will pursue what he conceives to be his own happiness; the next, that his only means of knowing what
will bring that happiness is the observation of the
consequences of his conduct.   In this pursuit the
first great motives to which he will give indulgence,
are the gratification of his natural appetites, and out
of this grow the parental relation, the maintenance
and care of children and the institution of the family.

> Hail, wedded Love! mysterious law, true source
> Of human offspring, sole propriety
> In Paradise of all things common else.
> By thee adulterous Lust was driven from men
> Among the bestial herds to range; by thee
> Founded in reason, loyal, just and pure,
> Relations sweet, and all the charities
> Of father, son, and brother first were known.[1]

The writer of a recent interesting and very valuable

[1] Milton's *Paradise Lost*, Book IV.

work, the benefit of which I have enjoyed during the preparation of the later of these lectures, makes the entire progress of man to consist in the development thus suggested, the development of what he calls "the Moral Instinct" beginning with the parental relation.[1]   He shows in great detail how the increasing care of offspring leads to self-sacrifice for others, develops by degrees the kindly and generous feelings, how it extends from the immediate family to a whole kindred, thence successively to a community and a nation and ultimately to the whole human race, manifesting itself in the cultivation of the higher individual qualities and in the improvement of society with all its intellectual appliances and charities.   I think this account of human progress in the main true, although sufficient importance may not be assigned by it to the purely intellectual element in our nature, the effect of that being more implied by the writer than expressed. It is the *mind* in man which conceives that the greater happiness which he finds in contributing to the happiness of others is *caused* by that contribution and which expects a still further increase from an extension of the contribution.   It is the mind, or reason, which forms an abstract notion of the quality resident in many different things of creating happiness and which it calls *goodness*, and which it presents to the will as the means of obtaining its desire, and this intellectual power is my more particular concern.

The law may have defects peculiarly its own, and these will be found in the administrative agencies by

[1] *The Origin and Growth of the Moral Sentiment,* by John Sutherland.

which the unwritten rule is ascertained and enforced, or in errors of legislation. The judicial tribunals may err in declaring what the true custom of society is, or the legislature may make an unwise attempt to create law not in harmony with custom. The remedy for such evils lies in improving the character of the courts by a better selection of judges and better training of lawyers, and in a repeal of the unwise enactments, and a selection of wiser and better legislators.

But if the judicial tribunals correctly declare and enforce custom all remaining social evils are evils in the customs and any improvement must be sought for in a reformation of custom itself, and custom being conduct it can be reformed or improved only by a reformation or improvement of conduct. Conduct, however, being caused by thought, can be changed and improved only by a change or improvement in thought. Here we come back to the conclusion reached in an earlier lecture that all substantial social reform must begin with individuals and by a change and improvement in their thoughts. The legislature cannot originate it, however it may aid it, and the sole function of the judicial power is to preserve the peace of society and leave its members to work out their own happiness and that of their fellows by a free exercise of their own powers. Men cannot be made better by a legal command. This conclusion is not a new one. How often have we been told from the pulpit and by moralists that reform must begin in individual life; but how often is the lesson forgotten in the multitude of legislative

enactments passed upon the notion that they will
in some manner execute themselves, and change
conduct without changing thought! and where a
reluctant compliance is compelled by a rigorous
enforcement of an unacceptable enactment, we are
apt to take the energy of prosecution as an evidence
of the triumph of law and of real progress, whereas
it will be quite as likely to breed more than counter-
balancing mischiefs and drive us back again to the
acknowledgment that no real advance is possible
except through the slow, gradual, unconscious, but
willing change of thoughts, and consequent changes
of conduct and custom. *Quid legis sine moribus?*

Accepting then the conclusion that progress and
improvement must in the main begin and continue
in the individual life, let us consider a little more
closely the method they must follow. Man seeking, as
by his nature he must, his own happiness, first thinks
to find it in the unrestrained gratification of his
original appetites and tendencies; but this leads him
into conflict with his fellows, and brings upon him
the miseries and suffering always attendant upon
self-indulgence. He finds no way of avoiding these
consequences except by self-restraint, and he soon
begins to learn that by postponing immediate indulgence and enjoyment he can gain a larger and
wider, though more distant, good. These lessons,
taught him by his observation of the consequences of
his conduct, unite with his affectionate tendencies
which find their activity in the formation of the
domestic relations. He not only observes the consequences of his own conduct, but the consequences

of the conduct of others and seeks by imitation to gain the happiness which others enjoy. Under this natural process, physical well-being and moral progress advance *pari passu* and the whole company of human virtues spring into action and propagate their influences in ever widening circles. This advancement is greatly stimulated by that co-operation which is attendant upon the increased peacefulness of society and the division of labour and effort. Men co-operate not only to increase wealth, but to enlarge social, intellectual, and moral well-being. Society takes on a more refined organisation, the institutions of government and law are more and more perfected, and a multitude of agencies and facilities for increasing happiness and diminishing misery are created by united efforts.

Ethical writers conceive the main question in morals to be, What is right, or What is right conduct? I do not mean to disparage the importance of this inquiry, but I would suggest that the progress I have indicated has begun and been carried forward to a high point, without an answer to this question, indeed, without asking it. The simple process has been to observe the consequences of conduct and to adopt such action as has seemed to be productive of happiness: and we may rest in confidence that those lines of conduct which conduce to what men in general feel to be happiness cannot be otherwise than in accordance with the profoundest conclusion concerning the ultimate highest Good. The light that has steadily guided us over the long pathway from primeval savagery into civilised society may be safely trusted during the continuance of our journey.

A crowning influence in the improvement of conduct comes from the further intellectual development. Though we may not be able to comprehend the cosmical plan and its ultimate aim to which all else is subservient, we may be able—we are able—to conceive of something better than we see. We may imagine a possible world fairer than the actual one. As we observe happiness to flow from different lines of conduct and from many different actions, we abstract from them the common quality which is the cause of the beneficent effects and give it a name. We thus form the abstract conceptions of kindness, gentleness, truth, charity, beauty, justice, liberty, and come to cherish these qualities for the happiness they conduce to bring and even to love them for their own sake. We form ideals of conduct, as the painter or the sculptor forms ideals of the beautiful in art, and these ideals are something fairer and better than we observe in actual life.

" Where, where are the forms the sculptor's soul hath seized?
    In him alone; can nature show so fair? "

These ideals furnish the stimulus which leads to higher forms of conduct. They have their home in *thought*, the fountain and guide of action. They are first developed with the more cultivated and enlightened, who are looked up to and imitated, and their influence flows down through all ranks of society and manners and morals rise in response. They become the themes of literature and the inspiration of art. They create the qualities we admire in the hero, the patriot, and the philanthropist. They are offended by everything low and mean, and gratified by the display of every virtue.

How is the improvement thus produced in conduct reflected or reproduced in the law? That it must be so reproduced is certain for it by degrees becomes customary and custom is law. But the principal agencies are manifest. The first and most important is that of the judicial tribunals. The judges are both by appointment and tradition the experts in ascertaining and declaring the customs of life. As the higher forms of conduct become customary they pervade all social and business life. Conformity with them is mutually expected by the parties to all transactions, and if disputes arise it is because this expectation has been disappointed, and it is the office of the judge to declare and enforce the fair expectation. But the expert is also an exemplar and teacher. The judges are the most enlightened of all. The study of justice leads to the love of justice, and thus they are the first to recognise and sanction the improving customs of life. Here is the process by which the unwritten private law recognises the advance in morals and manners and affixes upon advancing forms of custom the authenticating stamp of public approval. There is no head or topic in the law in which this process is not observable. Take, for instance, the law of sale. An early rule imposed upon the buyer the risk of loss arising from any failure of the thing bought to conform to his expectation. An improved sense of fairness led honest men to disclose defects known to them but not apparent to ordinary observation. This disclosure became so far customary that purchasers relied upon it and the courts recognised the custom and made compliance with it obligatory. Manufactured articles are bought and sold by a certain description and if they conform to that description the obligation of the seller is complied with; but where the product of a manufacturer is bought under the same description there has come to be an expectation that the product will possess certain qualities, and the custom has arisen for manufacturers to take care that the process of manufacture shall secure such qualities. This custom has been recognised by the courts and made obligatory, so that the manufacturer may be compelled to answer in damages in case of defects in the product caused by the want of the customary care. In similar ways the law of contracts has been expanded so as to be made to conform to the fair expectations attendant upon business transactions among the most honourable men. The jurisdiction which courts of equity exercise is marked by a like development in the obligations of truth and honesty which are enforced. The duties originally imposed upon actual and recognised trustees are extended to cases in which any trust or confidence has come to exist in whatever way, and also to cases in which one person has acquired a power over the property or pecuniary interests of another which he may exercise to his own advantage, and the detriment of such other, and fictions are indulged in, implications and presumptions made, in order to enforce under ordinary legal forms rights and obligations which spring out

of new customs. In short, it is the function of the
judges to watchfully observe the developing moral
thought, and catch the indications of improvement
in customary conduct, and enlarge and refine correspondingly the legal rules. In this way, step by
step, the great fabrics of common law and equity law
have been built up without the aid of legislation
and the process is still going on.[1]

[1] I borrow here the well chosen language of a very able and very
temperate writer, who felt that this consideration called for a sur-
render of the advantages which at one time he believed codification
might furnish. I refer to the late J. A. Dixon, a distinguished lawyer
of Glasgow: " This slow and gradual evolution or spontaneous
growth from judicial decision, and the slow operation of custom in determining organic changes in all the departments of the law, explains
how it is that there is a continuous process of refinement going on in the
Common Law of a country in all ages. As institutions undergo a silent
modification; as morality progresses; as new needs and new modes of
satisfying needs come to the surface, and as the countervailing facts
of new modes of fraud, oppression, and of crime also present themselves,
a demand for suitable laws or modifications applicable to the ever new
circumstances makes itself felt on every side, and is instinctively
responded to by judges, at once the sharers and regulators of public
sentiment. The change in laws so brought about is so exceedingly
minute from day to day, that it will only be noticed by comparing
classes of decisions made at tolerably long intervals of time, on the
same states of fact, and when no positive legislation has intervened.
Take a volume of Morison's Dictionary and look through it from this
point of view and you cannot fail to be struck with the evidences of this
slow but incessant process of organic change. You see whole sections
of law silently transformed, you see new regions arising and others
disappearing, not by violent revolutions, but by the astonishing
operation of some slowly-working causes, whose existence becomes
visible, and whose effects are to be measured only by generations
or centuries—like the stupendous geological changes—that continuous formation and destruction of strata—the submersion of
ancient continents—the upheaval of new—not by cataclysms and
earthquakes, but as the result of forces which are in active operation
around us day by day, and which produce so little disturbance that
their very existence is unperceived till we contemplate their vast
results over epochs and æons of time.

The scientific character of this process should be noted. The truths that man seeks his own substantial happiness, that he is taught what conduct to pursue by observing the consequences of previous conduct, and that what he has once observed to happen he expects will happen again under like circumstances are original and inherent in his constitution and are acted upon long before he reaches the abstract conception of them, and consciously employs them. The progress he makes, therefore, by unconscious action upon these truths is in a just

" What has been the great factor in the creation of the Mercantile Law? Not legislative intervention: our Mercantile Law has been the product almost entirely of custom and judicial decision, and in the various stages of its history it has moulded and adjusted itself with the most remarkable sensitiveness to the progress of commerce and civilisation. The progress in this particular department of law is perhaps nowhere better observed than in such a book as Mr. Langdell's collection of Cases on Contracts from the earliest period of English Law down to the present day. Another great region or tract of law which has undergone in a very remarkable manner this process of silent and imperceptible change, is the whole region of doctrines pertaining to Trusts and Fraud—the prominent matters of equity jurisdiction in England. The whole doctrines of equity, both as avowedly administered in the equity courts, and as they have in a less obtrusive way crept into and pervaded the decisions of the Courts of Common Law, all these doctrines have involved themselves into the state of high moral refinement in which they at present exist, not so much by the special moral elevation of particular judges, as by the concurrent onward impetus of the whole community, which all the judges have shared and felt the influence of. The history of the analogous Prætorian jurisdiction, and of the Prætorian doctrines in Roman law, is another instance—particularly in questions of *bona fides*, *culpa*, *dolus*, *fidei commissa*, of the same process by which the unwritten law of a country absorbs into itself the whole gradual refinement and elevation of advancing civilisation :—how, with the general advance in moral sensitiveness on the part of the community, there comes a demand in matters of contract and ownership, and legal duty, for fine and still finer shades of faithfulness, for absolute purity of intention, for the repression of all indirectness of aim and duplicity sense *scientific*, although not consciously so. The great general rule governing human action at the beginning, namely that it must conform to fair expectation is still the scientific rule. All the forms of conduct complying with this rule are consistent with each other and become the recognised customs. All those inconsistent with it are stigmatised as bad practices. The body of custom therefore, tends from the beginning to become a harmonious system. When the ascertainment and administration of custom are committed in enlightened society to learned

of purpose, for what has been called a superior refinement of moral scrutiny into the duties which the law will enforce, the negligences which it will punish, the frauds which it will defeat. The Prætorian Jurisprudence and the Equity Law of England developed themselves under widely different auspices, and I think the growth of both systems in gradual niceness and delicacy of perception of the subtlest shades of legal and moral distinctions, is a proof that an unfettered, unwritten law grows with a nation's growth, and refines itself with the national refinement. The writings of the Roman lawyers and the history of English Equity jurisdiction alike exhibit the exquisite accuracy and balanced moderation with which, in the hands of competent lawyers, an unwritten law succeeds in doing, by the slow process of adjustment and refinement of which I have been speaking, what no legislative effort ever could accomplish—I mean the work of reducing into scientific form, of fixing, circumscribing, limiting, getting into practical shape as instruments of justice, the apparently indefinite and indefinable principles of morality—of seizing, appropriating, and applying, day by day, and year by year, the insensible increment and product of the deepening moral sense. and conscience of the nation. This is what Savigny means when he says, in his remarkable Treatise on the Vocation of our Age for Legislation, that the largest portion of the unwritten Law of every nation is the exact product and measure of the national character and temper—a reflex of its life and progress. This also explains the immense importance, even in the case of a codified law, of not overlooking the difference between a process of codification that has gone on, as that of France, simultaneously, as it were, with the development of the law, and a Code to be framed at one stroke, and made absolute and final, such as ours might be.—"
—*Journal of Jurisprudence*, 1874, p. 312 *et seq.*

judges, who are men of science, improvement becomes more rapid and certain, but the process is the same. The means employed by the judge to determine the character of any piece of social conduct, as being legal or illegal, is, wherever there is no fit and acknowledged precedent to guide, to do precisely the same thing which primeval man did: observe the consequences of the conduct in question and approve or condemn it according as it appears to be or not to be in accordance with fair expectation. Nothing is more common than the practice of learned judges to say in rejecting some rule urged as being the law, that business could not be conducted as it actually is conducted if that were the rule. This is saying that the suggested rule does not conform to the fair expectation. Learned judges recognise the fact that all legal rules under whatever head of the law they belong must be consistent with each other, and this can be only when they are in accordance with fair expectation. Here is one of the chief methods of correcting and improving the law. Some particular act the legality of which is challenged may have occurred in many different transactions and thus have been considered under many different heads in the law, and have been sometimes regarded as innocent, sometimes as immaterial, and sometimes condemned. The judge compares the various groupings of fact in which the act is found and learns when it is permissible and when otherwise, and by this refining process numerous different rules are framed, all forming parts of a harmonious scientific system.

I am not aware that learned judges have ever

explicitly avowed that their determinations as to the legal character of novel forms of conduct were governed by the consideration of what was in accordance with fair expectation, but I think there can be no doubt that such is the fact, indeed, how is it possible to determine the character of conduct except by a regard to its *consequences* and if these consequences are such as fair-minded men in general would expect, the conduct must be approved, and if otherwise, must be condemned.

This identity between the scientific rule upon which legal tribunals act in determining the law with the one which the unlearned man naturally employs in determining upon his own conduct is the element, characteristic of the unwritten law, which creates in us the feeling that it is *just and right.* We are so incessantly asking and deciding every day, or rather every hour, what conduct is expected of us that we complete the process instantaneously, and decision seems like an immediate recognition of a truth, rather than what it really is, an inference. It is this which moved the classic jurists of Rome to declare the law to be self-existent, and identical with the right reason of Supreme Jove.

The other chief agency in the reform and improvement of the law is legislation. As has been shown, society cannot make law at will, the great causes which create law being self-operative; but it can aid in the process and give completed form to changes which are pressing for recognition. Its office is a supplementary one to that of the judges, designed to accomplish a work for which the judicial power is unfitted. The characteristic of custom is uniformity, and it is instinctive in the judge to pronounce the law the same to-day as yesterday. He hesitates ever to say that a change has taken place, even when one has in fact taken place. The great changes in custom relating to the treatment of married women received, and could only receive, a tardy recognition from the courts; but the legislative power, absolute in form, however limited in fact, can easily and with effect enact a change already existing or coming into existence in custom. Property was from the first recognised in all valuable things which were limited in quantity and susceptible of appropriation; but this limitation led to a definition which excluded the immaterial products of the intellect: but the principal reason which lay at the foundation of the custom of acknowledging private property in anything was that society cannot have a supply of those things which are the product of human labour or abstention without conferring upon the producer the rights of property in the fruits of this labour, and this equally applied to the products, if we may call them so, of the mind. The courts could not well change their definitions; but the legislature could easily and with effect extend to these fruits of intellectual industry the rights of property by enacting a patent law. The same progress has led to the bestowal upon authors of the right of property in literary works, through copyright legislation, and a further extension of the same privilege by one country to the citizens of another, by appropriate treaties—a form of international legislation—is likely to come in the near future.

Nowhere is the advance in morals and intelligence more manifest than in the criminal law. The harsh treatment of untried prisoners, the denial of counsel for prisoners upon trial, the practical taking of accusation as evidence of guilt have given way to just and even indulgent methods which never permit the punishment of the innocent. A great part of this improvement has been effected or made possible by means of legislation.

But the largest field for the employment of the conscious agency of society in the improvement of the law is to be found in the multiplied forms of legislation which a highly developed industrial life demands. When we consider the enormous mass of apparently necessary legislation found in modern societies, we are almost led to doubt the soundness of the maxim that the best government is that which governs least, as well as the soundness of the teaching that the sole function of government and of law is to secure to every man the largest possible freedom of individual action consistent with the preservation of the like liberty for every other man; but while these maxims are permanently and everywhere true, the actual amount of government control varies according to social conditions. In rural communities with their sparse populations engaged almost entirely in agricultural pursuits comparatively little legislative interference with the conduct of life is needed. A simple organisation of the civil power under officers such as sheriffs and constables, a suitable

provision of judicial tribunals for the determination
of civil disputes and the punishment of crime, simple
provisions for the maintenance of roads and bridges,
schools, poor-houses, and jails are all that is necessary. But the division of employments attendant
upon advancing civilisation and the consequent
increase of co-operation, and crowded populations
in cities, towns, and villages, present very different
conditions. Men touch each other in a vastly greater
number of ways and may consequently the more
encroach upon and abridge the individual liberty of
each other. These encroachments if left to the
natural mode of redress, would involve continual
strife. Moreover such populations have many common additional needs to which all must contribute.
Streets, pavements, sewers, light, police must be
provided for and these require many laws and regulations. Banking, insurance, and other methods of
business co-operation are demanded; but these would,
through the fraud or neglect of those entrusted with
the management, be perverted to the injury of the ignorant or unskilful, unless a system of government
supervision were maintained. Additional and more
complex legislation is therefore demanded as society
advances, but the principles which should guide that
legislation and determine its amount remain the
same. Where is the line to be drawn beyond which
compulsory laws should not be permitted to pass?
What are the maxims which should reconcile liberty
and restraint? There is no clearly perceivable line
which enables us in every case to clearly determine
how far society may go in limiting and directing

individual conduct. It changes with the changing conditions of life. But there is a guide which, when kept clearly and constantly in view, sufficiently informs us what we should aim to do by legislation and what should be left to other agencies. This is what I have so often insisted upon as the sole function both of law and legislation, namely, to secure to each individual the utmost liberty which he can enjoy consistently with the preservation of the like liberty to all others. Liberty, the first of blessings, the aspiration of every human soul, is the supreme object. Every abridgment of it demands an excuse, and the only good excuse is the necessity of preserving it. Whatever tends to preserve this is right, all else is wrong. To leave each man to work out in freedom his own happiness or misery, to stand or fall by the consequences of his own conduct, is the true method of human discipline. For myself I reject that view of the cosmical scheme which would regard society as the unit for the well-being of which our efforts should be immediately directed, even though individual happiness and perfection were thereby sacrificed. The society most perfect, as a whole, will be that alone which is composed of the most perfect and happy individuals.

Here then is the field of effort for the improvement at once of law and society. It is a strictly scientific field. It is the field in which the great laws of morality have their play and in which they are to be studied as those other laws of nature which are supreme in the physical world. Writers on law have frequently felt obliged to point out what they deemed

22

to be an error in the common expression the *laws of nature*, and to say that it was only by a not very appropriate metaphor that the great principles which govern the phenomena of the physical world should be called by the same name which is used to describe the rules of conduct; but the resemblances are more striking than the differences. In each case the phenomena obey original self-existing and unchangeable rules alike entitled to the designation of laws.

> All are but parts of one stupendous whole,
> Whose body Nature is, and God the soul.

There is a Science of Human Conduct which embraces the kindred sciences of law and legislation. To study the science of the unwritten law, to develop and apply its great principles is the work of every lawyer who aims to perfectly qualify himself for both the private and public duties which belong to his vocation, and it is no less his work to study the science of legislation and learn the ways in which man by conscious effort can furnish aid to the silently operating forces which are working for the good of mankind.

These views have a significant bearing upon the subject of Legal Education upon which I can bestow only a passing glance. They at once approve as correct the method of teaching now long established in the Law School of this University. The law being the science of conduct of men in their relations and dealings with each other, the facts of that conduct, that is, human transactions of every description are the arena of fact which that science embraces. The multitude of cases which have been adjudicated and reported are but the records of conduct, and the diligent study of them and of the numberless similarities and differences which they exhibit will disclose the landmarks which reason has followed in its search for the true rules. These volumes, however, are but a part of the great territory of fact which it is the business of the lawyer and jurist to explore. Life itself is a moving spectacle of numberless forms of conduct the study of which is necessary to the full equipment of the lawyer or the judge. They are the accredited and traditional experts in the great game of social life, and must carefully watch that game. Herein we find the reason why lawyers of sound practical sense and knowledge of affairs so often acquit themselves both at the Bar and on the Bench better than others who may be much more accomplished in the learning of books. They have been studying diligently and to good purpose the facts of human conduct as they are displayed in the great book of life. The actual methods and systems of trade, commerce, and finance embrace great realms of fact in which legal principles lie implicit and disclose themselves to careful investigation. All the actions of men—*quidquid agunt homines*— are the proper theme of the lawyer's study. And then too there is the internal world, the realm of consciousness, equally necessary to be studied and equally fruitful in results, for it is here that the secret springs, the real causes of all conduct are discerned. I do not disparage the learning of books. We find in them not only a great storehouse of the facts of human conduct, but the thoughts and workings of the great minds which in the past have made those facts a study. We learn the rules and principles which have governed human conduct through ages of the past, and are made the more certain that they will continue to guide it in the future. Nor is the study of literature other than that of the law to be neglected. In History we find the record of the great events which concern nations, the conflicts, not between individuals, but those larger ones which no pleadings can contain and no court adjudicate, but which are still examples of conduct full of instruction for the jurist, the legislator, and the statesman. Poetry also has the highest uses. It is here that we find our loftiest ideals of conduct. The Roman Horace says to a friend that he had been reading over again at his leisure in Præneste the poems of Homer, who taught him the lessons of moral wisdom—*quid sit rectum, quid turpe, quid utile, quid non,* better than those renowned philosophers, Chrysippus and Crantor.

There is another subject upon which the legal theories I have sought to maintain have an important bearing, that of politics. I have had occasion to point out that the functions of law and government are closely allied to each other. Law is indeed, one of the departments of government, that one which reveals, or frames the rules which the executive arm, the arm of power, is to enforce. What then is the best form of government? With us it is almost held to be treason to ask the question; but let us not be too confident. A wise and witty poet tells us with

truth, "Whate'er is best administered is best."
What that government is, be it an absolute monarchy, an aristocracy, a plutocracy, an oligarchy, or
a democracy, which secures to the citizen the largest
measure of individual liberty of action, the right to
freely work out his own destiny, at no peril save
that arising from the natural consequences of his own
conduct, is the best, for that particular society. The
first necessary condition of any society is *peace*, and
this must be secured at all hazards. If it can be had
only under the rule of a despot at the head of armed
men, that government is the best, for it is the only
possible one; but it is a tyranny. It is the reign
not of Order, but of Force. The domination of an
oligarchy may be no better, for it is still a tyranny,
but that may be the best for the particular society.
But be it ever remembered that whoever has power
over his fellow-men will use it in part at least for his
own purposes, and the misery he thus brings upon
those beneath him is the ordered penalty inflicted
upon those who fail to prove themselves worthy of
liberty. Nor does the oligarch wholly fail to render
a public service. The feudal baron asserted possession over all the land, compelled his serfs and
retainers to cultivate the soil, took from them the
whole product of their labour save enough to support
life, and compelled them to shed their blood in his private quarrels; but he defended them against all other
injury and secured for them no inconsiderable amount
of peace and happiness. And what would have been
the result, had he anticipated the justice and charity
of Howard, and measured out to every toiler the

full product of his industry? It would have been, there is much reason to think, expended in riot and debauchery with nothing left to support life for the making of another harvest. Many complain— none more than I—of schemes, such as protective tariffs, bounties, and subsidies, by which a government confers favours upon classes of persons which it cannot confer upon all alike and by which the greater part of the burdens of taxation are shifted to the shoulders less able to bear them; but I should be staggered for an answer if I were asked whether, on the whole, the result were not, at least in an economic sense, to place the surplus income of society in the hands of the best custodians—whether, if it were all divided with strict regard to supposed justice among those who contributed to produce it, it would not, to a prodigious degree, be wasted, and misspent, to the injury not only of society, as a whole, but to a vast number of the individuals among whom the distribution was made. When the workman has learned to exercise that *self-restraint* which will enable him to make a good use of the entire product of his labour, he will have acquired at the same time the intelligence and the courage which will enable him to win it. Perhaps he does not sooner deserve it. Absolute equality among men, however necessary we may deem it in our political systems, and however properly we may cherish it, is not regarded in the order of nature as the supreme good.

These reflections teach us that government is not an independent instrumentality, based upon original conceptions of right and justice for making men virtuous, prosperous, and happy, and equally applicable to all conditions of society. It is not primarily a *cause*, but an effect. It is that form of public authority which naturally comes into existence because it is the only form which will secure peace and something like order among the people over which it extends. There is, therefore, no form of government which is best for all political societies. Each one has its own merits. I have said that government was not primarily the cause of the advancement of society in virtue and well-being, but I am far from thinking that it has no effect in this direction. We have heretofore seen how social progress is the result of action and re-action, among many influences and that government which best preserves internal peace and order indirectly aids in promoting all those social utilities which are the fruits of peace and order.

We cannot, therefore, answer the question what form of government is best without knowing the society over which it is to be established; but as the function of Government is the same as that of Law—to mark out the line within which each individual can freely act without encroaching upon the like freedom in others, we can say that the best government is that which best performs this sole function. The best societies, that is, those composed of the best individuals, will, of necessity, have a government which for that reason, we call best, and therefore, the best and truest ideal government is that of the best society. This ideal is best represented by a representative Democracy, for in that is found the largest measure of individual liberty, and this, after peace is secured, is the first of human blessings.

The views I have presented have also an important bearing upon the question how far, in a democracy, the powers of government should rest with the central authority and how far they should be dispersed among the extremities. The cardinal test is the same. Which policy will secure the best performance of the function of Law and Government, that is, to maintain, first, peace, and next, individual liberty? Where the localities are able to perform the duties of local government the power should be lodged with them, and no occasional or partial failures constitute a sufficient warrant for taking it away; but there may be a local population so incapable as to be absolutely unable to perform the office of self-government, in which case the power should be withheld.

I have now completed the inquiries which were my object in composing these lectures, and stated some of the important consequences which seem to me to flow from the conclusions I have endeavoured to establish. I am almost painfully conscious how imperfect the treatment has been, but I shall be more than satisfied if I have succeeded in imparting clearer and more just conceptions than have heretofore been held of the true nature of Law and of Legislation, and of the respective provinces of each. I hope, at least, that I have done something to convince my hearers, that while Legislation is a command of the Sovereign, the unwritten Law is not a command at all; that it is not the dictate of Force but an emanation from Order; that it is that form of conduct which social action necessarily exhibits, something which men can neither enact nor repeal, and which advances and becomes perfect *pari passu* with the advance and improvement of society. Every human action has unvarying consequences, which will be repeated, *ceteris paribus*, whenever the action is repeated. To study these consequences and to follow the teaching they impart is the great duty of life. To arrange those acts which are social in their nature in their true order, and under their proper classes is the work of the complementary sciences of Ethics and the Law.

Index

A

Abrogation of private law does not occur after conquest of country, 85 *f.*

Alaric orders a compilement of the Theodosian Code, 93 *f.*

Alderson, B., on negligence, 76

Alemanni, code of the, 93; law of the, 96

Alfred, the laws of, 45, 61, 99

American law in Louisiana, 304

Ames, F., on justice, 162

Amos, S., on the Code Napoléon, 303; on the code of New York, 313 *f.;* on the codes of India, 307

Anglo-Saxons, customs of the, 97

Anti-Trust Act, the, 209 *ff.*

Apuleian enactments, the, 232

Arbitration, among early Germans, 53; the origin of, 47 *f.*

Aryan communities, the early, described by Maine, 198 *f.*

Assize, of Clarendon (1166), the, 63, 106; of Novel Disseisin, the, 63

Athens, early legislation in, 33 *ff.*

Austin, J., cited, 299; on codes, 313; of France and Prussia, 303 *f.;* definition of law by, agrees with canon law, 103; of positive law by, 7 *f.;* on the expediency of codification, 314 *f.;* on the lack of definitions in the French code, 305; on the purpose of codification, 309; theory of law by, 181 *f.,* 218, 268; of sovereignty by, 14, 193 *ff.,* 315

B

Banking department, the creation of a, is not law, 234

Barbaric man, the social conditions of, 16 *ff.*

Battle, judicial trial by, the origin of, 47

Bentham, J., on the authority of codes, 317 *f.;* on the common law, 266 *ff.;* definition of law by, 7; on the ethics of government, 222 *ff.;* theory of jurisprudence by, 235, 265 *ff.;* of law by, 180 *f.,* 217 *f.*

Blackstone, W., definition of law by, 8; on the digest of laws made by Alfred, 99; on the dominance of custom in governing conduct, 32; on early laws in England, 60 *f.;* on the functions of judges, 78 *f.;* on the law of nature, 11, 174

Brehons, the, referees in disputes, 51 *ff.;* the laws of the, 52 *f.*

Brooke, J., on compensation for murder among the Dyaks, 44; on custom among the Dyaks, 21

Browne, T., on the nature of God, 175

Burgundians, code of the, 93

C

Cæsar describes the Druids, 51

California, the code of, 307 *ff.*

Canon law, the, 101 *ff.*

Capitularies issued by Charlemagne and others, 109

Carlisle, the statute of (1309), 107

Carlyle, T., on Bentham's ethics of government, 222

Chancellor, the assumption of judicial functions by the, 64

Charlemagne issues Capitularies, 109

Charter, of the Forest (1217), the, 105; the Great, *see Magna Charta.*